Child Care, Parental Leave, and the Under 3s

CHILD CARE, PARENTAL LEAVE, AND THE UNDER 3s

Policy Innovation in Europe

EDITED BY Sheila B. Kamerman
AND Alfred J. Kahn

AUBURN HOUSE
New York • Westport, Connecticut • London

Library of Congress Cataloging-in-Publication Data

Child care, parental leave, and the under 3s : policy innovation in Europe / edited by Sheila B. Kamerman and Alfred J. Kahn.
p. cm.
Includes bibliographical references and index.
ISBN 0–86569–037–5 (alk. paper)
1. Parental leave—Europe—Case studies. 2. Child care services—Europe—Case studies. I. Kamerman, Sheila B. II. Kahn, Alfred J.
HD6065.5.E85C47 1991
331.25′763—dc20 91–14263

British Library Cataloguing in Publication Data is available.

Library of Congress Catalog Card Number: 91–14263
ISBN: 0–86569–037–5

First published in 1991

Auburn House, 88 Post Road West, Westport, CT 06881
An imprint of Greenwood Publishing Group, Inc.

Printed in the United States of America

The paper used in this book complies with the Permanent Paper Standard issued by the National Information Standards Organization (Z39.48–1984).

10 9 8 7 6 5 4 3 2 1

Contents

TABLES

Exhibits

Preface

This is a book about public policy support of parenting, with a focus on infants and toddlers. The words *Erziehung* in German and *education parentale* in French convey the focus best, as does *child rearing* in English. The authors and editors sometimes also refer to "child caring." Because of inconsistent country usage, the editors suggest "child care" as the generic program term covering day nursery, day care, crèche, kindergarten, and so on.

The important point is that in recent years, some European countries have inaugurated policy and benefit departures that are a challenge to the United States and other industrialized countries. Here we highlight Austria, Germany, France, Hungary, Finland, and Sweden.

This is more than a collection of commissioned chapters. The countries were selected after considerable on-the-scene exploration. The chapters were guided by a shared framework, individualized to clarify a country's unique orientations. Revision followed interchange among the authors and between them and a group of American experts and with the editors—a two-year process.

We are grateful to the European authors who undertook the scholarly tasks and continued their work through each stage. We appreciate the contributions of a group of American experts and of Shirley Gatenio and Susan Einbinder, who captured the interchanges at our major meeting. Sydney Van Nort managed the word processor, fax, and telephone with efficiency and good spirit throughout. We are especially in the debt of the Ford Foundation, as represented by June Zeitlin and Dr. Shelby Miller, and the Smith Richardson Foundation, represented by Dr. Kathryn Young, who made the entire project possible.

Child Care, Parental Leave, and the Under 3s

1

A U.S. Policy Challenge

Sheila B. Kamerman and Alfred J. Kahn

This is a book about the need for discussion, debate, and action in the United States in a much-neglected yet urgent public policy domain: social policy and children under the age of 3. The book particularly calls upon citizens, political leaders, and public officials to consider parenting policy—here defined as a concern with economic support, protection of parental time with their children, and child care services, all of which may help to ensure that infants and toddlers start their growth and development under decent circumstances. Measures now in place in European countries are reported and analyzed both to stimulate thought and to suggest options out of which we might construct our unique "package."

When we began to assemble the team that produced the chapters in this book, we talked of the troublesome policy vacuum for infants and toddlers in the United States and the lack of attention to the matter. To our surprise, by the time the book was in its final stages, we could document even more grounds for concern, but we also had reason to acknowledge important stirrings, significant program beginnings, and at least the outlines of a debate.

We begin with the stirrings to introduce some of the parenting policy issues now surfacing in this country but that are hardly resolved. Then we turn to a brief summary of the unsatisfactory situation facing many infants and toddlers. Later sections of this chapter clarify the interest in Europe and outline the country presentations in chapters 2 through 7. The final chapter in this book offers an analysis and some ideas for consideration in the United States.

The long-stalemated 101st Congress made small but significant breakthroughs in October 1990 in a last-minute cliff-hanger atmosphere as it passed a budget deficit reduction package and some noteworthy substantive legislation. Included was the most extensive child care legislation in decades. (The package was a major step but hardly solved the U.S. child care problem.) While most observers and advocates concentrated on the intra-party and inter-party political maneuverings and compromises that produced these results, it is also useful to highlight some relatively new themes in the policy debate.

In the past, opponents of federal child care legislation have opposed what they called "communal" and "institutional" arrangements for children as contrary to the American ethic, as when President Richard Nixon vetoed comprehensive legislation in 1971. Or they have opposed federal child care regulations and urged voluntary sector support for and operation of programs. But in 1989, an additional note was introduced by conservative, largely Republican opponents of an ambitious child care bill with broad support that was being reviewed at congressional hearings. Why, they asked, should taxpayers subsidize child care for children of mothers who want to work out of the home? In fact, why not use government resources to help those mothers who remain at home and forego the extra salary so that they themselves may care for their preschoolers? The first proposals called for limited $400 tax credits. Vice-President George Bush, campaigning for election as president, suggested $1,000.[1] Proponents of the pending child care legislation responded that they too favored cash aid to low-income families to help with child-rearing costs but that in their view, such aid was not a substitute for much-needed child care services. They cited European practice: provision of child allowances and other income transfers to share in child-rearing costs, as well as commitment to a basic child care supply, especially for preschoolers.

Europe received very little attention in the subsequent discussion, but from 1989, one of the visible issues in the child care debate was the desirable balance in legislation between an increased subsidized supply of child care services or funds to help low-income parents pay for care, on the one hand, and an expanded tax credit to make child care more affordable but also—and seldom said—to make the at-home option more affordable too.

The legislation passed addressed both components, each modestly, using the enhanced Earned Income Tax Credit (for low-income working poor in a specific income band) as its vehicle for the cash supplement option. In fact, the newly amended EITC also pioneered in innovative under-3 policy when it added a supplemental credit for children under age 1. This innovation, explainable only as a by-product of legislative bargaining, did not signal a formal decision to launch new policy.

Another episode during the 1989–1990 legislative battles is also relevant to the concern for the under 3s. After several years of hearings and debate and with strong support, the Congress enacted legislation for family and medical (parental/maternity/disability) leave, attempting to fill a statutory gap that only the United States and South Africa share in the industrialized world. Unlike legislation everywhere else, the U.S. proposal dealt only with unpaid leave and job protection, not with income replacement to cover a period of leave after childbirth. President George Bush vetoed that legislation, nonetheless, saying that this was a matter for private business to handle.

A difficult situation remains. For lack of maternity-parental leave, far too many American parents must seek child care arrangements for infants only a few weeks old, at a rate one does not see in Europe, where the maternity leave is a right and covers income replacement for at least twelve or sixteen weeks. And it has been widely reported and documented that the supply of infant and toddler care in the United States is inadequate, mostly informal and unregulated, and a cause for concern; it may be helped but not solved by the 1990 legislation.

We underline only one further point: the child care and parental leave discussions were never connected with one another by advocates, political leaders, or the media. Most of those involved apparently were not alerted to the connections. Others did not emphasize the relationships because it would have complicated coalition building. Still others simply accepted congressional committee jurisdictions and specialization. Parental-maternity leaves defer the day when parents must consider other-than-parental child care arrangements. The availability of reasonable paid or unpaid leaves affects the scale of needed infant and toddler child care. These are two of the major components of under-3 child policy—a domain in which there is a partial U.S. vacuum.

We say partial vacuum to acknowledge the 1990 enactments (only some of which apply to infants and toddlers): an improved Earned Income Tax Credit for the working poor and the supplemental credit for infants under 1 year old; more funds for child immunization; a child care block grant program that will concentrate on preschoolers but also serve infants and toddlers; another child care block grant for those in danger of needing welfare aid; improved mandates for Medicaid coverage of poor children; expansion of Head Start; and other valuable provisions—progress certainly, but there is still a long way to go. A sharply focused child policy debate that would clarify what direction is preferred is not visible.

NOT THE UNDER 3s

Leading child development experts continuously and unambiguously stress the importance of the first few years of life.[2] Most Americans are convinced that the experts are right. Since the mid–1970s, politicians have stepped up their pro-family rhetoric. Yet many young children are living in increasingly hazardous situations in the United States, and there is still too little attention to what could—indeed, should—be done.

If to some observers the United States does seem to be slowly stumbling toward a clearer and more coherent, if often only implicit and not at all comprehensive, national parenting policy for families with children, it is mostly for families with children aged 3 and older. Increasingly it is assumed that women with children of this age will be in the labor force, especially when income is modest, and public subsidies will be provided for child care for these children, in particular for those in low-income families and deprived groups. Out-of-home group experiences are increasingly viewed as important for adequate socialization and development of children aged 3 to 5, as well as to prepare them for primary school and eventual labor market success. Schools continue to expand their preschool programs, focusing first on handicapped, deprived, and poor children but gradually moving toward more universal coverage. More than one-third of the states have begun to provide preschool programs for 4-year-olds, and programs for the 3-year-olds seem likely to follow. Although part-day programs still predominate, kindergartens are moving toward a full-school day program, and prekindergartens and nursery schools are following a similar pattern. The 1990 child care and Head Start expansions should improve supply and quality.[3]

In contrast, children under age 3 and their families remain largely invisible in the U.S. social and family policy debate. The Family Support Act (FSA) of 1988 (P.L. 100-485, welfare reform) was directed primarily at poor families with children aged 3 and older. Federal child care legislation has been inadequate, and the existing supply has left its major gaps and its most unprotected programs in the infant-toddler category. There is no parenting-maternity leave as a national statutory right. Only about 40 percent of working mothers have leave and some income replacement at the time of childbirth, on the basis of legislation in five states, collective bargaining agreements, and employer fringe benefit plans. Infant and toddler care continues to be in short supply.

Beginnings have occurred for all young children in health care, a policy area that carries maximum human appeal and a minimum of ideological hang-up. Even the most extreme proponents of laissez-faire find it difficult to defend high infant mortality rates, the birth of handicapped children whose defects might have been avoided by prenatal and neonatal care, and uncontrolled infectious disease. At the very least, they have been impressed with the evidence that prevention and early treatment are far more economical than the horrendous costs of years of expensive hospitalization or home care of children who can be kept alive but not repaired if the medical intervention is too late. In recent years, the Congress has required states, through Medicaid, to provide prenatal and neonatal care to all poor pregnant mothers and their young children and has allowed even broader coverage at state options. Legislation enacted in 1990 increased the mandate. Medicaid now must cover all poor children born since 1983. Since the poverty threshold is very low, a threshold of 133 percent of the formal poverty line is now in effect, and states also have the option of reaching 185 percent of the federal poverty line for coverage.[4] (States are now also required to phase in medical coverage for all poor children up to age 18 by the turn of the century.) Also in 1990 the Congress created a child health insurance tax credit to help low-income families not eligible for Medicaid (intended largely to allow parents to pay for child coverage where an employer's health plan would not otherwise apply).

Other proposals by a presidential commission to decrease infant mortality have been deferred because of costs.

The situation presents a paradox. The United States is a major, perhaps the major, center of child development research. In scientific volumes and papers and in books addressed to parents, many leading child development psychologists, psychiatrists, and pediatricians have documented the importance of the first few years of life. While the research base may not be as strong for the 1s and 2s as for the 0 to 1 group, enough is known to suggest a serious program and policy lag. Good physical care, adequate nutrition, consistent upbringing by a loving adult, a stable environment, and verbal and sensory stimulation are all essential to normal cognitive, social, and physical growth. The alternatives of poor neurological, physical, intellectual, and interpersonal development create high hazards. At the least, they produce children, and then adults, who lack the social and cognitive skills and well-being essential to satisfactory (let alone, optimal) functioning. Where the deprivations are deeper and longer, perhaps interspersed with trauma, the price may be disability, handicap, pathology, defect, and high personal and social costs. Yet this profound, well-documented, understanding of the process, if not of all nuances and dimensions, has not yet moved the society to decisive action. There are the beginnings mentioned but not a full societal response. Or the understanding is put aside in the face of inhibitions and obstacles, as discussed in the final chapter.

One need not argue (although there are developmental psychologists who do) that the first three years are the most important—the definitive years. Perhaps all childhood years are of equal importance; all stages of childhood are certainly critical. In any case, the first years are too important to be ignored. Currently they are not ignored, but given what we know, not enough is done.

Apart from the modest health policy beginnings for all children, including the under 3s, the society falls back on family life education, self-help groups, and advice books for parents. Churches, community centers, schools, day care centers, and clinics conduct family life education courses and support groups to emphasize the under 3s (as well as other age groups) and what they require. For the stable working class and middle class and for the more affluent, the advice may seem real, however uncertain its efficacy, since they can afford the time to participate and can afford to follow through, or they purchase professional services. The working poor and the welfare poor can do less with these offerings. In recognition of this, a national movement stressing early childhood intervention both recruits the poor, the deprived, and the high-problem groups for available prenatal and neonatal medical care, an accomplishment in itself, and also seeks to involve them in early-intervention help where problems threaten.[5] And there are many problems ranging from teenage pregnancy, to severe child abuse and neglect, to grossly inadequate parenting, to personal disturbance, disability, or retardation in parent or child. The intervention may take the form of basic prevention or quick response to the manifestation of problems. Model

Table 1.1
Labor Force Participation Rates of Women by Single Year of Age of Youngest Child under 3 Years Old, March 1978, 1988, 1990

	(Age 1 & Younger)	2	Total Under 3
<u>1990</u>			
Total	53.5	58.4	54.8
Married Mothers	53.6	60.7	55.6
Single Mothers	44.0	54.1	46.9
<u>1988</u>			
Total	50.8	60.3	52.5
Married Mothers	51.9	61.7	54.5
Single Mothers	44.9	52.5	45.6
<u>1978</u>			
Total	35.7	47.0	39.1
Married Mothers	34.8	45.6	37.6
Single Mothers	43.2	54.4	48.6

Source: U.S. Bureau of Labor Statistics.

programs are widely publicized, but in fact coverage is very limited. The excellent models are available in few jurisdictions. The capacities of model programs are limited by budgets dedicated to experiment and demonstration, not to coverage.

But there is an even more basic concern: early intervention, admittedly a somewhat vague concept, cannot ensure a child an adequate parenting environment unless it attends to issues such as family income, parenting time (especially in the period right after childbirth), and child care services, as well as medical care. In short, it depends on the foundation of basic social policy and the component we would call parenting policy. Beginnings apart, and not to minimize the 1990 tax credit improvements for the working poor, the United States as a society has not yet undertaken to build that much-needed social policy foundation for the under 3s and their parents.

A PROFILE

There were approximately 11 million children under age 3 in the United States at the end of the 1980s, living in about 10 million families. About one-quarter of these children lived in single-parent families, overwhelmingly with their mothers. More than half of the under 3s, including even 1-year-old infants, have mothers in the labor force. Indeed, more than half of all mothers are back at work before their infants are 1 year old (tables 1.1, 1.2). And very young children in two-parent families are more likely to have working mothers than those in single-parent, mother-only families.

Table 1.2
Age of Children by Family Type and Labor Force Status of Mother, March, Selected Years, 1977–1990

	% of Mothers in Labor Force			
	1977	1982	1987	1990
All Children				
Under Age 3	33.5	43.4	51.3	50.1
Age 1 & Under	31.1	41.6	50.2	49.4
Age 2	38.4	46.9	53.6	51.5
Children in H/W Fam.				
Under Age 3	33.4	43.7	53.2	53.4
Age 1 & Under	31.2	42.2	52.1	52.9
Age 2	37.6	47.1	55.5	54.6
Children in Families Headed by Women				
Under Age 3	37.6	45.2	47.7	43.4
Age 1 & Under	32.4	42.2	45.7	42.2
Age 2	46.2	49.9	51.0	45.6

Source: U.S. Bureau of Labor Statistics.

According to U.S. Census Bureau data, almost one-quarter of the under 3s lived in families with incomes below the poverty threshold in 1988, the highest poverty rate for any age group. The child poverty rate was higher throughout the 1980s than at any other time since the mid-1960s and consistently higher the younger the child. The rate varies by race, by the mother's marital status, and by her employment status as well. For example, 18 percent of white children were poor in 1988, 44 percent of Hispanic children, and 50 percent of black children. Almost two-thirds of the under 3s living in mother-only families were poor as compared with 12 percent of those in husband-wife families. Thirteen percent of those with mothers in the labor force were poor (6 percent of those in husband-wife families and 45 percent of those in mother-only families) in contrast to 35 percent of those with mothers at home, caring for their young children (21 percent of those in husband-wife families and 83 percent of those in mother-only families). Black and Hispanic children are most likely to be living alone with their mothers, to be living with an at-home mother, and to be living in poverty whether or not their mothers work, although the rate is much higher among those with at-home mothers. Almost one in five white children under 3 is poor, primarily those with at-home mothers.

There has been a dramatic change in how very young children spend much of their days. More and more are cared for outside their homes by caregivers who are not members of their families. Almost one-quarter (about half of the more than 5 million with working mothers) are in out-of-home, nonrelative care for at least some part of the day. Slightly more than half of this group are cared for in family day care, largely informal and of unknown quality, and the remainder are in group care. The biggest shortages in child care services are in programs serving children of this age and these are also the most expensive programs.

INCOME SUPPORT

The Earned Income Tax Credit (EITC) offers modest supplementation for the working poor. The income question for many families in poverty, mostly for single mothers and their children, was addressed after long delay by the Family Support Act of 1988 (FSA). This most important reform of Aid to Families with Dependent Children (AFDC) in more than twenty years assumes that in the future poor mothers with children aged 3 and older will be in the work force. Except for a limited state option, however, it pays almost no attention to those with children under 3, leaving them in the same unsatisfactory situation that they are now in.

According to the FSA, all AFDC recipients except those specifically exempt will be required to participate in a job opportunities and training program, to the extent that opportunities are made available, and if they have or are ensured child care. Among the exempt are caretakers of children under age 3 (or at the option of the state, caretakers of a child younger than 3 but not younger than 1). Since states have limited resources and are mandated to cover specified proportions of parents of children aged 3 and older within certain time periods, they are not likely to create many additional opportunities for parents of younger children. Yet children under age 3 and their families constitute a large part of the AFDC population.[6]

Twenty-two percent of the 7.4 million children on AFDC in 1989 were under age 3. They are almost 14 percent of all children under age 3 in the United States and are the age group most likely to be recipients of AFDC. About 40 percent of all families receiving AFDC have a child under 3 as the youngest child in the family. Claiming AFDC for the first time, with a child under age 3, is highly correlated with long-term AFDC dependence and with poverty. Yet except for teenage mothers who have not finished high school, neither the under 3s nor their mothers (or their fathers) are targets of the new welfare reform legislation.

The purpose of the FSA is to transform AFDC from a long-term income-support program for poor single mothers at home rearing children into a short-term assistance program designed to help recipients (overwhelmingly single mothers) move into the labor market and manage on their own. The principal sections of the law deal with improved child support collections and the establishment of paternity; job opportunities and training; supportive benefits and services (child care, medicaid, work-related expenses) for families as they make the transition from AFDC to employment and independence; and the requirement that states offer AFDC to qualified husband-wife families.

The training and employment programs and the transitional Medicaid and child care services—to the extent that they are made available by the states and are effectively implemented—will be geared overwhelmingly to parents of children aged 3 and older. For those who remain, and overwhelmingly for the under 3s and their families, the inequities and inadequacies that have characterized AFDC since its beginning fifty-five years ago also remain. There are still no uniform national eligibility criteria, no way of ensuring that poor children in Alabama and Wisconsin, for example, will be treated the same. There is no minimum benefit provided for AFDC recipients (although two studies of a minimum benefit are mandated), and AFDC and food stamps together still will not bring the income of poor families with children above the poverty level in almost all jurisdictions.

Either the opportunities generated by the FSA are desirable for parents of infants and toddlers or not. If they are, they should be extended to them; if not, other alternatives should be offered. Instead the 1988 "reform" does neither. It exemplifies the neglect of the under 3s.

CHILD CARE AND PARENTAL LEAVE: A CLOSER LOOK

The champions of liberal child policy and gender equity responded to the labor market and demographic trends of recent years by concerning themselves primarily with the availability of affordable, good-quality child care and the enactment of a parenting (once "maternity") leave policy to allow a period for medical recovery after childbirth, followed, if possible, by some time for parenting, before a return to work. They also have urged flexible workplace policies (flextime, vacation, and sick-leave plans) to allow time for care of a sick child, meet daily emergencies, and manage the dual pressures of work and family life.

There are counterproposals from the right and the left. In 1989, conservative Republicans argued that rather than subsidize child care costs to encourage mothers to work, the federal government should enact tax credits to subsidize wives who remain at home to care for their preschoolers. Others, from the right and the left, have called for universal child or family allowances or tax credits, or for other forms of government subsidy to share in the costs of child rearing whatever the parental work status. At FSA hearings, some critics of welfare reform from the left attacked the new work programs proposed for FSA as creating a form of low-cost labor to benefit business and not offering real options or aid to the poor at all. They would prefer poor mothers to be at home, receiving improved AFDC benefits.

Child Care

Because the Congress, as it often does, enacted a compromise program, not a deliberative policy, the important child care legislation of late 1990, buttressing funding for child care program subsidies by the states and mandating that the states enact and enforce quality standards, does not ensure that the supply for infant-toddler programs will increase. As in the past, this is expensive care to deliver well. There are still child care supply needs among the 3- to 5-year-olds, in particular regarding expanded hours of care and improved quality. Even under favorable scenarios, it will be years before the infant-toddler child care supply will catch up either through development of quality-controlled (as contrasted with underground market) family day care or increased center care.

Because the 1990 legislation creates no coherent federal policy about these matters, much will depend on state initiatives and local market forces. The core federal role remains to provide funding for child care through a variety of programs, many of which also fund other activities. The effects are incremental and in fact avoid the choices required by policy coherence.

Despite some efforts at recruitment of family day care providers in some states, there still is a major shortage of child care places for children under age 3. Parents of infants and toddlers often express concern about the quality of the care available and the extent to which they can afford the good-quality care that was estimated at the end of the 1980s to cost about $5,000 a year or more for care for a child under age 3.[7]

Another issue has recently entered the discussion: the debate about the developmental impacts of infant care (care for children under 1). In reviewing the research on the impact of out-of-home child care on infants, a recent National Academy of Science report concludes that there are "unresolved questions concerning full-time care [more than twenty hours a week] in the first year of life."[8] Some children experiencing such care show certain differences in their patterns of relationship with their mothers that raise questions for some researchers. The report urges further research in order to clarify the significance and implications of this finding. Recent research, although limited, buttresses similar concerns.[9] With the situation blurred, some observers see here a case for ensuring availability of parental options at least until children reach their first birthday. The research issue apart, clearly many parents would rather have more at-home time with their newborns than they can afford.

Parental Leave

In its lack of federal policy concerning parental (or maternity) leave for working parents, the United States is almost unique in its negligence—neither statutorily ensuring a mother opportunity for physical recovery after childbirth nor providing parent and child some minimum of time thereafter to get started together.[10] The Pregnancy Discrimination Act was enacted in 1978 as an amendment to Title VII of the Civil Rights Act of 1964 to prohibit discrimination against pregnant workers. The law requires that pregnancy and childbirth be treated the same way as any other short-term disability or illness. If an employer provides benefits (including the right to a paid or unpaid leave) to his or her employees for temporary medical conditions, the same benefits must be provided with regard to pregnancy and maternity. If, however, an employer provides no such benefits, none need be provided to women at the time of childbirth.

Almost half the states have passed some kind of family and medical, parenting, or pregnancy-disability law, most within the last few years. Six of these apply to state employees only. Only five states (California, Hawaii, New Jersey, New York and Rhode Island) include a partially paid leave, and these provisions were all enacted as part of a much earlier wave of state temporary disability legislation (TDI) to which the Pregnancy Discrimination Act now applies.[11] It is estimated that as the result of employer benefit packages, union contracts, and state TDI legislation, about 40 percent of employed women have job- and benefit-protected leaves and an entitlement to a cash benefit that would replace some of their earnings (at about the unemployment insurance level) for about six to eight weeks following childbirth.[12]

There is no evidence to suggest that rates of coverage of paid leaves increased significantly over the 1980s, although there has undoubtedly been some increase in formal policies providing for unpaid job- and benefit-protected leaves. Recent research has shown that women workers who are especially likely to be without the right to such a leave are unmarried and part-time workers,[13] low-wage workers,[14] and young and/or less educated mothers.[15] Furthermore, women workers who do not have job-protected postchildbirth leaves are more likely to experience additional unemployment solely attributable to lack of leave and/or to experience a disproportionate loss in earnings within the first two years after childbirth.[16]

With regard to the family leave legislation vetoed by the president, the General Accounting Office (GA0) in 1990 estimated the cost of a slightly more generous, earlier version of this act at about $4.50 per year per covered employee, clearly a modest cost. It would have mandated the right of employees to an unpaid family leave at the time of childbirth, adoption, or a serious health condition of a child or parent, and to temporary, unpaid medical leave at the time of an employee's own serious health condition, with adequate protection of the employees' employment and benefit rights.

The proposed legislation reflected some basic premises as elaborated in extensive hearings in the Congress. The numbers of working parents (both married and single) have increased significantly and are likely to continue to do so in the 1990s. Good child development requires the active participation of parents during the first years. Overly restrictive employment policies can force working parents to choose between job security and parenting. Given the greater probability of women carrying the primary child care and child rearing responsibilities in a family, a policy that focused exclusively on mothers alone would be likely to lead to discrimination against women in the workplace, so the leave should be "parental."

The recent and extensive National Academy of Science report limits its recommendation for federal action to mandating a one-year unpaid leave.[17] It states further that the panel members hoped that in the long term, six months of this leave would be partially paid, but they viewed such a recommendation as unrealistic at present and insufficiently supported by existing research. In short, this recent, important report refers to research highlighting the economic costs to women and families (and the potentially detrimental developmental problems for young children) of the existing limited provisions yet recommends unpaid leave for one year. No effort was made by the NRC panel to review the European experience and research concerning paid leaves and more extensive unpaid leaves.

An inadequate, stigmatized AFDC is the only alternative open to most poor mothers other than a full-time job and unsatisfactory child care, and middle-class parents increasingly see themselves as having no alternative except to remain at their jobs despite inadequate child care. Neither option enhances the development of children or benefits the society. Parental leave is not available to most and, at best, is limited. There are good beginnings with medical care and some good directional signs in the recently augmented EITC. Social service programs to support parenting are developing but offer limited coverage and lack the social policy foundations on which they must build.

The U.S. policy response is grossly inadequate, and the debate is clearly too constricted. In contrast, the European countries have been confronting this issue for the past decade or more. It may be worth exploring what some countries are doing and whether any of their policy and program initiatives might be appropriate for or stimulating to the United States.

EUROPEAN POLICY AND PROGRAM DEVELOPMENTS

Propelled by different priorities but responding to similar demographic and social trends, many West European countries are beginning to target special policies on families with very young children. Among the similar demographic and social changes and the resulting issues affecting these children and their families (tables 1.3, 1.4, and 1.5) are the increase in the proportion of mothers in the labor force, the decrease in fertility rates, the increase in the use of out-of-home child care, the high and rising costs of good-quality care, the increase in mother-only families, and the continued economic vulnerability of families with young children. Some countries have been led to their particular policy responses for families with very young children by their major concerns about adequate time for parenting and optimal child rearing, low birthrates, or the costs of infant and toddler care, as well as by the search for effective measures of economic support, labor market trends, and awareness of the impacts of work patterns on family life.

While the West European developments are recent and are offered here as a stimulus to U.S. thinking, the notion of a child-rearing allowance as an alternative to work by a parent during the child's first two or three years of life has an earlier East European history. In our 1981 book, *Child Care, Family Benefits and Working Parents*, we introduced the case of Hungary, which from 1967

Table 1.3

Demographic, Economic, and Other Social Trends for Major Industrialized Countries

COUNTRIES	POPL. SIZE 000'S	% OF POPL. UNDER 15	% OF POPL. OVER 65	FERTILITY[a]	FOREIGN RESIDENTS AS % OF POPULATION	FEMALE LABOR FORCE PARTICIPATION RATE[b]	PART-TIME (P.T.) EMPLOYMENT AS % OF ALL: BOTH SEXES	PART-TIME (P.T.) EMPLOYMENT AS % OF ALL: WOMEN	FEMALE (P.T.) EMPLOYMENT AS % OF ALL P.T	UNEMPLOYMENT RATES (1989)	INFANT MORTALITY (1987)
AUSTRIA	7,595	17.5	14.9	1.6	NA	53.7	7.4	18.8	91.5	3.6[e]	9.8
DENMARK	5,130	17.5	15.4	1.6	2.3	78.3	24.2[f]	53.3[f]	79.2[f]	7.2[e]	8.3
FINLAND	4,946	19.3	13.1	1.7[f]	NA	73.0	8.0[f]	16.7[f]	68.6[f]	3.4	6.2
FRANCE	55,873	20.4	13.6	2.0	6.7	55.7	12.0	28.4	83.6	9.6	7.6
F.R. GERMANY	61,451	14.6[f]	15.3[f]	1.4[g]	7.6	54.4[f]	13.2	33.9	90.5	5.5	8.3
ITALY	57,441	15.0	14.8	1.4[h]	NA	43.9	5.6	16.8	62.2	10.9	9.6
JAPAN	122,613	15.0	14.8	1.5	NA	58.4	16.9	15.7	73.2	2.3	5.0
NETHERLANDS	14,765	18.4	12.6	1.7	4.2	50.6	25.1[f]	71.9[f]	76.1[f]	8.3	6.4[g]
SPAIN	38,996	21.6	12.6	1.6	5.9	39.4	4.8	15.5	77.2	16.9	8.7
SWEDEN	8,438	17.8	17.8	1.9	5.0	80.1	24.4	50.8	85.3	1.4	6.1
UNITED KINGDOM	57,065	18.9	15.5	2.0	3.1	63.5	21.9	51.6	85.7	6.4	9.1
UNITED STATES	246,329	21.6	12.3	2.1	NA	66.9	17.2	38.2	67.3	5.2	10.1

Sources: Except as specified below, all data from 1990 edition of *OECD in Figures: Statistics on the Member Countries* (Paris: OECD, 1990). Data are for 1988 except as otherwise specified. All German data are for West Germany, before unification. To the extent that data in chapter tables vary, the explanation is differences in definitions, methods of compilation, and dates.

[a] Fertility = average number of children born per woman at current age-specific fertility rates. The replacement rate is around 2.1.

[b] Defined as female labor force of all ages divided by female population ages 15–64.

[c] Not standardized for Austria, Denmark, and Netherlands.

[d] The standardized data are for OECD countries. Where available, we provide comparable Hungarian statistics, with the caveat that our author urges caution.

[e] Figure for 1988.

[f] Figure for 1987.

[g] Figure for 1986.

[h] Figure for 1982.

Table 1.4
GDP per Capita, Government Expenditures, and Social Expenditures for Major Industrialized Countries

COUNTRIES	1989[a] GDP AT MARKET PRICES	PER CAPITA GDP 1988 (current prices) USING EXCHANGE RATES	PPP[b]	GENERAL GOVT EXPENDITURES AS % OF GDP (1985)[c]	TOTAL GOV'T SOCIAL EXPEND-ITURES AS % OF GDP (1985)[c]	TOTAL TAX RECEIPTS AS % OF GDP[c]
AUSTRIA	$ 126.7	16,748	12,506	47.4	28.8	42.3
DENMARK	105.3	20,912	13,555	57.3	33.9	52.0
FINLAND	114.7	21,266	13.792	35.9	22.8	35.9
FRANCE	948.5	17,002	13,603	49.4	34.2	44.8
F.R. GERMANY	1,200.2	19,581	14,161	43.1	25.8	37.6
ITALY	864.0	14,430	12,985	46.1	26.7	36.2
JAPAN	2,812.1	23,190	14,288	27.2[d]	16.2	30.2[d]
NETHER-LANDS	225.0	15,461	12,832	53.3	30.7	48.0
SPAIN	376.3	8,722	9,343	36.1	15.2	33.0
SWEDEN	189.3	21,546	14,772	57.8	32.0	56.7
UNITED KINGDOM	831.6	14,413	13,428	41.2	20.9	37.5
UNITED STATES	$5,165.8	19,558	19,558	34.8	18.2	30.0

Sources: Except as specified below, all data from 1990 edition of *OECD in Figures*. Data are for 1988 except as otherwise specified. All German data are for West Germany, before unification. To the extent that data in chapter tables vary, the explanation is differences in definitions, methods of compilation, and dates.

[a] In billions of U.S. dollars at current prices and exchange rates.
[b] Adjusted for purchasing power parities.
[c] Includes personal income tax, corporate income tax, social security contribution, and taxes on goods and services.
[d] Figure for 1987.

offered a child rearing grant at a time of labor surplus to encourage unskilled women to remain at home for three years after childbirth.[18] Recognition of the high costs of good-quality child care was part of the picture. This pattern spread throughout eastern Europe, usually including a two-year-leave provision and a grant either more or less generous than the Hungarian one, then equal to about 40 percent of the wage of an unskilled woman in the labor force. In many of the countries, pronatalist goals were added. (We have revisited Hungary in this

Table 1.5
Labor Force Participation Rates of Women[a] with Children under Age 3 in Selected Countries[b]

Country	All Women	All Women With Children Under Age 3	Lone Mothers With Children Under Age 3[c]
United States	68.5	52.5	45.1
Canada	66.8	58.4	41.3
Denmark	79.2	83.9	80.9
Germany	55.8	39.7	50.4
France	60.1	60.1	69.6
Italy	43.3	45.0	68.0
Sweden	80.0	81.0	81.0
United Kingdom	64.3	36.9	23.4

Source: Constance Sorrentino, ''The Changing Family in International Perspective,'' *Monthly Labor Review* (March 1990): 53. Published data from U.S., Canadian, and Swedish labor force surveys; unpublished data for other countries provided by the Statistical Office of the European Communities from the European Community labor force surveys.

[a] Women ages 60–64 are included in Canada and Sweden. Lower age limits are 16 for the United States and Sweden, 15 for Canada, and 14 for all other countries. For participation rates of women with children, no upper limit is applied for the United States or Canada. These differences do not distort the comparisons because very few women under 16 have children, while few women over 60 live with their children.

[b] Data for the United States are for March 1988; Canada and Sweden—annual averages for 1988; data for all other countries are for spring 1986.

[c] Includes divorced, separated, never-married, and widowed women.

book both to recall the East European initiatives and see what has occurred in the interim years.)

In the late 1970s and early 1980s, it appeared that the West European parenting strategy was moving to a norm of five to six months of paid maternity-parental leave, some further job-protected unpaid leave, and efforts to ensure access to an adequate supply of child care thereafter. It is the appearance of a variety of extended paid leaves—in some ways more like the earlier East European child rearing grants, in some ways quite different—that makes one pause and pay attention to the significance of the new developments.

The differences of the West European countries from the United States go beyond the presence or absence of the new types of leave, however. In contrast to the United States, the European countries long ago established an extensive social infrastructure for families with children that includes national health insurance or services and cash benefits to families based on the presence and number of children (child or family allowances). Many of these countries also provide guaranteed minimum child support payments (when the noncustodial spouse does not pay support or pays it irregularly or at an inadequate level)[19] for children in single-parent families, housing allowances for low- and middle-income families, health visitors (who visit new mothers in the hospital following childbirth and monitor the children's development at home as well), and special family life and parenting programs.

Child care for children aged 2½ or 3 to primary school entry is close to universal in much of Europe.[20] It is provided in preschool programs usually under educational auspices and is free and voluntary to children whose parents want them to attend regardless of their mothers' employment status.

European child care for the under 3s involves almost as diversified a delivery system as in the United States, includes both family day care and center care, and serves a wide-ranging proportion of children—from about 10 percent in most of Europe to 33 percent in France and about 50 percent in Denmark, Finland, and Sweden, largely 1- to 2-year-olds.

The take-off points for new parenting policies in Europe vary depending on the country, as do the specifics, but all seem to share a common goal: support for parental care for very young children at home for some time following childbirth. This involves provision of financial support to make a period of parental care possible. The Europeans seem to be moving toward a policy package that defines infant care as care by a parent who is home on a paid and job-protected leave from his or her job for much of the first year following childbirth and a menu of policy options for toddler care (care of 1- to 2-year-olds). The components of the policy package vary significantly in detail but include to some degree the following core elements:

- A paid, job-protected leave lasting five to six months on average but ranging from a three- to four-month maternity leave to a one-year parental leave, depending on the country.
- An extended or supplementary job-protected parental leave for an additional six months to three years, paid as either an earnings-related cash benefit or as a modest flat-rate benefit, designed by various countries either to acknowledge the value of family work and child rearing or to compensate for an inadequate supply of child care services (or both).
- The right to work part time for some time after the postchildbirth leave ends or perhaps at some point during the leave.
- An expanded (subsidized) supply of family day care homes and center care, available at income-related fees to toddler-aged children of working parents.

Countries may design one policy for all children or set different policies in accord with the child's specific age, or they may offer multiple elements, stressing choice or further differentiations. A few country-specific illustrations follow:

- A West German parent (overwhelmingly a mother) may stay at home for up to one and a half years after childbirth or work part time (at her previous place of employment only) and receive very modest financial support. The benefit is helpful for married-couple families primarily as a supplement to family income; it is not adequate to support a single mother at home unless child support, welfare, or other income also is available.

Of the countries covered, Germany is closest to Austria in the policies described in Chapter 3, yet there are differences too. Written before the late 1990 German reunification, chapter 3 focuses on three major instruments of parenting policy in the Federal Republic in the context of the broader social infrastructure of family allowances, tax exemptions, housing allowances, health insurance, and universal kindergarten.

These measures are: a paid maternity leave for employed women and an extended job-protected leave for parents with partly universal, partly income-tested, child rearing benefit. The original maternity benefit was wage related and available only to employed women. The subsequent extended leave is also available to at-home mothers and to either parent and is paid as a flat-rate grant for six months (minus the eight-week postchildbirth maternity period for the employed) and income tested for the subsequent year. While modest, the new benefit and leave are used by almost all who are eligible and for most of the time allowed.

In a formal sense, these new policies equate at-home child rearing (''family work'') with labor market participation and acknowledge its value. Benefit levels have quite different effects for the two-earner family (for whom the income replacement is minimal), the one-earner family (which obtains a small income supplement), and the single mother who cannot manage the at-home choice without social assistance in addition. The child rearing benefit and leave policies are not designed to constitute an attack on poverty or a response to the specific costs of child care. The grant levels encourage traditional intra-familial gender roles. There is limited availability of part-time work, limited child care service for infants and toddlers, and limited sharing between parents of the at-home role permitted once the initial choice is made. Although early modifications are not expected, the author reviews proposals for improvement made by various political groups.

French family policy (chapter 4) reflects yet a different historical tradition. Unlike a number of other countries represented in this book, the French program does not consist of a single, recently enacted measure to permit or induce an interruption of labor market activity in favor of a period of at-home parenting for one or several years. Rather, French family policy has had a long evolution and consists of a complex list of incremental, categorical measures currently attempting to satisfy at least three policy motives: to encourage child bearing (especially a third child), to facilitate labor force participation of women with children, and to provide adequate income to families rearing children, especially young families, single parents, and large families.

The two programs most relevant to this book's focus, the child rearing or parenting (''parental education'') leave and the Young Children's Allowance, are particularly instructive, as is the rich family policy backdrop. Furthermore, apart from Finland and Sweden (among the countries covered here) and Denmark, France has the most extensive provision of child care services for the under 3s of the Western countries.

The policy strategy France has tried to follow is one of supporting choice for parents of very young children with regard to labor market or at-home roles. There are those who would argue, however, that the policy does not really support either choice adequately and that despite acknowledgment of the value of both options, French policy does not appear to be fully committed to either.

While many Western readers will focus on Hungary's pioneer three-year child care leaves and benefits established first in 1967 and the alternative or supplementary child rearing policy of 1985, the author, writing in the context of the monumental social and economic changes and disruptions of 1989–1990, points as well to the "contradictions of the society that created it, used it, operated it, and shaped its character." As it describes effects, intended or not, and poor implementation, chapter 5 raises fundamental questions about infant-toddler care and preschool; labor market and family roles of men and women; and the relationships between child rearing benefits and leaves and the rest of the social infrastructure, as well as the labor market. Clearly when wage levels are inadequate, cash benefits linked to earnings cannot be assigned their intended functions of supporting an at-home role. Nor when the economy is in upheaval, can a modest flat-rate benefit play its supportive role either.

Finally, this chapter, chosen to represent Eastern Europe (because Hungary's child care grants became a model for all of Eastern Europe), provides insight into the complex task facing those who would engineer economic, social, and political change and who cannot expect any element of the heritage of recent decades to escape major questions, challenges, and interdependencies.

Finland's political history from World War II to the end of the Cold War required consensus government. Indeed, the annual budget must have a two-thirds parliamentary majority. As a result, the governing coalition typically includes two central parties and one large party from either the right or the left. The result, explored in chapter 6, is a coalition of parties committed to both universal flat-rate and earnings-related income transfers and grants and to both public child care services and financial support for at-home care. The emerging parenting policy has favored choice—first as a necessity and then as a doctrine. In the area of focus, the main instruments are maternity-paternity-parental leaves with cash benefits replacing wages, job security, and parental choice of either subsidized child care or a home care (child rearing) allowance. Recently, leave has been extended to the child's third birthday, and work hours may be shortened until the child is 4; those home on leave may work part time if they wish and receive a prorated benefit. Benefits are paid to both employed and at-home parents. There is also a well-developed framework of other social benefits and tax considerations for families. All of these family policies were either significantly expanded or initiated in the 1970s and 1980s, decades of dramatically increased economic growth for the country.

Long before other countries had begun to consider child rearing leaves, beyond the briefer maternity-parental insurance benefits, Sweden had pioneered with its unique parenting insurance and was discussing it in the context of gender equality goals. As seen in chapter 7, Sweden, clearly pleased with the results and public reception of its parenting policies, views them as promoting both parenting and gender equity, at home and at the workplace. There is an emphasis on context: economic growth, low unemployment, separate taxation of each adult, and high levels of government expenditures. The policy instruments are the still-unique, pioneering, extended parental insurance program, large investments in high-quality child care, a well-defined priority system for use of that child care, and a firm social infrastructure, including child allowances, health care, housing allowances, and guaranteed child support. These are reinforced as well by a variety of benefits that facilitate the balancing of work and parental responsibilities, including the strongest right anywhere to part-time work when one has young children and an ideology that stresses fairness and equity across income, class, and gender lines. The system clearly engages men in child rearing and parenting more than elsewhere, attenuates potential negative consequences for women, and tries to be protective of the needs of children. It does not, however, end occupational segregation or open private sector management jobs to women on a equal basis with men.

The country chapters provide readers and editors with the data for analysis and the raw material for debate. In chapter 8, we offer our views of where the action now stands and of the issues to be faced. We ask about possible relevance to the United States and take a stand.

NOTES

1. House Committee on Education and Labor, *Hearings on Child Care*, April 21, 1988; Senate Committee on Finance, *Federal Role in Child Care*, Hearing, September 22, 1988; House Committee on Labor and Education, *Hearings on Child Care*, February 8, March 6, April 5, 1989.

2. Michael and Sheila Cole, *The Development of Children* (San Francisco: W. H. Freeman, 1989); Sandra Scarr et al., eds., *Understanding Development* (Orlando, Fla.: Harcourt Brace Jovanovich, 1986); Alan Sroufe and Robert Cooper, *Development in Childhood and Adolescence* (New York: McGraw-Hill, 1988); Samuel J. Meisels and Jack P. Shonkoff, eds., *Handbook of Early Childhood Intervention* (New York: Cambridge University Press, 1990).

3. Especially the Child Care and Development Block Grant, constituting Subtitle F of the Deficit Reduction Package of 1990.

4. Deficit Reduction Package. On earlier Medicaid improvements to cover pregnant poor women and infants, see House Committee on Ways and Means, *The 1990 Green Book: Background Material and Data on Programs within the Jurisdiction of the Committee on Ways and Means* (Washington, D.C.: GPO, 1990).

5. Meisels and Shonkoff, *Early Childhood Intervention*; Sharon L. Kagan et al., eds., *America's Family Support Programs* (New Haven: Yale University Press, 1987). Also see Family Resource Coalition, *Report* (Chicago: Periodic Newsletter).

6. For details on child poverty, AFDC, and family trends, a valuable compilation is Committee on Ways and Means, *1990 Green Book*. Also see U.S. Bureau of the Census, Current Population Reports, Series P–60, No. 163, *Poverty in the United States: 1987* (Washington, D.C.: GPO, 1989).

7. The most recent child care supply and demand surveys and among the most comprehensive ever are reported by Sandra Hofferth, *National Child Care Survey, 1990* (Washington, D.C.: Urban Institute Press, publication pending). Also see Alfred J. Kahn and Sheila B. Kamerman, *Child Care: Facing the Hard Choices* (Dover, Mass.: Auburn House, 1987); National Research Council, *Who Cares for America's Children*? eds. Cheryl D. Hayes, John L. Palmer, and Martha J. Zaslow (Washington, D.C.: National Academy Press, 1990); Martin O'Connell, "Maternity Leave Arrangements: 1961–1985" in U.S. Bureau of the Census, Current Population Reports, Series P–23, no. 165, *Work and Family Patterns of American Women* (Washington, D.C.: GPO, 1990).

8. National Research Council, *Who Cares*, p. 77.

9. Nazli Baydar, Roberta Paikoff, and Jeanne Brooks-Gunn, "Effects of Child Care Arrangements on Cognitive and Behavioral Outcomes in 3-to 4-Year-Olds: Evidence from the National Longitudinal Study of Youth," *Developmental Psychology* (forthcoming).

10. Sheila B. Kamerman, "Child Care Policies and Programs: An International Overview," in Sandra Hofferth and Deborah Phillips, eds., *Child Care: A Policy and Research Perspective*, Special Issue, *Journal of Social Issues* (forthcoming); Sheila B. Kamerman, "Child Care Policies and Programs: An International Overview," *Journal of Social Issues* (special issue on "Child Care: A Policy Research Perspective," eds. Sandra L. Hofferth and Deborah Phillips, forthcoming).

11. Sheila B. Kamerman, Alfred J. Kahn, and Paul W. Kingston, *Maternity Policies and Working Women* (New York: Columbia University Press, 1983).

12. Ibid. A more recent analysis suggests that the coverage rate may have reached 44 percent. Roberta M. Spatler-Roth et al., *Improving Employment Opportunities for Women Workers: An Assessment of the Ten-Year Economic and Legal Impact of the Pregnancy Discrimination Act of 1978* (Washington, D.C.: Institute for Women's Policy Research, 1990).

13. Eileen Trzcinski, "Employers' Parental Leave Policy: Does the Labor Market Provide Parental Leave?" in Janet Shibley Hyde and Marilyn J. Essex, eds., *Parental Leave and Child Care: Setting a Policy Agenda* (Philadelphia: Temple University Press, 1991): 209–228.

14. Roberta Spalter-Roth and Heidi Hartmann, *Unnecessary Losses: Costs to Americans of the Lack of Family and Medical Leave* (Washington, D.C.: Institute for Women's Policy Research, 1990).

15. O'Connell, "Maternity Leave Arrangements."

16. Spalter-Roth and Hartman, *Unnecessary Losses*.

17. National Research Council, *Who Cares*.

18. Sheila B. Kamerman and Alfred J. Kahn, *Child Care, Family Benefits, and Working Parents* (New York: Columbia University Press, 1981).

19. Alfred J. Kahn and Sheila B. Kamerman, eds., *Child Support: From Debt Collection to Social Policy* (Beverly Hills, Calif.: Sage Publications, 1988).

20. Kamerman, "Child Care Policies."

2

Austria: Family Work, Paid Employment, and Family Policy

Christoph Badelt

Parenting policies for young families in Austria consist of several programs explicitly focused on mothers (and fathers) of newborn children, including maternity benefits and leave for working mothers. These programs are embedded in a broader system of family policy that includes regulatory social policy, financial support to families, and in-kind transfers to children and parents. The programs are independent of the work status of mothers or fathers. Parenting policies are a controversial issue in Austria; however, major improvements (and the addition of new programs) have been realized recently and are planned for the future.

BACKGROUND OF PARENTING POLICIES

The Political Background

Parenting policies are formulated and implemented on both the federal and the provincial levels. From a macroeconomic standpoint, the financially most important programs are federal, as are the regulations on family matters. However, recently, six of the nine provinces have begun additional income transfer programs for parents that may have a considerable impact on the economic situation of the participating families. Moreover, support for services such as nursery schools and family counseling has always been under the jurisdiction of the provinces. Consequently, although Austria is a country of only 7.5 million residents, parenting policies may differ from province to province, depending on the local influence of the various political groups.

The political landscape of parenting policies is complex. First, there are the well-established political parties, operating on both the federal and the provincial levels: the Social Democrats (SPÖ), the Christian Democrats (ÖVP), the Greens, and the ''liberals'' (FPÖ). It should be noted that *liberal* as used here is a literal translation of the German word *freiheitlich* and that *liberal* in Europe is used differently than in the United States. In Europe, liberal indicates a leaning toward free-market and minimal governmental interference. Also, the FPÖ is a party consisting of a liberal and a national wing. Consequently, this party is not comparable to the Free Democrats in the Federal Republic of Germany (FRG). On the federal level, SPÖ and ÖVP have formed a coalition government, with an SPÖ representative as chancellor. In the provinces, the political majority varies. Second, in addition to the political parties, a number of interest groups are engaged in family policy matters. The largest and most influential is the Catholic Family Association (*Katholischer Familienverband*). Other groups, such as *Familienbund* (family alliance) and *Kinderfreunde* (friends of children), operate in close relationship to the large political parties.

In general, the Christian Democrats and the Catholic Family Association promote a more conservative view of family policy, while the Social Democrats emphasize concern for the evolving role of women. Yet one should be cautious with these generalizations. The substantial changes in the roles of women and families over the last twenty or thirty years have resulted in the advocacy of conservative and progressive positions throughout the political spectrum. The traditional distribution of values among the political groups is not valid at all times in regard to this issue.

Parenting policies are a controversial issue in Austria. The debate about legislative measures ultimately can be traced back to several basic questions. Some of these issues were more controversial twenty years ago than they are today; others may not even have existed at that time. The most important political issues include the following:

- The value attributed to traditional families (married parents plus children) compared to other kinds of families, especially unmarried couples and single parents. In the 1970s, the Social Democratic federal government implemented a number of important legal reforms that led to an equal division of rights and duties between husband and wife in civil law. Moreover, discrimination against children whose parents were not married was reduced. While these issues were controversial for a long time, the political parties now officially subscribe to the equal rights of married and unmarried couples and their children, although the conservative groups are quite often suspicious of ''privileges'' that unmarried parents have now.
- The role of women in society and in the family. Equal rights for husband and wife in the legal sense do not determine the roles women actually play in society. Although few politicians will explicitly say that primarily women should be responsible for family work at home, implicit value judgments of this kind do have a significant influence on

the discussion of parenting policies. Sometimes the traditional division of labor between the sexes is promoted by stressing the need for a better appreciation of women's worth within the family, perhaps even in monetary terms. On the other hand, the same argument can also be raised from a feminist perspective. Although advocates of traditional sex roles are most likely to be found in the Christian Democratic party or the Catholic Family Association, there are conservative politicians in other political groups as well.

- The freedom to choose between family work and paid work. Practically every political group concerned with family policy subscribes to the view that women should have a real chance to choose between unpaid family work and paid work on the labor market. Seemingly this is also a good compromise between "progressive" and "conservative" views of the role of sexes. Yet the practical implications illustrate that such a compromise is only superficial. While the conservatives generally consider the choice as permanent, progressive groups tend to emphasize the possibility of doing family work for a limited period of time and then returning to the labor market. Verbally, there is broad consensus that males also have the freedom to choose. In reality, conservatives are not interested in this option.
- The economic situation of young families. Parenting policies are also seen as a package of measures to improve the economic situation of young families, which are usually rather poor. Again, the issue of freedom of choice becomes relevant. It is argued that families' financial need for two incomes does not permit a parent to give up paid work even when maternity benefits are paid. This position would imply the need to increase benefits close to the earned income of mothers (or fathers). An alternative point of view—held particularly by conservatives—tries to deliver high transfer benefits to parents independent of their previous work status. This position holds that the family work itself deserves public support rather than emphasizing the loss of income that follows from a (temporary) absence from the labor market. Moreover, the economic situation of families is a function of the number of children and the number of incomes per household. This contention is the starting point for another controversy: Should parenting policy progressively support families with more children, or should every child receive the same support?
- Parenting policy and population policy. Support that increases progressively with the number of children is sometimes advocated in reaction to the economic problems of large families; sometimes it is seen as an element of population policy that, with birthrates declining, is another controversial issue. There is even debate as to whether population policy should be undertaken, whether it is feasible, and whether family policy should be used as a vehicle of population policy. In general, the more leftist political groups are opposed to active population policy and consequently oppose every measure of parenting policy that they believe is a vehicle of population policy. Conservative groups do not see this problem in the same way. Some of them support population policy, while others see it as a possible side effect of family policy to which they would subscribe in any case.

Demographic Background

The demographic background of parenting policies in Austria is similar to that in other West European countries: a decline in marriage, birth, and fertility rates that is interrupted only by occasional special developments.

In 1988 the Austrian population was estimated at 7,596,100. Marriage rates have declined considerably in Austria since the 1960s (from a rate of 103.2 per 1,000 unmarried women over age 15 to 50 in 1960 to 44.1 in 1988). Also, in 1988, 62.8 percent of the males and 54.6 percent of the females (age 15 and over) were married, while the respective figures in 1971 were 68.3 percent for males and 57.0 percent for females.[1] At the same time, the number of divorces has risen steadily, from a rate of 13.9 in 1960 to 29.5 in 1988 per 1,000 married women.

In addition to the decreasing number of marriages and the rising marriage age, the number of unmarried, cohabitating couples has grown substantially. Living together without being married is usually seen as a test phase. To illustrate this point, data for the first six months of 1989 show that 47.5 percent of the couples who register for marriage already live at the same address.[2] This tendency is also supported by longitudinal studies undertaken in the 1970s.[3]

The Central Statistical Office publishes estimates of the probability that cohorts of couples who marry in a particular year will divorce. According to these estimates, the divorce rate increased until those marriages that took place in the late 1970s. For those cohorts, the divorce probability is estimated at 29 percent—a level currently seen as a ceiling.

The demographic trends are also characterized by declining birthrates and fertility rates, with 1963 generally seen as the year in which this development began. In 1963 134,809 children were born in Austria compared to 86,503 in 1987. During the same period, the fertility rate declined from 2.82 to 1.43, the lowest such rate ever reported in Austria. Since 1963 some minor countertrends can be observed. In the late 1970s and also recently, fertility rates have increased marginally. This tendency is much stronger in other European countries (particularly in northern Europe). Whether this trend will become marked in Austria cannot yet be determined.

The overall fertility trend is also confirmed by an analysis of the fertility of particular yearly cohorts. The cohorts born over 1933–1935 had the highest fertility rates in Austria (2.45 children on average per woman). Estimates for the youngest cohort available (born in 1961) are for 1.59 children per women on the average. Given the current mortality rate, this latter rate implies only a 76 percent reproduction of the parents' generation.

From the standpoint of parenting policy, it is worth noting that the overall decline in fertility rates is primarily the result of the smaller number of children to which the average mother gives birth and less an effect of the number of women who become mothers at all.[4] Currently 34 percent of all children are second children, and 48 percent are first children.

The reasons for the demographic trends have been heavily debated. Changes in attitudes, improved contraceptive methods, legal abortion, and the increase in female labor force participation are usually mentioned as possible explanations. There is no doubt that each of these factors has some influence on fertility rates, yet the weight of the particular factor and sometimes even the direction of causality can be debated.

Two interesting trends should be noted for Austria. First, female labor force participation increased much more in the 1950s than in the 1960s when the birthrate declined. In an international comparison, female labor force participation is still relatively low, particularly so in comparison to countries like Sweden, which also has higher fertility rates. Second, family size has declined in those subgroups of the population where female labor force participation is not relevant, for example, in farm households and in families where wives do not participate in the labor force in any case.[5] This decline in family size is consistent with survey results indicating that individuals and couples are reluctant to carry the economic and personal burden of more than one or two children. As the number of children per family remains rather small, the probability of females' engaging in paid labor increases. In this view, labor force participation by women is to be interpreted as an indicator of changing attitudes and as a consequence rather than a cause of lower birthrates.

Economic Situation of Families

Parenting policies have a strong economic aspect. The economic situation of couples is likely to influence their decisions about whether to have children at all and whether a parent should stay home for a particular time period.

Since 1955 the total female labor force participation rate (over all age groups) has risen by approximately 5 to 7 percentage points but is still rather low compared to most other West European countries (with the exception of the Federal Republic of Germany) and with the United States. In 1988, out of the total female population in Austria, some 35.6 percent were in the labor force. The rate was 59.2 percent for women ages 15 to 59 (table 2.1).

The overall labor force participation rates are misleading since they disguise the important effects of the rates of specific age groups. The most significant increases in the participation rate can be observed in the age groups between 35 and 44 years (more than 15 percentage points), an increase even more pronounced in other West European countries. On the other hand, labor force participation of women between 25 and 34 years increased only a small amount.

It seems doubtful that the age components of the changes in the labor force participation rate and the changes in fertility are directly linked. To give an example, the strong decline in the fertility of females aged 20 to 34 that took place in the 1960s was accompanied by a reduction in the labor force participation rate of this age group, while participation of women older than 45 years went up. In the 1970s and early 1980s, the fertility of women ages 25 to 29 was rather stable, while labor force participation rose.[6]

The comparatively low female labor force participation rates in Austria coincide with a relatively small percentage of part-time workers. (Part-time involves over thirteen hours and fewer than thirty-five per week.) The part-time work rate of women in Austria is currently about 17 percent, while the total part-time work rate (out of total employment) was 7.4 percent in 1987. This rate is 25.2 percent

Table 2.1
Female Labor Force Participation Rates by Number and Age of Children (percentages)

	Women	Married Women	Single Women
Total	58.2	53.5	71.3
No Children	63.2	61.2	/
With Children	53.8	50.8	/
Number of Children Under Age 15			
1	61.3	57.1	79.4
2	46.3	44.5	71.3
3 or more	39.2	38.7	42.1
1 or more	53.8	50.0	76.8
With Youngest Child			
Under Age 3	51.9	48.5	73.2
Ages 3-5	52.3	48.1	76.9
Ages 6-14	55.0	51.7	79.0
15 and Over	54.5	52.4	64.3

Source: Microcensus, 1988.

Note: Includes women ages 15–59.

for Sweden, 17.3 percent for the United States, and 12.9 percent for the FRG, (although it should be kept in mind that the definition of part-time work varies from country to country).[7] Although more opportunities for part-time work have been pointed to in the political arena in Austria, there are still too few such opportunities available. For example, a recent empirical survey of women in the province of Vorarlberg doing family work for their children under age 3 indicated that 97 percent were interested in working part time when they returned to work.[8]

The typical part-time worker is a married woman over the age of 30. In 1987 77 percent of women who worked part time were married, and 65 percent were between the ages of 30 and 50. Most women working part time have one or two children under the age of 15.[9]

Reliable income data are available only for those families in which the "head of the household" is not self-employed. It should be noted that the term "head of household" is a category of household statistics, not a social evaluation of family structures. In the Austrian census, one household member has to declare himself or herself as head of the household. In family statistics, the husband is always defined as "head of family." Per capita incomes of families are calculated by use of equivalence scales. A number of general trends can be observed on this basis. For example, the income situation of families deteriorates dramatically with the number of children, the occupational status of the head of household, and the number of incomes per family, which can be illustrated by the following data.

The median income (per capita) of all households with an employed head was AS (Austrian shillings) 8,870 per month in 1987. (As reported by OECD the average exchange rate for 1989 was AS 13.23 = $1.00. The monthly figures shown here are for one-fourteenth of annual net after taxes and including transfer payments. The self-employed are not included.) This income varied between AS 3,980 (for a household with a blue-collar worker, housewife, and four children) and AS 11,540 (white-collar employee as husband, wife employed, and one child). These figures indicate an extremely unequal income distribution among families, an effect that would be even stronger if comparisons to households without children were made. In that case, median per capita income rises to AS 13,350. For this reason, 26.6 percent of the families with one income, 17.5 percent of the single-parent families, but only 2.3 percent of the dual-income families are poor or near poor.[10] Given these facts, parenting policies automatically have broader social policy implications.

The unequal distribution of income between families is also mirrored on the expenditure side. According to the 1984 consumer survey, per capita expenditures of families quickly decline with the number of children and number of incomes in a family. The average per capita expenditures in 1984 of all households with an employed head were AS 11,080 per month. In contrast, for one-income families with three children, expenditures were AS 8,363.[11]

It is conceivable that the decline of per capita expenditures in large families is a result of economies of scale connected to the number of children. Currently a controversial political debate on this point is underway. Two facts cannot be ignored. First, for some kinds of expenditures, such as housing, economies of scale obviously exist. Second, the large consumer expenditures that large families are compelled to make place serious restrictions on these incomes. There is no empirical answer to the question of the relative size of these two effects.

There are, however, some indicators that show that the restrictive element is rather strong. One example is expenditures on food. For dual-income households without children, the per capita expenditures for food are 46 percent larger than for one-income households with three or more children. Clearly economies of scale do not have much impact in this instance.

The other example of the relatively poor economic situation of larger families in Austria is provided by the data on expenditures for children ("costs of children"). Austrian households spend between 25.7 percent and 55.8 percent of their total expenditures for children. This proportion increases not only with the number and age of the children but also with the total level of household expenditures. While the first two effects are obvious, the last is not obvious at all. Just as richer families spend more for their children not only in absolute but also in relative terms, less-wealthy families are apparently strongly constrained in their ability to spend money for their children.

A comparison of income data and expenditure data shows that families generally spend more money than they earn. Some of this discrepancy is only a matter of bookkeeping.[12] Yet the existence of a gap cannot be denied. There are basically three explanations for this discrepancy, all of which are relevant for parenting policies. The first is the relevance of the shadow economy. Second, transfer payments between generations obviously play a significant role in the budgeting plans of young families. Third, young families spend more than they earn while their children are small. They either use up savings accumulated in a dual-income period before their children were born, and/or they make use of consumer credits. In either case, from an economic standpoint, existing on a single income is seen as a time-limited period in a family's existence. This perception is also consistent with empirical survey results that show that the dominant reason for female labor force participation is the income gain.[13]

CORE PROGRAMS

The core programs of parenting policies are focused on parents of newborn children. In most cases, the support given is work related, although general financial and in-kind support to young parents is a growing issue in the policy debate.

Maternity Benefits and Leave for Working Mothers

A law for the protection of expectant mothers and nursing mothers (*Mutterschutzgesetz*) prohibits work by employed women during the last eight weeks before the expected delivery date and during the first eight weeks after delivery. During these prenatal and postnatal periods, women are entitled to claim maternity benefits (maternity leave pay) (*Wochengeld*) under the compulsory health insurance system. Maternity benefits, which are intended to compensate in full for the loss of earnings, are calculated on the basis of the net earnings over the previous three months. The insured woman's entitlement to claim maternity benefits is suspended while she is in the hospital, and costs are paid by an insurance company. In cases of premature birth, multiple births, and delivery by cesarean operation, maternity leave and benefits are extended to twelve weeks. Moreover, if an expectant mother cannot be employed during her pregnancy because of the risk to her life or the life of her child, leave and benefits may be granted during the complete pregnancy.

Self-employed mothers (in industry, trade, or under the farmers' health insurance system) are entitled to analogous financial support to finance the temporary employment of a substitute (*Betriebshilfe*).

Due to the compulsory membership of employees in the public health insurance system, the utilization rate for these benefits by employed mothers is nearly 100 percent. Since maternity leave is not an option for the employee but a legal responsibility for both the employee and the employer, the utilization rate has never been a problem for this program and is not subject to political debate. The strict obligatory character is seen as the only way to protect employees. The situation, however, is different for the self-employed. Here, again, application numbers for maternity benefits indicate universal utilization, but there are only sporadic cases where a work substitute is actually employed. Consequently, although self-employed and dependently employed mothers receive the same financial support, they do not actually receive the same health benefits.

Maternity benefits are paid by health insurance organizations. Yet health insurance finances only 50 percent of the benefits. The other 50 percent is covered by a fund that administers family-related transfer payments (Family Allowance Fund, *Familienlastenausgleichsfonds*). The total expenditures for maternity benefits amounted to approximately AS 2.2 billion in 1987, which is about 2 percent of the total public expenditures for families in Austria. In 1987, the total budget of the health insurance was about AS 60 billion. Total federal budget expenditures were about AS 510 billion.

The protection of working mothers has a long tradition in Austria. A law with that intent was passed in 1957 and was seen as particularly modern and far-reaching throughout Europe. Originally benefits and leaves were granted only for twelve weeks. They were extended to sixteen weeks in 1974; however, the protection was limited to mothers employed by others. While this protection was not very controversial, comparable protection for self-employed mothers did become the subject of debate.

From 1957, the ÖVP tried to include self-employed mothers in the program. Apart from the financial implications, the main argument against such a regulation usually was that maternity benefits would make sense only if mothers were required to stay away from work. Since this practice cannot be enforced for the self-employed, the Social Democrats were always skeptical. A political compromise was finally reached in 1982: mothers have to prove that they will use the benefit to employ a substitute.[14]

Extended Maternity (Parental) Benefit and Leave

In addition to the regular maternity benefits and leave for sixteen weeks, employed mothers other than the self-employed (and, since 1990, fathers) of newborn children are entitled to a parental leave for two years. Extension of this period from the first to the second birthday of the child became effective for children born after July 1, 1990. During this leave, a special maternity benefit (*Karenzgeld*) is paid out of the funds of the federal unemployment insurance system. Unlike the regular maternity benefit, this payment does not generally depend on the previous wage. It is a flat payment of AS 4,524 per month for married women or AS 6,725 per month for single parents or for mothers or fathers where the other parent either earns a very low income or does not pay maintenance. Since in 1988 the median wage was AS 16,372 before taxes and the female median wage was AS 12,868, this is a low benefit compared to the full wage replacement of the maternity benefit. Nonetheless, for the single parent, it is 52 percent of a median female wage. The extended maternity benefit payments are to be increased every year by the same factor by which retirement pensions are increased annually.

Eligibility for the extended benefit is linked with the right to receive unemployment compensation. In practice, this means that extended benefits for the first child are paid only to individuals who have been employed for at least fifty-two weeks within the two years preceding the date of application. Starting with the second child, twenty weeks of employment are sufficient to qualify. The twenty-week period is also relevant for mothers of first children who are under 20 years old or who have received unemployment compensation. Special regulations are applicable for women who are still at school. Since the sixteen weeks of regular maternity leave are credited for this twenty-week time period, a mother who returns to her workplace for four weeks after the end of her first maternity leave is entitled to a second year of leave if she is expecting a second child.

Surveys by the Austrian Statistical Office (*Mikrozensus*) and the Austrian Institute of Demography indicate a high utilization rate for the extended parental leave. An estimated 60 percent of women are eligible for an extended parental leave, and 95 percent of the eligible women make use of it.[15] Both the eligibility rate and the utilization rate have increased substantially during the last twenty years. For example, in 1962 the rate of eligibility was estimated at 37 percent and the utilization rate 73 percent. Two of three ''available'' parental leaves are taken after the first child; 27 percent are taken after the second child. There is no significant difference in the utilization rate between mothers of different social or economic statuses.[16] It is likely that financial reasons are not a crucial factor in the decisions of mothers not to make use of the parental leave. Usually mothers who make this decision either have a high degree of autonomy over their working hours or are afraid that staying away from work could endanger their careers.[17]

Only a minority of mothers who take the parental leave return to work immediately after the leave ends. According to a longitudinal study by the Austrian Institute of Demography,[18] only 24 percent of the mothers returned to work after the leave ended, 16 percent stayed away from work until the child's third birthday, and 11 percent until the sixth birthday of the child for whom they received the leave. On average, women stayed away from paid work for three or four years. Yet the median value of the leave is only seventeen months, which implies that the decision to stay home or return to work is made rather soon after the end of the parental leave. (All of these empirical results refer to the time during which the parental leave lasted for one year.)

Since there has been a strong tendency of mothers to extend their leave beyond the official period, the official increase to two years may in fact increase the opportunities of women to return to their previous workplaces. About two-thirds of the women who return to paid work before the first birthday of their child actually return to their former employers. More than 80 percent of those who returned to their former workplace stayed there for at least two more years.[19]

In 1988 44,066 women made use of the extended maternity (parental) leave. (The average number of women who were on leave at a particular day during the year was about 9 percent lower than this figure.) The total expenditure for this program was AS 3,229 billion. Recipients are paid their basic benefits through the unemployment insurance system, and 50 percent of the cost is refunded by the Family Allowance Fund (*Familienlastenausgleichsfonds*). Given the total volume of the family-related transfer payments in Austria (approximately AS 105 billion), the macroeconomic weight of the program is rather small. Again, the program is a good case in point that macroeconomic relevance and individual impact may differ significantly. Bearing in mind the high utilization rates (and the increase of the utilization rate over time), there is no doubt that extended maternity benefits plus leave heavily influence the living conditions of young parents and substantially increase the freedom of choice of parents to stay home with their children at least during the first (and in the future also during the second) year after birth.

The current system of extended paternal benefits and leave has been developed since 1957, when a maternal leave (first for six months and, after 1961, during a child's first year) was granted. Yet the relevance for parenting policies really began in 1961, when the first maternal benefit was introduced. Both the SPÖ and the ÖVP endorsed this system at that time, although the business wings of the ÖVP complained about the burdens imposed on business. The extended parental benefit and leave were always considered an incentive for parents to stay home with children. They were also seen as an appreciation of child rearing and family work. The benefit, which was linked to wages and family size until 1974, is intended to serve as a partial compensation for lost income.

Recently two aspects of the system have come under intensive debate. First, the idea of partnership within the family implies an extension of the program to fathers. In the early 1980s, this idea was viewed quite skeptically by some political groups in both large parties. Conservative groups argued against ''progressive'' views of the role of women, and unions opposed the idea because they were afraid to lose one of the few privileges for women at work. Furthermore, the whole program was criticized as an unfair privilege for employed persons, in contrast to those who were self-employed.[20] The criticism disappeared in the late 1980s; not until 1990 was the parental leave actually introduced.

The second issue, still under debate, is an extension of the program, combined with the right of employees to do part-time work in a later phase of the leave (similar to the provision in the FRG). The two-year period of leave and benefit will be available to parents of children born after July 1, 1990. As an alternative to taking the second year of the leave, parents have the option to do part-time work until the child's third birthday. If the employer refuses to grant this option, the case will be settled by a labor court.

Several regulations have been introduced to improve the possibilities of reintegrating women (or men) after the two-year leave. First, parents may now work part time on a limited basis (maximum monthly income of AS 2,658) during their leave without losing the right to receive the benefit. Second, employers whose employees make use of the two-year leave may get wage subsidies for the weeks immediately following the leave if they guarantee to employee the returning worker for at least one year (the legal protection covers only four weeks). These wage subsidies are granted only to smaller firms. Larger ones can use free training courses organized by the government for returning employees.

These arrangements followed from a compromise by the political parties, unions, and management. Business representatives were under strong pressure to accept improvements of the leave regulations. Basically, the conflict had to be resolved within the ÖVP, since both the minister of family affairs and the business representatives belong to this party. Additionally, benefits for certain groups of self-employed parents, including farmers, have been introduced. These groups are now entitled to a special payment that is half of the parental benefits provided to employees on leave. Finally, a further extension of the leave arrangement up to the third birthday of a child is now increasingly mentioned as a goal.

Special Assistance for Single Mothers and Additional Maternity Leave for Low-Income Families

Extended maternity (parental) benefits and leave for two years after the birth of a child are programs directed toward every employed mother (and, in the future, father). They are independent of the social or economic situation of the beneficiary. The program has always had the primary goal of enabling mothers to stay home with their children at least for a limited time after birth. There is no doubt, in the Austrian view, that for the child's benefit, it would be desirable to extend this period even beyond the second birthday. Since this problem is particularly severe for single mothers, an additional program for single mothers was introduced in 1974. Before that time, mothers sometimes could receive unemployment compensation after the first birthday of the child. In practice, the matter was handled differently in various Austrian provinces, since local labor offices interpreted a mother's "willingness to work" in various ways. Since 1974, single mothers who can prove that they cannot find appropriate day care for their child that would enable them to accept a job may receive a special additional maternity benefit up to the child's third birthday (*Sondernotstandshilfe*). Like an unemployment compensation payment, the amount depends on the original wage. In practice, beneficiaries receive 45 to 70 percent of their previous net income depending on the regional costs of living. In 1987 the average payment was AS 4,402 per month (quite like the married woman's benefit under the two-year extended maternity benefit).

In 1988 10,574 women—about 25 percent of the recipients of the one-year benefit—received this payment. In the reference period, before the extended maternity benefit covered two years, *Sondernotstandshilfe* was paid for two years. The overall figures therefore indicate that 12 to 13 percent of the recipients of the one-year benefit made use of the additional program. The expenditures amounted to AS 664,287 million in 1988, about 20 percent of the expenditures for the one-year program.

The utilization rate is difficult to estimate because it is hard to know how many women theoretically qualify for benefits. It is common knowledge that proving an inability to find day care is easier or more difficult in various provinces. Although applications are sometimes rejected, figures on the number of rejections are not available. If, however, the regional distribution of unmarried mothers is compared with that of grant recipients, it becomes obvious that some provinces (in particular, Vienna and Lower Austria) are rather strict, while in others (Salzburg, Tirol, and Kärnten) it seems to be easier to have one's application approved.[21] The longitudinal study by the Institute of Demography indicates that 53 percent of the unmarried mothers actually received the benefit during the early 1980s.

The political debate on the *Sondernotstandshilfe* long focused on the effects the program may have on marriage rates. Critics accused the program of giving couples strong incentives not to marry in order to qualify for the full three-year payment. In general, this effect was very likely, although it would be incorrect to attribute the decreasing marriage rate completely to these benefits.[22]

In 1984 family policy reacted to these effects by making unmarried mothers who live in the same household with the father of the child ineligible for the benefit. Exceptions were made if the father had no income or a very low income. Now, however, the policy has changed again. As of 1990, married women may get the grant under the same conditions as unmarried women who live with the child's father. Although this new development will probably affect only a small number of beneficiaries, it indicates a general change in the program's emphasis. What started as a special program for single mothers now seems to be evolving into a broader program to support low-income families during a child's first three years whenever day care is unavailable.

Despite this new development, a basic problem with the *Sondernotstandshilfe* still remains. Eligibility depends on the eligibility for the one-year (in the future, two-year) regular benefit, which means that the program is helpful only to mothers who have worked long enough to qualify for the whole chain of supports in the first place. Those who did not manage to enter the system because they became pregnant before they had any or sufficient prior employment history are not eligible for any of the programs and often must resort to welfare. Because of this situation, a number of charitable organizations that work with single mothers have offered employment contracts for pregnant women to enable them to qualify.

This problem has sparked considerable controversy. For those on the left of the political spectrum (not necessarily the SPÖ as such) and also for the Greens, the situation simply provides an additional argument for the need for a general basic income, perhaps in the form of a negative income tax. Catholic and conservative groups jump to the conclusion that a general child rearing "salary"

(*Erziehungsgeld*) would be appropriate for mothers or fathers who stay home to rear their children. They criticize the preferential treatment of employed persons and lobby for support of parents regardless of their previous work status.

Provincial Parenting Allowances

Monetary support for young parents has always been the domain of federal family policy. Yet the focus and the goals of this kind of family policy have become increasingly controversial. Since the ÖVP lost its majority in the federal parliament in 1970, the Christian Democratic party and the Catholic Family Association have not had an opportunity to implement their policy positions directly. Specifically, efforts to move toward extended parenting allowances that are independent of previous work status, such as a ''mother's [or father's] salary'' (*Erziehungsgeld*) as introduced in the FRG, have not been enacted. Under the current administration, although the family minister is a member of the ÖVP, this goal is not feasible.

Several Austrian provinces in which the ÖVP holds the majority, however, have introduced monetary parenting allowances on their own. Two goals can be identified as motivating this decision: (1) the desire to provide a model of the prevalent family policy if the ÖVP won the majority on the federal level and (2) the desire to exert political pressure on the other provinces and on the federal government to initiate the kind of allowances the ÖVP has in mind. The province of Vorarlberg took the first initiative in 1988. Tirol, Oberösterreich, Niederösterreich, and Steiermark soon followed although with somewhat different programs. In Carinthia, a program started in 1990. The example of Carinthia is particularly remarkable since the FPÖ and ÖVP form a coalition there and the ÖVP is only in third place in its number of representatives in the provincial parliament. Salzburg plans to start a program in 1992.

One political development common to all the relevant provinces deserves attention. While on the federal level the SPÖ opposes and prevents this kind of family support, on the provincial level, it has never rejected the programs in principle. In some cases, the Social Democrats have voted for them; sometimes they competed politically concerning which party would be more generous to the families. Only in a few cases did they vote against a program because of opposition to its main features.

The common denominator of the programs is the payment of an allowance to parents of young children regardless of the work status of mother or father before the child's birth. Payments are made for a maximum of three years and, in many programs, for only one year. Which year of the child is selected depends often on a mother's (or father's) eligibility for federal (extended) maternity benefits. In all cases payments are made only to families up to a maximum determined by their weighted per capita income. The weights used to calculate this income differ among the provinces. The absolute level of the income ceiling is typically AS 5,000 (net income per month). In most provinces, the amount paid to the families varies with family income. Only Oberösterreich has a flat payment. The maximum monthly allowance is AS 3,675 per child (Vorarlberg).

The programs differ substantially enough to indicate different philosophies behind them. One difference concerns the ordinal position of a child for which a payment is made. The pioneers of the program, Vorarlberg and Tirol, give allowances starting with the second (Vorarlberg) or even third child (Tirol) in a family. The others start with the first child. Oberösterreich originally started with the third child and switched in 1990 to supporting the first child. The second difference concerns the work status of parents during the support. Tirol and Vorarlberg pay allowances only to mothers or fathers who are not employed during the time of support. In official terminology, support is made only to parents who decide to dedicate themselves completely to child rearing (''family work'') during their newborn children's first years. Special arrangements are made for single parents and for couples who do part-time work. Third, some provinces restrict their allowances to Austrian citizens, while others do not discriminate against foreigners who have lived in the province for a certain period of time.

The economic relevance of the programs have to be viewed on both the micro- and macrolevels. From a macroeconomic standpoint, the expenditures are of marginal relevance compared to those of the big federal programs. The provinces spend up to AS 70 million per year for these allowances. Yet on the microlevel, there may be a significant effect on a family's economic situation. For example, the household income of a Vorarlberg family that is eligible for the program is raised on average by more than 20 percent.[23]

It is still too early to make a final evaluation of the programs' results. For Vorarlberg, I have begun a related evaluation for which data on the recipients of the allowances in 1988 and 1989 have already been collected and recorded.[24] From these data, it can be already concluded that (1) the utilization rate for eligible Vorarlberg families is extremely high (close to 85 percent), although the rather restrictive eligibility criteria should be kept in mind, and (2) the program considerably improves the economic situation of low-income families with two or more children. Yet this improvement holds only until the third birthday of the youngest child. Analogous data for the other provinces are not available.

Possible long-run effects of the programs are subject to speculation. Advocates and opponents of the programs argue particularly about those provinces where support is given only for second or subsequent children and where support is linked with the requirement not to do paid work. These program elements are criticized for their pronatalist character and for their conservative incentives to keep women out of the labor market. Although in Vorarlberg all the allowances can be given to fathers as well as mothers, only 0.5 percent of the recipients are male. The pronatalist aspect of the policy is a good example for the more general debate on whether financial incentives will influence families to have children. In this respect, the provincial allowances can be considered as similar to the general family allowances—maybe even as having less effect—since the provincial benefits are paid for only three years, while the federal family allowance may be paid for as long as twenty-five years.

It is not surprising that some of the programs provoke debate about whether they try to support or reactivate traditional roles of women in the family. There is no doubt that conservative values have influenced requirements for grant recipients to stay home with their children during the period of support. Yet this intent does not necessarily imply that the programs actually affect the behavior of women, in particular their decision to join the labor market. In fact, two pieces of evidence indicate that such a conclusion is questionable. First, it is known from empirical work in another context that the decision to give up paid work is usually made after the birth of a first child, while the program in Vorarlberg starts support with the second child and the program in Tirol with the third child.[25] Second, results of the survey of recipients in Vorarlberg indicate that only 35 percent of the recipients have done paid work immediately before receiving the allowance. In other words, it seems likely that the allowances are experienced much more as an appreciation by the society of family work than as an immediate factor influencing a woman's decision between paid work and family work. Also the substantial increase in family income that results from the benefit in Vorarlberg, for example, may even lead women to increase their interest in joining the labor market after the allowance has expired because they may become accustomed to a higher income.

The impact of the provincial programs should not be seen only in terms of female labor force participation or population policy. There is also the effect on the climate for having and raising children. All of the programs are viewed as not only explicitly supporting young parents in an economic sense but also as support in their struggle to combine their individual goals of having a family and—in the long run—doing paid work. In this view, the provincial payments can be seen as one of a number of steps to increase the range of choices young parents have without asserting that this range of choices is already as broad as would be desirable. Combined with the political pressure to give additional help to mothers and fathers who want to return to paid work after a period of family work, the provincial programs may turn out to be very effective in broadening the range of choices. It is not coincidental that this political pressure is also strong in the provinces where parenting allowances are linked with the requirements that recipients restrict themselves to family work.

CONTEXTUAL PROGRAMS

The situation of young families cannot be understood outside the context of general family policy, which includes monetary support programs (transfer payments), social services for parents and children (in-kind transfers), and regulations.

Monetary Transfers to Families and Children

It is not easy to calculate the exact amount of direct and indirect transfer payments that are either explicitly given to families or are at least partially motivated by family-related matters. In the "Report on the Situation of the Family in Austria," published in early 1990 by the Federal Ministry for Family Affairs,[26] all family-related transfers reached an estimated AS 113 billion in 1987,[27] which comes to about 27 percent of total social expenditures and about 7.2 percent of the gross domestic product (GDP). About 70 percent of this amount is spent on general family allowances (AS 31 billion) and family-related social security payments (AS 47 billion), primarily pensions for widows and orphans. The core programs described in the previous section are not included here; they are comparatively small from a macroeconomic standpoint.

General Programs for Families. The most important single transfer payment for families is the family allowance. Parents who are residents (not necessarily citizens) of Austria are entitled to receive a family allowance for minor children (or for children up to 25 years if they are enrolled in higher education programs) who share their household or for whose maintenance they are responsible. In 1990, the basic allowance was AS 1,300 per month; additional payments are granted for children over the age of 10 (an additional AS 250 per month) and for handicapped children (an additional As 1,550 per month). Starting in 1990, an additional allowance of AS 200 per month and child was paid to low-income families.

Apart from this supplemental payment, family allowances are not income related. Since they are not subject to taxation, there is also no indirect recognition of the family income. They have been constructed as a means of horizontal redistribution to support individuals who assume the economic burden of raising children. Despite the constant demands of the Christian Democratic party and the Catholic Family Association, allowances are not progressively increased with the number of children. Social Democrats oppose this position, arguing that every child should receive an equal payment. Family allowances are currently financed by employers' wage-related contributions, which are paid into the Family Allowance Fund (*Familienlastenausgleichsfonds*), created to administer the allowance system and other family-related expenditures. Moreover, a certain percentage of income tax revenues is used as an additional source of funds. As of 1987, family allowances were paid to about 1.8 million children, with expenditures amounting to AS 28 billion.

Family allowances provide long-term basic financial support to parents. The monthly payment is significantly lower than those provided by the core programs already described. Yet because of their long-term nature, their effect on a family's economic situation should not be underestimated. Since the calculation of exact figures on child-related expenditures is a controversial issue, it is not possible to determine the precise percentage of family expenditures covered by the allowance. Depending on family income and the ages and number of children, the percentage can vary between 14 and 40 percent for one child. Coverage per child increases considerably with the number of children and decreases with income, an effect that mirrors the statistical picture of expenditures.[28]

A second program of family-related income transfers is the birth allowance. Since the 1970s, birth allowances have combined elements of health policy with family policy goals. The family policy aspect consists of financial support to cover the additional expenses that accompany the birth of a child and his or her first years. For health purposes, most of the payments are made only on the condition that pregnant mothers and their children have regular medical checkups, which must be documented. The total birth allowance is AS 15,000, which is paid in four installments: at birth and on the child's first, second, and fourth birthdays.

Birth allowances are not a subject of political debate. This was not the case, however, when the system was introduced, particularly since the direct payments were constructed as a substitute for tax benefits that could be claimed when a child was born. Moreover, birth allowances are one of the few social programs where payments have been slightly reduced recently for budgetary reasons. In 1989, approximately AS 1.2 billion was paid for about 87,000 children.

Grants for Special Groups and/or Situations. In addition to the general monetary transfers, a number of small targeted programs are important for special subgroups of young parents. In most cases, they support families or parents in emergency situations.

Under certain circumstances, the federal government will grant advance maintenance payments to minors, that is, to single mothers of newborn children, if the father who is legally obliged to make these payments has failed to do so and court proceedings have proved ineffective. Courts responsible for guardianship and trusteeship are empowered to approve advance maintenance payments in speedy and simplified proceedings. These payments are financed by the family allowance fund (*Familienlastenausgleichsfonds*). Currently about AS 550 million per year are spent for this purpose.

Advance maintenance payments are one of the most important programs for the support of single mothers. The program has turned out to be an effective means of overcoming financial difficulties in emergencies. Yet from a social work perspective, the program still suffers from substantial deficiencies, particularly that a mother is not entitled to advance payment of the maintenance (alimony) she herself is legally entitled to receive from the father. Since maintenance payments for the child plus family allowance usually are not sufficient to cover living expenses, mothers are often forced to apply for welfare payments on top of the advance maintenance payments they receive for the child.

If unforeseen circumstances, such as the death of the breadwinner or a natural disaster, create an emergency that threatens the livelihood of a family or an expectant mother, special assistance allowances are provided by the Ministry of Family Affairs (*Familienhärteausgleich*). This program was introduced in 1984 and is financed by the Family Allowance Fund (*Familienlastenausgleichsfonds*).

About AS 20 million is used for this purpose every year. In 1989 1,638 applications were made to the ministry; in 518 cases, positive decisions were made. The average payment has decreased steadily over the years because the budget has remained constant while the number of cases has increased. In 1989 the average payment was still AS 27,000.

While advance maintenance payments and special assistance allowances are elements of family policy targeted to particular groups of needy parents, there are also some general social policy programs that may become relevant to parents of young children. The two most important examples are survivors' pensions in the context of the general social security system and family-related payments in the general welfare system (*Sozialhilfe*). These programs need not be elaborated. Under the "principle of finality," welfare payments, which are under provincial jurisdiction, may be the last resort for young parents or single mothers. In 1988 33,314 individuals in private households received permanent welfare payments. An estimated 15 percent of the recipients of welfare payments are single mothers with little or no other income. Moreover, foster children and children living in institutions are usually recipients of welfare payments. The reasons that mothers receive welfare payments have been documented in some Austrian provinces. For example, 20 percent of the mothers in Salzburg never held a paid job and therefore could not enter the maternity benefit system. Additionally, 30 percent of the single mothers had incomes from job or unemployment compensation (including *Sondernotstandshilfe*) that were low enough that they could qualify for welfare payments.[29]

Tax Expenditures. Monetary transfers need not be provided by direct payments but can consist of tax privileges or reduced fees for publicly provided services. From an economic point of view, these indirect payments can be characterized as tax expenditures. Some of the tax expenditures in Austria are granted for family-related matters.

The tax system's treatment of families in Austria has always been controversial.[30] The question of individual income tax filing versus household filing and the balance between tax privileges and direct transfer payments for families, in particular, are seen differently by the Social Democrats on one side and the Christian Democrats and Catholic groups on the other.

The main features of the tax system's current treatment of families were introduced by the Social Democratic government during the 1970s. In 1973 the tax system was changed from household-oriented taxation to individual taxation. In 1978 tax privileges for families were cut dramatically and replaced by greatly increased family allowances. Advocates of the change emphasized that because of progressive income tax rates, tax deductions would assist higher-income families more than low-income families, an argument that can hardly be ignored. Under the current system, only a few privileges still exist. These include a lower tax rate, depending on the number of children, for special income components (for example, bonuses, which are very popular in Austria); a nontaxable single income allowance for married parents and an equivalent allowance for single parents (AS 4,000), which increases by AS 1,800 for every dependent child; and certain extra income tax deductions for children (for example, for private health or life insurance premiums). Moreover, bonus-linked savings deposits at a building society reflect the number of children.

A recent estimate of the economic relevance of these remaining tax privileges indicate that in 1987, the total volume of tax expenditures was figured to be about AS 10 billion.[31] This is less than 10 percent of the value of direct transfer payments to families and indicates the marginal relevance of this policy in the context of total public family support.

Indirect monetary transfers to families are also provided through reduced fares for public transportation and low-priced tickets for cultural and leisure programs financed by federal or local governments. Although it is impossible to calculate the total economic implications of these reductions, family fares on the federal railways and the local transportation companies in the provincial capitals lead to tax expenditures of not more than AS 25 million.[32]

Despite the relatively small amount of total expenditures, reduced fares and other price reductions for families may have a significant economic impact on an individual family's expenditures for cultural and social activities. Some provinces have realized this effect and have started to issue family passes that list all possible reductions or provide coupons for reduced prices. Still, it is likely that the lowest-income families will not make much use of these reductions because they have too little discretionary income for nonbasic expenditures.

Social Services to Families and Children

Parenting policies are not confined to financial assistance. Social services—either free of charge or sold to families at income-related prices—are an important complement to the monetary transfers. In some respects, services and monetary transfers can also be viewed as substituting for one another. This has to be mentioned particularly against the background of political discussions in other countries, for example, the United States and Sweden, where this type of trade-off is made much more explicit. Social services (including day care) are under the jurisdiction of the provinces, while most transfer payments are federal programs, so the issue also involves cost shifting in politicians' eyes, however seen by clients.

Given the trend of increased female labor force participation, access to day care and kindergarten facilities is a key issue in parenting policy. Every political group that addresses family policy endorses the basic right of parents and their children to a place in a preschool educational institution. [Since the discussion includes infant, toddler and preschool care (usually ages 3–5), we have substituted *child care* for *preschool* at several points in this section. However, it is noted that there is minimal coverage for infant and toddler care. Family day care in the U.S. sense does not figure in this report.—Ed.] Yet positions differ when it comes to deciding the age at which children should enroll in programs and whether half-day or full-day programs should be offered. While Christian Democrats and Catholics emphasize the role of the family in preschool education and prefer half-day programs, Social Democrats and unions more strongly support the idea of full-time programs. They also direct attention to the need for day care opportunities for children under 3 whenever this is necessary for particular families.

Some provinces have defined explicit goals concerning participation rates in preschool programs. Typically, these goals specify that a number of places should be available for children between ages 5 and 6.[33]

Currently there are about 4,400 schools and day care facilities in Austria that offer about 8,500 classes in preschool education; 71 percent of the schools are sponsored by public sector institutions, mostly by localities or, as in the case of Niederösterreich, by the province governments themselves. Approximately 24 percent of the schools are operated by private nonprofit institutions, with the Catholic church as the largest single sponsor. Only 6.7 percent of all schools are run by secular nonprofit organizations. Private market organizations are of only marginal relevance, operating 4.5 percent of schools.[34]

These figures provide aggregate information. Yet the area of child care education is much more complex since a number of different services are provided. The main categories include the following:

- Infant and toddler care centers (*Kinderkrippen*) (KR): day care for children up to the age of 3.
- General nursery schools (*Allgemeine Kindergärten*) (AKG): preschool classes for children between ages 3 and 6.
- School day care centers (*Allgemeine Horte* (AH): afternoon day care for children who attend school in the morning. This service is not strictly preschool education, yet it is included in all the statistics of preschool education that cover all forms of voluntary institutional care for children in Austria. (Compulsory school starts at age 6 and runs only a half-day.)
- Special nursery schools for the handicapped (*Sonderkindergärten*) (SKG).
- Special school day care centers for the handicapped (*Sonderhorte*) (SH).

The providers vary for the different services (table 2.2). Infant and toddler care centers are the domain of the public sector; churches, on the other hand, are not active in this area, reflecting their political values. There are also interesting differences in the number of hours they provide service. The private market organizations react strongly to the need for full-day programs, an effect that can be proved by econometric tests.[35]

The participation rate in preschools and other services for children varies with the age of the children. Table 2.3 gives an overview of the respective rates for 1985. Enrollment for those from birth to 3 years is very low, and family day care in the U.S. sense is limited according to the latest reports (table 2.4).

There are substantial regional differences in participation rates. In eastern

Table 2.2
Child Care Services in Austria by Sectoral Distribution, 1985–1986 (Percentage distribution of number of children)

	All	KR	AKG	AH	SKG	SH
Total number of children (100 %)	203,777	6331	171,570	21,028	1,249	885
Public Sector total (GOs)	72.0	84.9	72.8	64.2	43.8	79.1
Voluntary Nonprofit Sector total (NPOs)	25.0	9.5	24.2	33.2	49.9	20.9
Out of which secular (SNPOs)	4.9	6.9	3.9	11.7	30.2	5.5
Cath. Church (CNPOs)	19.4	2.1	19.7	19.6	19.6	15.4
Prot. Church (PNPOs)	0.7	0.4	0.6	1.8	0.0	0.0
For-profit Sector total (PMOs)	3.1	5.6	3.0	2.7	6.3	0.0

Source: Ch. Badelt, and P. Weiss, ''Specialization, Product Differentiation and Ownership Structure in Personal Social Services: The Case of Nursery Schools,'' *Kyklos* 43, fasc. I (1990): 75.

KR infant and toddler care centers
AKG general nursery schools (preschool)
AH school day care centers (after school)
SKG special nursery schools for handicapped
SH special school day care for handicapped

Table 2.3
Child Care Services: Participation by Age, 1985

Age	Population	Number of children enrolled	Percentage
0-1	87,328	114	0.1
1-2	88,815	1,865	2.1
2-3	91,369	4,419	4.8
3-4	93,162	26,534	28.5
4-5	92,001	56,035	60.1
5-6	88,085	72,825	82.7
6-7	83,931	22,429	26.7

Source: H. Fassmann, E. Aufhauser, and R. Münz, *Kindergärten in Österreich* (Wien: Bundesministerium für Umwelt, Jugend und Familie, 1988), p. 41.

Austria (Vienna, Niederösterreich, Burgenland), up to 75 percent of the children ages 3 to 6 attend a preschool program; the rates are as low as 34.3 percent in Carinthia and between 42 percent and 48.8 percent in Styria, Vorarlberg, and Tirol. These differences indicate substantial shortages (quantitatively and qualitatively) of preschool programs in certain Austrian provinces. To give an example, 85 percent of all infant and toddler care places are in Vienna; these facilities do not exist in Vorarlberg at all. Additionally, 92 percent of full-day programs are in Vienna and only 5 percent in Tirol and Vorarlberg.[36]

Table 2.4
Children in Infant and Toddler Care Centers and Nursery Schools

	INFANT AND TODDLER CARE CENTERS					NURSERY SCHOOLS					
Year	No. of Children in Infant and Toddler Care	Out of Which Children With full Day Care in %	Out of Which Children With Working Mom in %	Enrolled children out of total population (ages 0-3) a	b	No. of children in nursery schools	Out of Which Children With full Day Care in %	Out of Which Children With Working Mom in %	No. of Children (Ages 3-6) in Nursery school	Enrolled out of total population a	b
1970	4800	---	---	1.3	100	120,339	---	46.4	104,280	27.9	100
1971	4800	---	---	1.4	104	126,641	---	46.3	109,880	29.5	106
1972	4888	97.1	90.5	1.5	112	133,406	74.0	43.4	114,443	31.3	112
1973	4674	95.9	90.0	1.5	113	141,103	72.7	43.0	120,196	34.4	123
1974	4787	96.0	89.2	1.6	120	149,221	70.8	42.1	125,765	39.3	141
1975	4723	94.4	86.0	1.6	123	154,318	68.4	39.9	130,445	41.4	148
1976	4664	93.7	86.5	1.7	124	156,278	66.2	38.8	133,494	44.2	159
1977	4737	92.5	82.4	1.8	131	160,081	64.0	38.1	137,663	47.2	169
1978	4931	92.4	82.0	1.9	142	161,711	62.4	37.8	139,358	49.4	177
1979	5073	91.6	75.9	2.0	148	162,502	61.0	38.0	141,023	51.8	186
1980	5137	91.1	77.5	2.0	148	160,948	60.1	38.2	140,671	53.9	193
1981	5417	90.1	76.5	2.0	152	159,186	59.1	38.9	139,445	55.0	197
1982	5690[c]	88.5	72.7	2.1	154	158,923	59.8	38.7	138,119[d]	54.2	194

Source: Östz, Kindergarten/ Kindertages-Statistik.

[a] in percent

[b] index (1970 = 100)

[c] By 1988 the enrollment was 6,604 children of whom 80.5 percent had working mothers (1988/89 kindergarten stat.).

[d] By 1988, the enrollment was 180,546 of which 43.6 percent had working mothers (ibid.).

In a 1983 survey of parents, the shortage of places became evident. Parents wished to have a place for about half of the preschool children who were not enrolled in a program.[37] Yet in western Austria, the excess demand was substantially lower than average, which implies that low utilization rates in that area partly reflect preferences of the population.

The financing of preschool education varies among provinces. In some provinces, places are either heavily subsidized (Oberösterreich) or even offered free of charge (Niederösterreich). Other provinces have no systematic regulations, which means that the school can determine its own policy. Often there is a sliding-fee scale, based on the social and economic status of the parents.

In summary, the provision of day care, nursery school, and kindergarten services varies considerably among Austrian provinces. It is evident that there is a general and substantial shortage of places, particularly for the under 3s. But parents also differ in the kind of care they prefer and select for their children. In family policy, the connections between day care facilities, monetary transfers to parents, and increased female labor force participation are discussed quite frequently. Nevertheless, there does not seem to be a coherent overall policy largely because the political responsibilities are shared by the federal, provincial, and sometimes even municipal governments. Although a number of steps have been taken on the federal level to improve the possibilities of combining paid work and raising children, the shortage of group care for young children presents an obstacle to this goal. There are also various experiments with alternatives to group care, for example, family day care. Since most of these arrangements are made in the private sphere, reliable data do not exist. According to a survey in 1983, only one out of fifty children receives day care from a paid person outside the family.[38] It is likely that this percentage has increased in the interim.

Regulatory Family Policy

A number of core programs for young parents are based on labor market regulations. Maternity leave and general protection of expectant mothers especially fall into this category. Additionally, a number of more general regulations have bearing on the situation of young parents.

One example is the special nursing leave for employed persons, which provides an important opportunity for combining paid work with responsibility for children. An employee who produces evidence that his or her absence from work is unavoidable because of the need to nurse a close relative or dependent living in the same household is entitled to special nursing leave at full pay. For this purpose, the term *close relative* includes children and grandchildren, parents and grandparents, husband or wife, adopted and foster children, and common-law wife or husband. In any one year, the maximum time allowed for special nursing leave on full pay is the equivalent of one regular working week per employee. This rule applies to men and women alike. In families in which both parents do paid work, the man and the woman may take special nursing leave alternately.

The general law on the Protection of Expectant Mothers and Nursing Mothers (*Mutterschutzgesetz*) also includes a regulation specifically concerning working mothers who are still breast feeding their baby. Depending on the length of the workday, nursing breaks must be granted and may not be subtracted from other regular breaks to which the mother is entitled. Her pay must not be curtailed because of this time off.

The nursing leave has become well utilized, although parents are often under social pressures not to use it. However, the nursing breaks have not gained comparable acceptance among mothers. Currently unions are suggesting an extension of the nursing leave beyond the one-week period. Thus far, there has not been intensive political debate on this issue.

SUMMARY: ACHIEVEMENTS AND FAILURES OF PARENTING POLICIES IN AUSTRIA

Any general evaluation of parenting policies in Austria must begin with the fact that there is not a consistent goal behind these policies. The actual policies result from a partially implicit compromise among conflicting goals. Across the ''classical'' political groups that are active in family policy, both progressive and conservative views of the role of women and the role of families in society can be observed. The superficial compromise between the two positions can be defined as the goal of freedom of choice for each woman and also every father to do paid work in the labor market and/or to do family work. This compromise is indeed superficial since both parties seem to assume that if individuals are really free to choose, they will choose the specific ideology that the party endorses. In other words, it is not the idea of choice per se that makes the compromise sound but rather the hope for a particular result of the choices that will be made.

There is no doubt that the system of core programs has advanced the opportunity to choose between paid work and family work, and particularly for individuals to combine both aspects in their lives. Opinion polls make clear that women do not see paid work and family work as mutually exclusive alternatives but wish to combine both options in the long term. Maternity (and parental) leaves from paid work plus financial assistance during the leave are important steps in the right direction, as will be the new extension of this arrangement. However, these steps are not far-reaching enough to achieve the goal. Although the *Sondernotstandshilfe* has turned out to provide important help to single mothers and low-income couples, this program is not intended to serve a broader clientele. In other words, political decisions are pending concerning whether maternity leaves can and should be generally extended until children are ready to enter a preschool or day care program. If the age of 3 is the point decided upon, there will need to be additional efforts to gain another extension of the leave, unless the political choice is that society cannot relieve parents who want to combine paid work and family work of all the risks. If an extended leave up to age 3 were to prove possible, the problem of the shortage of preschool places would still have to be resolved.

While the cluster of leave arrangements is impressive, it must be recognized that the financial assistance element of the programs is accessible only to women who entered the labor force early enough before the birth of their first child to qualify for maternity benefits. Consequently, two groups of mothers are often excluded from the advantages of the program: very young mothers (although improvements have been made here by special arrangements) and mothers who stay home after their first child for at least two years and would need financial assistance after the birth of a later child.

This problem can be generalized to demonstrate another key issue in family policy: the core programs of parental policies are not for parents or children in general but specifically for employees with children. If a goal of parenting policy is a public appreciation for and support of family work and work with children, then support for parents and children should not be linked to previous work status. The consequence of such a position would be the generalization of the benefit side of the core programs toward a parent's salary or child-rearing grant (*Erziehungsgeld*). The first steps toward such a goal are being taken at the provincial level; little emphasis beyond the family allowance has been placed on it by federal parenting policies so far. There are, however, indications that this matter will become a high-priority and controversial issue during the next few years.

The issue of work-related benefits in parental policy is closely linked to another goal of family policy: the improvement of the economic situation of young families. In this area, the results of current parenting policies are ambiguous. Although substantial transfer payments are made to families, the economic situation of large families with only one breadwinner with a low social status, measured either in terms of income or in terms of expenditures, is poor. From this viewpoint, freedom of choice is obviously restricted. There is evidence that the vast majority of mothers in the paid labor force are working primarily out of economic pressure. They hardly have a choice between staying home and doing paid work. As a consequence, financial assistance to families must be much more directed to low-income groups. The most recent development in family allowances may be interpreted as a step in this direction.

Finally, population policy must be addressed. It is not clear whether parenting policies are intended to serve the goal of increasing fertility rates. At first sight, demographic developments seem to indicate that parenting policies have failed in this respect. Yet a deeper investigation brings up the question of how birthrates would have developed in Austria without the parenting policy. It is possible only to speculate on this point. There is no doubt that recent developments in parenting policies (in particular the extension of maternity leaves, the improvements for single mothers, and the provincial allowances) have contributed to a generally more favorable climate for raising children. However, the idea that incremental changes in family policy could directly lead to additional childbearing remains questionable, whether or not such a policy is seen as desirable.

NOTES

1. R. Gisser, "Familienstandsgliederung," in R. Gisser et al., *Lebenswelt Familie, Familienbericht 1989* (Wien: Bundesministerium für Umwelt, Jugend und Familie, 1990), p. 62.
2. Ibid., p. 66.
3. A. Haslinger, "Ehe ohne Trauschein," in *Demographische Informationen*, no. 1 (1981), pp. 13–35.
4. P. Findl, "Familie und Bevölkerungsentwicklung," in Gisser et al., *Lebenswelt Familie*, pp. 479–501.
5. P. Findl, "Geburtenentwicklung und Kinderlosigkeit," in *Statistische Nachrichten*, 1, no. 1, 1984, pp. 9–14, 206.
6. G. Biffl, "Der Wandel im Erwerbsverhalten in Österreich und im Ausland," in *Monatsberichte des Österreichischen Instituts für Wirtschaftsforschung*, no. 1, 1988, p. 44.
7. *OECD Employment Outlook* (Paris: OECD, 1988).
8. Ch. Badelt, *Familienzuschüsse des Landes Vorarlberg: Eine Analyse der zweiten*

Generation des geförderten Personenkreises (Bregenz: Amt der Vorarlberger Landesregierung, 1990), p. 48.

9. A. Klein, "Teilzeitbeschäftigung: Ergebnisse des Mikrozensus 1974–1987," in *Statistische Nachrichten*, no. 6, 1989, pp. 408–14.

10. Ch. Badelt, "Die ökonomische Situation der Familien in Österreich," in Gisser et al., *Lebenswelt Familie*, p. 175.

11. Ibid., p. 160.

12. Ibid.

13. Ibid.

14. R. Münz and G. Neyer, "Frauenarbeit und Mutterschutz in Österreich, Ein historischer Überblick," in R. Münz, G. Neyer, and M. Pelz, *Frauenarbeit, Karenzurlaub und berufliche Wiedereingliederung* (Linz: Österreichisches Institut für Arbeitsmarktpolitik, 1986), pp. 58–60.

15. R. Münz and G. Neyer, "Mutterschutzleistungen für unselbständig Beschäftigte: Wochengeld, Karenzurlaub, Sondernotstandshilfe," in Münz, Neyer, and Pelz, *Frauenarbeit*, p. 151.

16. Ibid., pp. 150–59.

17. R. Münz, "Beruf oder Familie?" in Münz, Neyer, and Pelz, *Frauenarbeit*, p. 249.

18. Ibid.

19. Ibid., pp. 254–55.

20. Münz and Neyer, "Frauenarbeit und Mutterschutz in Österreich," pp. 62–63.

21. Münz and Neyer, "Mutterschutzleistungen für unselbständig Beschäftigte," *Sondernotstandshilfe*," pp. 184–85.

22. Ibid., p. 194.

23. Ch. Badelt, "Finanzielle Familienförderung auf Landesebene-Erste Erfahrungen mit dem Vorarlberger Modell," in *Familienpolitik auf dem Prüfstand* (Wien: Zeitschriften Verlagsgesellschaft, 1989), p. 48.

24. Badelt, *Familienzuschüsse des Landes Vorarlberg.*

25. Münz, "Beruf oder Familie?"

26. Gisser et al., *Lebenswelt Familie, Familienbericht 1989.*

27. Badelt, "Die ökonomische Situation der Familien in Österreich," p. 200.

28. Ibid., pp. 170–72.

29. F. Köppl and H. Steiner, "Sozialhilfe—ein geeignetes Instrument zur Bekämpfung sozialer Not?" in Kammer Für Arbeiter und Angestellte, *Sozialhilfe* (Wien: Verlag des ÖGB, 1989), pp. 60–62.

30. R. Münz, *Familienpolitik, Gestern-Heute-Morgen* (Salzburg: Amt der Landesregierung, 1984), pp. 86–88, 92–93.

31. Badelt, "Die ökonomische Situation der Familien in Österreich," pp. 202–3.

32. Ibid., p. 204.

33. H. Fassmann, E. Aufhauser, and R. Münz, *Kindergärten in Österreich* (Wien: Bundesministerium für Umwelt, Jugend und Familie, 1988), pp. 14–18.

34. Ch. Badelt and P. Weiss, "Specialization, Product Differentation and Ownership Structure in Personal Social Services: The Case of Nursery Schools," *Kyklos*, 43, fasc. 1 (1990): 73.

35. Ibid., pp. 84–86.

36. Fassmann, Aufhauser, and Münz, *Kindergärten*, p. 38.

37. Ibid., pp. 51–53.

38. Ibid., p. 79.

3

GERMANY: RECOGNIZING THE VALUE OF CHILD REARING

Christiane Schiersmann

This chapter offers a survey of family policy measures in the Federal Republic of Germany (FRG). Because the greater part of this chapter was written in 1989, before the social upheaval in the German Democratic Republic and the subsequent reunification of the country, the situation in the East has not been considered.

To clarify and to interpret the political and policy strategies adopted, the first section outlines developments in both family structure and female labor market participation. The second section describes the history and evolution of family policy in West Germany. The chapter then focuses on the Federal Child Care Benefit Act (and Leave) (*Erziehungsgeld und Erziehungsurlaub* [child-rearing benefit and leave]), its development and its effects. This act, which grants mothers or fathers a child care benefit of DM (deutsche mark) 600 a month for a limited period during which their jobs are held for them, represents the most significant innovation in family policy in Germany during the 1980s and is the central element in this discussion of German family policy. The act can be regarded as an expression of a new political strategy to focus family policy primarily on families with very young children. The topic of the final section is family policy proposals and strategies for the future, which build on the innovations of the Child Care Benefit Act.

Inla-Marleen Gonzales, a research associate at the Institute of Women and Society (Hanover), assisted on this chapter.

CHANGES IN LIVING CONDITIONS IN THE FRG

Changes in Family Structure

In 1988 there were 23.4 million married couples and families in West Germany. Of these, 12.9 million (55 percent) were married couples or widowed, divorced, or separated people with no children. Some 10.5 million (45 percent) were married couples and single parents living with children. Of these 10.5 million, 52 percent had one child, 35 percent had two children, and 13 percent had three or more children.[1]

Paralleling a decline in the number of marriages, the number of divorces increased steadily from the mid-1960s. In 1987 there were about 530,000 divorces.[2] The risk of divorce is greatest in the first years after marriage and is much higher in urban than in rural areas.

The birthrate has also declined steadily since 1965, when 85.2 children were born per 1,000 women between the ages of 15 and 44. In 1985 this number was only 44.1; the birthrate was reduced by half. Additionally, the average age of the mother when giving birth to her first child rose from 24.9 in 1965 to 26.2 in 1985, and the average length of time the parents were married at the birth of their first child increased from 1.9 to 2.6 years. These statistics indicate that women are postponing childbirth for a longer time. In 1988 nearly 4 million families had one child, approximately 2.4 million families had two children, 585,000 families had three children, and 161,000 families had four or more children.

Participation of Women in the Work Force

In the last two decades, fundamental changes in the life situation of women have led to a clear increase in their orientation toward and participation in the work force. Younger women, in particular, now assign equal weight to the areas of career and family when planning their lives. Economic considerations are not the only reason that women have become increasingly likely to work, although an ever-increasing percentage of them can no longer depend on their husbands to support them during their whole lives. Alongside economic motives such as ensuring their own or the family income or becoming entitled to their own pension, they also desire to break out of the confines of their familiar surroundings. Longer life expectancy, the declining number of children, higher levels of education, increased self-assertiveness, and a greater claim to participate in society as a whole are relevant causal factors.

Nonetheless, German women, who in 1989 constituted only 39 percent of the labor force, have relatively low labor force participation rates compared to European women in general. The rise in the proportion of women between 15 and 65 who worked in West Germany from 49 percent in 1970 to 54 percent in 1984 was primarily a consequence of the increased labor force participation of women

Table 3.1
Hours of Work, Women and Men, March 1987

Length of work week	Female	Male	Total
Less than 21 hours	17.7	1.4	7.8
21--39 hours	27.2	22.7	24.5
40 or more hours	55.1	75.9	67.8
Total	100.0	100.0	100.0
Numbers (in 100s)	10,525	16,548	27,073

Source: Statistisches Bundesamt, Fachserie 1, Reihe 4.1.1, 1987. Results of Microcensus, 1987.

between 20 and 55, which has increased on average by about 10 percent. Among both 15- to 20-year-olds and 60- to 65-year-olds, labor force participation has actually decreased. In the first of these age groups, the decline has occurred because of longer schooling or training periods. In the latter, it is due to both an earlier retirement age and a decrease in the number of female family members who help out at home.

Clearly the number and ages of their children affect the labor force participation of women. With a total of working women of 32 percent in 1985, 47 percent of the women with a child under 15 were gainfully employed compared to only 41 percent in 1971 and only 37 percent in 1961.[3]

The rise in the proportion of working women can be seen most clearly in the changed labor force behavior of married women, a large contributory factor in the increased labor force participation of women in general. Between 1961 and 1984, the proportion of married women in gainful employment rose from about 35 percent to 49 percent.[4] The increase was particularly notable among married women between 35 and 55. It is generally accepted that with higher standards of education, fewer children, and a longer life expectancy, the labor force participation of women will increase even more in the future and also increase the ranking in comparison to other Western industrial nations.

In 1987, of more than 10 million employed women, 40.7 percent had children. Of all women with children under the age of 3 (about 1.5 million), 32.4 percent were gainfully employed. This total includes 31.9 percent of the married women with children under 3 and 38.2 percent of single women. Of all women who have children and who are part of the labor force, 12 percent have children under 3.

Because of the necessity of coordinating family responsibilities and gainful employment, many women work part time. In 1987 some 17.7 percent of employed women worked less than twenty-one hours a week and 27.2 percent less than forty hours a week (table 3.1). Women do not always choose part-time work of their own accord; in many cases this decision results from the lack of suitable public or private child care facilities.

The labor market behavior of West German women is influenced by the number and age of their children, their level of education (completion of vocational training), their present or previous profession, family social class, and household income.[5] (See table 3.2.) The husband's attitude to his wife's participation in the labor force is also a significant factor.

Although for women in West Germany, labor force participation represents self-sufficiency and economic independence and has also become an essential component of women's plans for their lives, this does no mean that the desire to have children is no longer significant. The realization of the desire to have children has totally different implications for men and for women. Women become confronted with two contradictory sets of role expectations. The situation in West Germany is characterized by the fact that, on the one hand, "the new image of female self-reliance" has established itself.[6] On the other hand, the traditional role of the woman as primarily concerned with her children and her family is still as relevant as ever. Especially when there are young children who need to be cared for, this traditional image with its implicit demands comes strongly to the fore.

Thus, women who consider confinement to one area of society—be it their job or their family—to be unacceptable are confronted with serious conflicts. As well as bearing a double burden, a working woman must come to terms with her guilt about the inadequate care her children may be receiving. On the other hand, there are the so-called only housewives, who are excluded from relevant areas of life and are thus permanently dissatisfied with their confinement to the family.

As a result of these conflicts, now as in the past, almost half of the working women in West Germany temporarily give up their jobs to take on family responsibilities. Younger women clearly tend to take much shorter leaves of absence. Among women up to 35 years of age, the average length of leave is currently three years.[7] Furthermore, it seems, in general, that marriage no longer provides the occasion for a leave from work, which is instead postponed until the birth of the first child and in some cases the birth of the second child. Similarly, the number of women who want to return to work after a leave is on the increase. A survey by the Institute for Labor Market and Job Research showed that 10 percent of women who were not working stated their desire to return to work, and 20 percent answered the question with "perhaps."[8] From 1980 to the end of 1985, almost 2 million women returned to work after a time away.

Facilities for Child Care

In view of the growing interest in gainful employment among women, it has become increasingly clear that the number of child care facilities for younger children in West Germany is totally inadequate. The number of available kindergarten places in 1987 could accommodate only 80 percent of the children between the ages of 3 and 6 (table 3.3). In general political discussions, and particularly in connection with the reform of the *Jugendhilfberecht* (Youth Services Law), which deals with the provision of kindergartens (for 3, 4, 5 year olds), demands were recently made for a law that would entitle every child between the ages of 3 and 6 to a kindergarten place. This demand foundered, however, mostly because of the

Table 3.2
Female Labor Force Participation by Family Status and Presence and Age of Children, 1987 (Women Ages 15–65)

	Number 000s	Total	Not in Labor Force	In Labor Force All	Full Time	P-T 21-39 hrs.	P-T up to 20 hrs.
All Women with Children			(%)	(%)	(%)	(%)	(%)
under Age 15	5,571	100%	58.3	41.7	15.9	11.4	14.5
under Age 6	2,746	100%	64.4	35.6	14.3	8.9	12.4
under Age 3	1,590	100%	67.6	32.4	___	___	___
Married with Children							
under Age 15	4,944	100%	59.9	40.1	14.6	10.7	14.8
under Age 6	2,481	100%	65.4	34.6	13.4	8.5	12.7
under Age 3	___	___	___	___	___	___	___
Single, with Children							
under Age 15	628	100%	45.0	55.0	25.8	17.0	12.1
under Age 6	265	100%	55.0	45.0	21.9	12.8	10.2
under Age 3	13	100%	61.8	38.2	___	___	___
Married, but separated with Children							
under Age 16	104	100%	57.9	42.1	___	___	___
under Age 6	50	100%	___	___	___	___	___
under Age 3	23	100%	___	___	___	___	___
Widows, with Children							
under Age 16	69	100%	45.5	54.5	___	___	___
under Age 6	13	100%	52.2	47.8	___	___	___
under Age 3	___	100%	58.8	41.2	___	___	___
Unmarried, with Children							
under Age 16	174	100%	39.2	60.2	___	___	___
under Age 6	123	100%	54.5	45.5	___	___	___
under Age 3	80	100%	62.0	38.0	___	___	___
Cohabiting, with Children							
under Age 16	280	100%	___	___	___	___	___
under Age 6	79	100%	___	___	___	___	___
under Age 3	29	100%	___	___	___	___	___
All Women	21,628	100%	51.2	48.8	27.2	___	___
All Men	29,292	100%	43.5	56.5	76.9	___	___

Source: "Population and Labor Force Participation." Specialist series 1, vol. 3 *Haushalte und Familien* (Households and Family) (1987), p. 170 (Stuttgart: Federal Statistics Office, 1989); author's calculations.

Note: Empty cells indicate unavailable data.

Table 3.3
Kindergartens and After-School Day Care Centers for Children Ages 3 to 6, 1960–1987

	Kindergartens[a]		Day Care Centers	
Year	Total Places Thousands	Places per 1000 Children	Total Places Thousands	Places per 1000 Children
1960	817.2	328	67.4	22
1965	952.9	327	73.6	21
1970	1160.7	384	72.9	18
1975	1478.9	655	82.7	21
1976	1463.0	705	85.0	23
1977	1441.0	755	87.6	25
1978	1396.9	773	101.7	31
1979	1390.7	784	104.5	35
1980	1392.5	787	105.7	38
1981	1396.5	793	107.4	41
1982	1335.0	769	86.8	37
1983[b]	1410.0	800	94.0	40
1984[b]	1435.0	801	98.0	42
1985[b]	1465.0	800	100.0	44
1986	1438.4	790	102.9	44
1987[b]	1415.0	790	100.0	44

Source: Federal Ministry of Education and Science, *Basic and Structural Data*, 1988/89 ed.

[a] Including kindergartens in Bavaria from 1980.

[b] Estimates.

opposition of the states with conservative governments; the determining factor was that the states are responsible for the financing of kindergartens.

It is almost more difficult for mothers of school-age children than for mothers of preschool-age children to pursue even half-day employment because there are fewer day care centers for school children outside school hours. Schools in West Germany, apart from the comprehensive schools, are almost without exception half-day schools, and primary school children in particular have irregular school hours, sometimes attending only two or three periods a day.

The provision of places in child care centers for the under 3s is totally inadequate. In 1982 1.5 percent of the children in this age group were provided for. According to the minister for culture in Lower Saxony, this figure has not substantially increased since then. Public provision for infant care has always been regarded as an emergency solution for families in crisis, not as an ongoing and normal service.

GENERAL FAMILY POLICY MEASURES

Various family policy measures are currently in place to augment the incomes of families with children. The costs of raising children are taken into consideration in a dual system of tax relief, largely by tax exemptions for children, and cash payments, including children's allowances and children's allowance supplements made by the state. The specific strategies of family policy have changed several times since 1945.

In 1953 the Ministry for Family Affairs was established in West Germany for the first time. The chancellor, Konrad Adenauer, explained that this ministry was created because of "the increasing percentage of old people in the population," that is, for demographic reasons.[9] The family policies of the first minister for family affairs were directed to bolstering the income of large families. The eight-point program covered, among other things, building houses for families, a monthly allowance for families with three or more children, tax exemptions for families with children, reductions for families on the Federal Railway, and more protection for wives and children who had been deserted.

From January 1955, a children's allowance of DM 25 was paid, starting with the third child. The funds came from contributions from employers and the self-employed, on the basis of a certain percentage of wages, and were paid out by the Family Burden Compensation Funds (*Familienlastenausgleichkasse*). Employers were critical of this form of taxation; resistance was especially strong among middle-sized and small businesses, which had a particularly heavy burden because the tax was based on wages. They also argued that because these costs had to be passed on by means of higher prices, the advantages to be gained by families with several children were greatly diminished. Moreover, the principle that industry had to raise the necessary funds was undermined from the beginning. Because families of unemployed people could not be excluded, funds for them had to be raised by the government. The Social-Democratic Party (SPD) also opposed this act and demanded that children's allowances be financed by federal resources.

When the payment of children's allowances was extended to the second child in 1961, industry was no longer willing or able to raise the funds. For this reason, the payment of the money for the second child was assumed by the government, and payment was made through the Federal Employment Agency (*Bundesanstalt für Arbeit*). Due to a shortfall of financial resources, an income limit was also set on money for the second child. Because the previous provision for the payment of the money for the third child and additional children was still valid, the system became extremely complex. The calculation of children's allowances was transferred to the Federal Employment Agency, and the Family Burden Compensation Funds were dissolved. The income limits were eliminated for families with three or more children and raised for two-children families. The total amount of the children's allowance was increased several times.

In 1975, the monthly allowance was DM 50 for the first child, 70 for the second, and 120 for the third and subsequent children. There were modest increases for second, third, and subsequent children from 1979. Children's allowances from 1982 were DM 50 a month for the first child, DM 100 for the second, DM 220 for the third, and DM 240 for the fourth child. The children's allowance for the second child was increased on July 1, 1990, from DM 100 to

DM 130. Since 1983 the children's allowance for parents with higher incomes has been gradually reduced to DM 70 for the second child and to DM 140 for the third and every additional child. (As reported by OECD, the average exchange rate for 1989 was DM 1.88 = U.S. $1.00) Thus, for a family with three children not in the higher income group, a 1987 child allowance monthly payment of DM 370 would have been equal to 9.5 percent of an average white-collar worker's monthly wage and 12 percent of the blue-collar worker's wage.

In 1974 only 9 percent of children's allowances were claimed by women. Currently about 80 percent of claimants and recipients are men. According to the 1974 Federal Pay Law (*Bundesbesoldungsgesetz*), children's allowances are granted only to the father and are granted in halves only on application of both parents; women and men are not equal in making claims even here, according to the law. The mother receives the children's allowance when she alone has the right to custody.[10] The children's allowance is not purpose specific; recipients can use it as they please.

Tax exemptions for children play a central role in family policy. From the beginning of the Federal Republic, an exemption of DM 600 each was granted for the first, second and third child. The size of the exemption was again increased, mainly for second and third children (e.g., in 1963, the tax-free allowances amounted to DM 1,200 for the first, DM 1,680 for the second, and DM 1,800 for the third and additional children). Because these exemptions reduced taxable income and thereby lowered the tax rate, families with higher incomes benefited most. Families with smaller incomes either did not benefit from these exemptions or did so only to a small extent. This effect was criticized as early as 1968 in the *First Family Report* of the federal government.[11] The conservative government found even the disproportionate advantages to higher-income families to be desirable and justified them with the argument that upper-income families have greater costs associated with a more expensive education and other expenses in keeping with their higher social standing.[12]

Following the changeover from a conservative to a social-liberal government, family policy changed dramatically. Some of the important changes included an effort to arrive at a more flexible definition of family; the Illegitimacy Act of 1969 and the Adoption Act of 1976 represent important legal steps in this direction. Additionally, family incentives were to be targeted less to the family as a whole and more to the needs of the children. Those aspects of the family incentives that favored higher-income families were also done away with, an aim largely achieved by the Children's Allowance Reform of 1975. The reform abolished the tax-free allowances and all other tax-related advantages for children. Instead, a children's allowance that was not dependent on income was now paid for the first child. The SPD was in favor of a reverse proportional children's allowance: the lower the income, the higher the amount of the children's allowance. They were opposed by their liberal partners in the coalition.

Since the beginning of the 1980s, a new system of family supports has been introduced by the federal government, which is headed by the Christian Democratic Union (CDU), together with the Free Democratic Party (FDP). This system consists of a complicated combination of children's and tax-free allowances and combines elements of the universal strategy with the policy thrust that favors higher-income families.

The current children's allowances have been summarized. The income tax exemption for children that was eliminated in 1975 was reintroduced in 1986 and raised to DM 2,484 per child. On January 1, 1990, the exemption was raised again to DM 3,024 per child. This allowance is intended to compensate for the fact that child-related expenses substantially reduce family income. (DM 3,024 on an annual basis may be compared to DM 3,384, the median white-collar monthly salary in 1987, and DM 2,875, the median blue-collar monthly woman's salary in 1987.) Since 1986, low-income parents who receive no or little advantage from the tax allowance for children have received a supplement of DM 48 a month per child to their children's allowance as compensation.

The combination of child allowances, a child allowance supplement (not available at upper-income levels), and tax allowances (for high-income families) had the result in 1986 of providing identical levels of subsidy to parents below the tax threshold and those with typical family incomes of DM 36,000 (DM 96 per month with one child, DM 242 with two, and DM 508 with three). Parents with high incomes, such as DM 100,000 taxable, received DM 141 with one child, DM 300 with two, and DM 528 with three.

Since January 1, 1990, the costs of employing household help, for whom a social insurance contribution is required, can be deducted from taxes as a work-related expense of up to DM 12,000 in households with at least one person needing care, or in the case of a single parent, at least one child, and for married couples two children, each under 10 years old. However, only very well-off families can benefit from this; the others cannot afford to employ household help.

Families with children who build or renovate property for their own living purposes may claim a tax deduction under the Children' Building Allowance (*Baukindergeld*). This allowance, introduced in the 1950s by the first minister for family affairs, has been greatly increased since 1986. For every child who is a member of the household during the period of construction, the income tax is reduced by DM 600. (Before 1987 this allowance was granted only to families with two or more children.) Within the framework of the Tax Reform Act of 1990, the children's building allowance has been increased to DM 750 a year per child for property acquired or built for living purposes after December 21, 1989. This tax measure also is of greatest advantage to upper-income families, the only ones in the Federal Republic who can afford to buy their own owner-occupied dwelling.

In comparison to the building allowance, rent assistance for needy families is a less impressive benefit. Because assistance can also be claimed by single or childless people, it is not primarily an aspect of family policy; however, the number of people in the household does affect the income ceiling on the rent allowance.

In 1986 the rent allowance was made somewhat more accessible to families in that households with several children are now treated more favorably than smaller households. The rent allowance for a four-person household was increased by more than DM 60 a month by the Sixth Rent Allowance Amendment, which became effective on January 1, 1986. A family allowance was introduced as an extra family policy measure to encourage the cohabitation of several generations and to facilitate the care of old people within the family rather than in a nursing home. This additional family allowance increased the rent allowance by DM 45 a month. Also, children between the ages of 16 and 25 who have their own incomes receive an allowance of DM 100 each in the calculation of the income limit for receiving the rent allowance. Finally, one might mention training allowances as another family policy measure, but these are reserved for families with older children (starting from the eleventh school year) and will not be discussed in greater detail here.

In a sense, the principle of married-couple tax splitting (*Ehegatten-Splitting*) can also be regarded as relevant to the family in that it is intended to ensure that marriage is the predominant form of cohabitation. Couple splitting has its origins in a change in the tax laws of 1958, which resulted from a ruling of the Federal Constitutional Court declaring that the tax law was unconstitutional because of the insufficient protection it provided to marriage and family, as well as to the equality of the wife. Under the old tax law, because of tax graduation, married couples with a double income paid much higher taxes than two single people with the same income. Under the splitting procedure valid today, the two incomes are added together, halved, and then taxed separately. This provision particularly favors families where the wife is not working. The more the husband earns, the more advantageous this is. This is based on the idea that married couples living together form a partnership in which each partner should share equally in the income and the expenses of the other.[13] It also expresses the equal status of the work of husband and wife in regard to both household tasks and gainful employment.

Since 1980 the Advance Maintenance Act has assisted the increasing number of single parents (in 1987, 86 percent were women) with maintenance advances (child support) or compensatory payments to single mothers and fathers of children up to 6 years old. The state assumes the minimal child support payment, which the noncustodial parent would otherwise have to make. Certain amounts are deducted, including previous payments made by the parent responsible for payment and, in general, half of the children's allowance payable for the first child. The base amount paid is adjusted periodically to changes in circumstances. Since July 1, 1989, it has amounted to a maximum of DM 251 a month for a maximum period of three years, or until the situation regarding the right to child support has been clarified. If possible, the amount paid is later recovered from the parent responsible for payment.

In addition to the standard family policy benefits, single parents receive a household tax exemption, which in 1988 amounted to DM 4,752 and was subsequently increased to DM 5,616 on January 1, 1990. A single parent can claim only half of the tax exemption for children if the other parent pays the required amount of child support. The deductibility of child support payments in taxation was extended in 1986 by raising the maximum amount from DM 3,600 to DM 4,500 and the tax exemption from DM 4,200 to DM 4,500 a month. As a result of the Fourth Act of Amendment of the Federal Social Welfare Act, single parents who are dependent on public assistance (those who cannot support themselves by paid employment and/or child support payments) have received an additional supplement of 20 percent since 1985. The Rent Allowance Act grants an allowance of DM 1,200 for every child under 12 in assessing the yearly income of single parents if they are absent from the household for a longer period of time to engage in employment or training.

Under certain conditions, child care costs are taken into account in assessing the income tax of single parents. Substantial expenditures for the care of children up to 16 years old that arise because of employment, handicap, or chronic illness are tax deductible as an extraordinary burden up to DM 4,000 for the first child and up to DM 2,000 for each additional child. Without supplying documentation, a flat rate of DM 480 per child can be deducted. Since January 1, 1990, single parents have been eligible for this deduction and can deduct DM 12,000 a year for household help requiring social insurance payments. However, only a few single parents can benefit from this provision because most cannot afford household help.

The Surviving Dependents' Pension and the Period of Child Care Act that became effective in 1986 allows mothers (or fathers) born after 1921, who have been drawing a disability or an old age pension, to receive credit in the official pension insurance plan for one year of care for each child in either starting a pension or increasing an existing one. During the child care year—the twelve months starting at the end of the month in which the child is born—mothers (or fathers) are considered equal to employed people, with 75 percent of the average wage credited to them. In cases where the person rearing the child has already received social security benefits at a level of at least 75 percent of average wage, the period of child care is not added into the benefit computation. In individual cases, child care can substantiate a claim for a pension; the minimum period of pension insurance was reduced from fifteen to five years, so that five years of child care (the care of five children) would entitle the parents to a minimal pension. In 1988 each child care year credited increased a monthly pension by DM 28 per child.

On the basis of the Undertaking of Child Care Act (*Kindererziehungsleistungsgesetz*), mothers born before 1921 are gradually becoming entitled to in-

Table 3.4
Family Policy Expenditures through Direct Payments and Tax Exemptions, 1989 (DM Millions)

Tax free allowance Kinderfreibetrag:	7,900
Other family-related tax reductions Andere familienbezogene Steuerermässigungen:	4,485
Child-care benefit Erziehungsgeld:	4,000
Consideration of child-care time in pension Kindererziehungszeiten in der Rente:	2,990
Children's allowance and Children's allowance supplement	14,100
Training allowance Federal Part Ausbildungsförderung Bundesanteil:	1,520
Federal Foundation "Mother and Child" Bundesstiftung "Mutter und Kind":	130
Maintenance Advance Federal Part Unterhaltsvorschuss Bundesanteil:	96
Married couple tax splitting Ehegattensplitting:	25,700
Total:	60,921
Subtotals:	
Money Transfers Geldleistungen:	22,836
Tax allowances Steuerbereich:	38,085

Source: Federal Ministry of Youth, Family, Women and Health, *Materials on Family Policy* (Bonn, 1989).

clude in their pension claims the child care they provided. It was generally regarded as being unjust to limit the entitlement to those born after 1921 and was justified by the government on fiscal grounds. Eligible persons receive a contribution toward child care, currently DM 28 a month, regardless of whether they were previously eligible for a pension, that is, whether or not they were employed during the child's first year.

Table 3.4 summarizes the federal financial expenditure for family policies. Since the 1950s, there has been a shift in emphasis from support for larger families to assisting all kinds of families. In certain respects, during the 1980s, the conservative-liberal government took new notice of the fact that marriage and family do not have the same binding power as they did in the past. This awareness is expressed, for example, through increased assistance to single parents. Moreover, there seems to be an emerging tendency to align family policy measures more closely to certain phases of life, reflected, for example, in the passage of the Federal Child Rearing Benefit Act of 1986.

MEASURES SUPPORTING THE CARE OF VERY YOUNG CHILDREN

Provisions of the Child Care Benefit Act (FCCBA)

The introduction of child care (or child rearing) benefits and child care leave (*Erziehungsgeld und Erziehungsurlaub*) is a central theme in any discussion of family policy measures. The Federal Child Care Benefit Act (FCCBA) (*Bundeserziehungsgeldgesetz, BErzGG*) came into effect on January 1, 1986. On the basis of the Protection of Mothers Act (*Mutterschutzgesetz*) of 1974, which is still in effect, working women are granted leave for six weeks before and eight weeks after the birth of their child (twelve weeks for multiple births). Furthermore, this act prohibits the dismissal of an employee from the time her pregnancy is announced until four months after delivery. The amount of the maternity benefit is determined by average earnings and comes to DM 25 per day or DM 750 a month, with the difference between the maternity benefit and the possibly higher previous average monthly income to be paid by the employer. The act also protects pregnant women and new mothers by various regulations. For example, women who produce a medical certificate cannot be expected to perform strenuous physical tasks in the first months after delivery, and they must be allowed to breast-feed during working hours.

The recent child care and leave act (FCCBA) produced several significant advances over the Protection of Mothers Act. First, the act extends the entitlement to all mothers and fathers, while the Protection of Mothers Act applied only to working women. Additionally, the act provides for protection against dismissal for a longer period of time (twelve months up to mid–1989, fifteen months from July 1, 1989, and eighteen months from July 1, 1990). It also guarantees a child caring or child rearing benefit of DM 600, independent of the family income for the first six months and on a means-tested basis thereafter. (DM 600 was 15 percent of a median white-collar monthly wage in 1987 and 25.8 percent of a median blue-collar female wage.) The shorter periods for the guaranteed benefit were initially explained ''by the poor state of the economy,'' not by the aims of family policy. A three-year period is now being sought, with the intention of allowing a transfer of benefits from at-home care to a preschool program.

Before examining the provisions of FCCBA in greater detail, we should consider the motivation for and objectives of this piece of legislation. It is based on the principle of freedom of choice, advanced primarily by the CDV, that people rearing children should be given a choice between working and staying home, as well as which parent should assume responsibility for child care. The ability of both parents to claim child care benefits or leave reflects the partnership principle introduced in 1977 in marriage and family law to support the equivalency of paid work and work in the home. The legislation is also intended to ensure that one parent takes primary responsibility for child care because the legislators considered consistency of care to be important to children during their early years.

The plan for implementation of FCCBA referred to the beneficial side effect that it would have on the labor market during periods of high unemployment by leading to the temporary employment of workers to replace women on child care leave. It was also expected that some of the women who use the leave would not return to their jobs, providing their temporary replacements with the opportunity of permanent employment. (This argument is deceptive, however, from the perspective of labor market policy. At a time when unemployment averages 2 million, the only employment benefit that results is a substitution of one worker for another rather than the creation of new jobs.) Finally, the FCCBA was expected to encourage pregnant women who were uncertain about whether to continue their pregnancy to do so.

Those entitled to the benefit must live in the Federal Republic, care for the child themselves, and not have a full-time job. Eligibility applies not only to persons with natural children but also those with adoptive and stepchildren. Unmarried natural fathers cannot claim the benefit because it is assumed that there is no close relationship between him and the child and the natural mother. This exclusion corresponds with family law, which also excludes unmarried fathers as a matter of principle. Persons belonging to the European Community may also claim the benefit if they are employed in the Federal Republic. A one-time change from mother to father as claimant is permitted for a very good reason if both are eligible to claim the benefit. Persons who are employed for fewer than nineteen hours a week are also eligible. (From 1991, nineteen hours of work will ensure full eligibility for social benefits.)

Those eligible for the child care benefit receive DM 600 a month for six months. Payment after the sixth month is dependent on an income test. An income of up to DM 23,700 for single parents and DM 29,000 for married couples does not affect eligibility; the full amount is still paid. In calculating a family's full eligibility, a further allowance of DM 4,200 is granted for every additional child. The income test applies to family income, excluding the earnings of the parent who will stay at home to provide the care (table 3.5).

The child care benefit is tax free. Means-tested social payments are discounted up to DM 600. Social payments such as social assistance or the rent allowance, which are made according to need, are not taken into account. Receipt of the child care benefit does not rule out the entitlement to unemployment insurance if the person caring for the child was previously employed; however, unemployment insurance and the child care benefit cannot be drawn simultaneously.

Employed mothers do not come under FCCBA in the first two months after the birth of their child. They receive wage compensation according to the Ma-

Table 3.5
Income Ceilings for Child Care Benefit Eligibility (in DM)

INCOME CEILINGS (NET)

Married couples with one child	Single parents with one child	Benefit
-2,450	-1,975	600
2,800	2,325	460
3,150	2,675	320
3,500	3,025	180
3,850	3,375	40

Source: Federal Minister for Youth, Family, Women, and Health: ''Child-care Benefit, Child-care Leave and Crediting Periods of Child-care in Annuity Insurance,'' document series of the Federal Minister for Youth, Family, Women, and Health, vol. 243. (Stuttgart, 1989), pp. 36ff.

Note: Add DM 350 for each child beyond the first.

ternity Act, which is based on their previous earnings and is usually higher than the child care benefit. Only in special cases where wages are very low would the maternity benefit need to be topped off by the child care benefit.

FCCBA and the Protection of Mothers Act, which is still in effect, pursue different aims. The intention of the Protection of Mothers Act, according to the Federal Constitutional Court, is to resolve the conflict between the woman's responsibility as a mother and as a member of the work force in the interests of preserving the health of mother and child.[14] Consequently, the maternity benefit serves the function of preserving the mother's standard of living before her pregnancy began. In contrast, the payment of the child care benefit is based exclusively on providing for the upbringing and care of children.

As a result, the act has different effects on mothers who worked before the birth of their child and those who did not work. The family income of women who were not working before their child was born is increased by DM 600 net; that is, they are ''rewarded'' for not working by the payment of the child care benefit. Financially there is a danger that this benefit will encourage traditional marriages, in which wives remain economically dependent on their husbands. Particularly in times of high unemployment, this provision could lead women of childbearing age to have a child because of the difficulty of finding a job rather than continuing to seek employment.

The act is particularly inadequate for those who must rely on their earnings to cover their living expenses. This group, which primarily includes single parents, must earn the amount in addition to the child care benefit they need to cover their expenses. If they cannot earn enough during the nineteen hours a week they are allowed to work while receiving the benefit, they must then decide whether to forgo the child care benefit altogether and work full time, an enormous burden for single parents, or claim social assistance, which at most will allow them to live at the subsistence level. (The poverty line or social help eligibility threshold is about DM 1,451 monthly for a single mother with two children, including DM 492.20 for the mother, DM 287 for the children, and about DM 665 for housing. Housing and heating grants, as well as clothing lump sums, vary somewhat.)

Furthermore, as a precondition for claiming social assistance, applicants must consider the question of whether other persons, especially their parents, have an obligation to support them (relative responsibility under social assistance). Because many young women do not want to ask their parents for financial assistance, a sizable percentage of those eligible do not claim social assistance. The limit on the amount of permissible work, which also applies to single mothers, clearly shows that the law is based on a traditional definition of the family as a married couple with children and is not oriented primarily toward the child and his or her caretaker.

Even more of a problem for parents who are dependent on their jobs for their income is the FCCBA regulation that permits parents to work part time only for their former employer. The justification offered for this regulation is that during child care leave, the employee's obligation to work and the employer's obligation to pay wages lie dormant while the secondary obligations continue. The employer could not be expected to keep jobs vacant for women who are employed by another employer during their time of leave.

This regulation is considered unfair because employees are not legally entitled to part-time work during their child care leave, which essentially provides financial support to stay home during their child's early childhood, with the ability to work part time only if the employer agrees. Should the employer refuse to reduce the work week to a maximum of nineteen hours, then the women concerned have no chance of obtaining part-time employment.

In any case, employees who work part-time in West Germany are at a grave disadvantage regarding career advancement. Therefore FCCBA's stipulation that women can work only on a part-time basis while they are looking after their young children and claiming the benefit places them at a greater disadvantage in the workplace and also limits the role of the wife to that of a secondary income earner.

By allowing a maximum of only nineteen hours of employment per week, the act makes a reduction of the workweek a precondition to claiming the benefit. Thus, women cannot receive child care benefits if they do not wish to or cannot interrupt or reduce their hours of work because their jobs are so responsible that the hours cannot be shortened or because their employers will not permit them to do so. However, women who continue to work full time after their child is born also take on child care responsibilities, which in many cases entail a greater burden and greater costs than do mothers in part-time employment or mothers who are not working. By means of their tax payments, they also contribute toward the children's allowance for the other mothers. This clearly shows that the child care benefit is not intended to pay for the child care and the expenditure involved. Instead, it is meant as an incentive to take a leave from work. From the point of view of the government, the personal care of the child is of greater significance than the mother's paid employment.

The second component of FCCBA beyond the cash benefit is a child care leave for men and women in the work force for up to eighteen months after July 1, 1990. Those eligible to claim this leave include men and women in jobs with social insurance deductions, as well as women whose maternity protection has expired, on the condition that they claim their child care benefit whether or not they actually receive it. The employer must be informed of the child care leave and its intended duration at least four weeks before the leave is taken. An extension after the agreed period of leave is possible only if one parent was expecting to turn over the responsibility for child care to the other but was unable to do so for a good reason. Employees normally come back to work on the same terms on which they left. From the perspective of labor law, only the major responsibilities are dormant (the performance of work); the minor obligations (loyalty and right to payments) are not.

FCCBA can, however, also be criticized for its inadequate protection against dismissal, which in many respects is a watered-down version of the protection granted by the Maternity Leave Act. The ban on termination in the Maternity Leave Act covered the period of maternity leave as well as the two months that followed. In contrast, FCCBA's ban on termination covers only the period of child care leave. Moreover, the highest state authority (in most cases the Trade Supervisory Office) can grant permission in exceptional circumstances for the dismissal of the person taking child care leave. Permission can be granted, for example, to small companies with fewer than six employees or if the employer is in a difficult financial situation or cannot find a suitable replacement for the employee. This last aspect particularly affects women in highly skilled jobs or managerial positions for whom a replacement cannot easily be found, especially because many employers do not believe that a temporary worker can satisfactorily assume managerial functions. To what extent these exceptions are actually granted is not yet clear; so far, experience has been limited, and few dismissals have yet occurred.

All things considered, the general ban on termination does not provide full security for employees who want to return to their former jobs. Only when the relevant employment contract specifically mentions the performance of a particular task can the persons concerned make a claim to return to this job.

Claiming of the Child Care Benefit

In 1987 the child care benefit was claimed by 97 percent of those eligible, which would seem to indicate that this measure is very widely accepted. In 98.5 percent of the instances, however, the benefit is claimed by women; it is claimed by men in only 1.3 percent of instances. In 0.2 percent of the cases in 1987, one parent turned over responsibility for child care to the other at some point.

The reason that mainly women claim the benefit is that they generally fulfill their traditional gender-related roles, which still include the lion's share of family and child care responsibilities. Furthermore, the amount of the benefit, DM 600, does not provide full compensation for wages, and it is more advantageous financially for women, who generally earn less than men, to claim it because the resultant drop in income for a married couple is usually not so severe.

The child care benefit fulfills the intention of the federal government of recognizing the child care contribution of one parent and the value of family work as compared to the paid employment of women. However, there is no connection made in the discussion between the size of the benefit and the actual costs of rearing a child.

In 1987 45.9 percent of the total number of people receiving the child care benefit were employed prior to receipt, and 54.1 percent were not employed; a similar proportion of working women (46.1 percent) and nonworking women (53.0 percent) received the benefit. A surprisingly high number (70.3 percent) of the relatively few men receiving the benefit were unemployed. Claiming the child care benefit is clearly attractive to men only if it is not accompanied by a decline in living standards caused by either fewer working hours or temporary unemployment. For unemployed men, the child care benefit provides extra money, just as it does for nonworking women, and does not entail any material or immaterial sacrifice.

Of the 271 thousand women claiming the benefit in 1987, 95 percent used the leave without part-time work, 2.5 percent also worked part time, and 2.5 percent worked part time and did not receive the leave. Of the 2 thousand men drawing the benefit, 78 percent took the leave without part-time work, 8.3 percent also worked part time, and 13.6 percent had part-time work without the leave.[15]

In the first three years since the introduction of FCCBA, 97 percent of all parents of newly born children—1.8 million—including about 20,000 fathers, received child care benefits; about 84 percent of single parents received the benefit, with single parents comprising 9.7 percent of all recipients. Only 6 percent of the claimants in 1987 returned to their jobs before their leave expired. Only in a very few cases did the Trade Supervisory Office permit a dismissal. In fact, the number of dismissals permitted during child care leave was even lower than under the Protection of Mothers Act. According to the ministry press office, after the sixth month, when the benefit becomes income-tested, 79 percent of the recipients continued to receive the full benefit, 11 percent received a reduced amount, and 10 percent received no payment at all. There has been some surprise at the large proportion of young families with modest incomes.

In 1986, the first year of the program, expenditures were DM 1,653.7 million, rising to DM 3,170 million in 1987 and DM 3,800 million in 1989. The 1990 preunification estimate was DM 3,650 million.

Child Care Leave and Part-Time Work in the Public Sector

The public sector has a long tradition of limited leave taking—reducing working hours to permit child care. In 1969 regulations were passed granting child care leave to women judges and state officials; the first draft gave women child care leave of up to twelve years, according to family situation and age and number of children to be cared for. In 1974 the range of eligible persons was extended to include men to comply with the equality principle of the Constitution, and the period of leave was extended first to fifteen years and in 1984 to eighteen years and, in exceptional circumstances, to twenty-three years. Since 1974 other dependents in need of care, as well as children, are included in the group of persons for whom leave can be claimed. Along with these increasingly generous provisions of leave for dependent care, the provisions of FCCBA also apply to women state officials and judges and enable them to receive the child care benefit.

The introduction of the regulations for child-rearing leaves and part-time work in the public services was motivated by changes in the social status of women, particularly by the declining role of marriage as the principal means of support for women, the growth in the number of working women, and the resulting demands to make work responsibilities more compatible with family responsibilities. The first draft of the law, however, implicitly assigned responsibility for family duties to women, making them the only people eligible to claim the benefits.

The available data concerning the use of the part-time work and leave-taking provisions do not break down the claims according to either sex or career groups. What is clear is that there is a higher rate of claiming in individual authorities, such as the Federal Post Service and Federal Railway, in the Ministry of Finance, and among women teachers. There has also been a clear reduction in the number of women civil servants who leave public service because of marriage or child care. Higher management positions were regarded as being generally incompatible with claims for child care benefits, and employers can turn down applications by managers for part-time work and child care leave in the interest of the efficiency of the organization.[16]

The part-time work and child care leave regulations apply only to women state officials and judges. For workers in the public sector, the respective federal or state regulations for child care leave and receiving the child care benefit apply. Possibilities for taking long-term child care leave are included in the wage regulations of the government. Additionally, a ruling by the Federal Labor Court has made it possible since 1989 to take unpaid special leave to care for children so long it does not conflict with the needs of the employer. The conditions surrounding leave taking are regulated by the state, and the specifications concerning length of leave are based on the provisions for state officials but are basically left to the discretion of the employer.

A Pilot Project in Lower Saxony and State Provisions

A Pilot Project in Lower Saxony. Even before the FCCBA became law, the state of Lower Saxony tested a model with somewhat different benefit levels, no job protection, and including only those with labor force attachments. Claim totals were smaller than under the subsequent federal law.

The regional differences were interesting. In structurally weak areas, more women gave up gainful employment in order to draw the child care benefit because this money was necessary to maintain their standard of living. The scientific advisory board suggested that mothers be allowed to work part time.[17] Basically the experience indicates that married couples with one breadwinner need child care benefits to compensate for the loss of the wife's earnings; single parents without another breadwinner cannot afford to claim it.

State Provisions. Individual states have introduced extra provisions to complement the current federal provisions. For example, the state of Baden-Württemberg has had a family benefit plan since 1983, which lasts for a maximum of two years and provides a maximum payment of DM 4,800 during that time. In keeping with the state government's aim that one parent provide comprehensive personal care while the child is young, leaving work completely was initially made a condition of eligibility for benefits. In 1984 not quite 19 percent of the claims made by eligible parents were made on this basis (excluding multiple births).[18]

Since 1986, in coordination with the Federal Child Care Benefit Act, the state family benefit is paid for twelve months after the Federal Child Care Benefit. However, the state benefit in Baden-Württemberg is DM 400 a month, lower than the federal benefit, and it also carries a lower income ceiling. Receiving benefits in Baden-Württemberg after the Federal Child Care Benefit has ended does not rule out limited work with an income limit of under DM 450 a month.

These state provisions tend to disqualify parents who are considered eligible for FCCBA benefits. Furthermore, the period during which a worker claims state child care benefits is not taken into account in calculating pension benefits. Protection against dismissal is not extended beyond the period of time covered by the Federal Child Care Benefit Act.

There have been earlier variations as well in Berlin (from 1983) and Rhineland-Palatinate (from 1984).

Company Agreements and Wage Agreements

Company Agreements. Along with the countrywide provisions for child care leave and the complementary provisions of the states, there is a tendency for companies, and especially large ones, to make company agreements that are similar in intention but cover a longer period of time than do the provisions for child care leave. Through company agreements negotiated between work councils and management, benefits can be provided at the company level that are not covered exclusively by legislation or by wage agreement between the parties involved.

The first large company to make such an agreement was the firm Messerschmidt-Bölkow-Blohm GmbH (MBB). This agreement is still valid today in a more contemporary form, and many other firms have followed this example.[19] The central theme of these company agreements or programs is a more or less binding assurance of reemployment after the employment relationship has been interrupted in order to take on child care and/or the possibility of continuing the employment relationship in part-time form at the end of the legal child care leave.

In examining the wording of these agreements with regard to their binding force, we see that the agreements vary considerably in their value to employees. Not all employees of a company are always entitled to take advantage of its agreement. In some cases, only women are eligible, although most company agreements now refer to mothers and fathers. Some firms such as BASF set a certain length of employment as a precondition for receiving benefits, while in others only certain groups of employees are included (e.g., permanent employees who have completed vocational training at AUDI) or certain groups of employees are excluded (e.g., the managerial staff at BOSCH). As a rule, the leave granted from work is valid only for the first years of child care. In some firms, however, employees can also be granted leave for special family or social duties (e.g., in the Leonberger Bausparkasse and the Volksfürsorge). The length of the leave is limited, according to each company's specifications, to between three and seven years after the birth of the child. The actual value of an agreement facilitating the return to work after a leave depends on the binding force of the commitment to reemployment.

Only in exceptional cases (e.g., Leonberger Bausparkasse or MBB since 1990) is there a provision to suspend the employment relationship when leave is granted. Normally the employment relationship is dissolved if mothers or fathers resign so that a new employment contract must be negotiated when they return to their jobs. Many company agreements contain relatively vague language; for example, they talk of favoring the reemployment of women who are returning to their jobs, which implies that no legal claims can be made. What happens if a company has no available employment for women returning to their jobs or if a company goes bankrupt is not clear.

Generally the commitment to reemployment refers to a job that is equivalent to the earlier one or utilizes the vocational knowledge and ability of the person concerned. It does not refer to the job previously held. Receiving the same wage scale as before the job break is not always guaranteed; that is, in some cases less favorable wages cannot be ruled out.

Most of the company agreements contain provisions for part-time work, but whether part-time work is actually allowed depends on the company. It is also repeatedly and explicitly stated that no claim can be made to change a full-time employment arrangement to a part-time one after returning to work (e.g., Wüstenrot and BASF).

Qualifying for company agreements in some cases is bound by certain conditions that must be fulfilled during the leave—for example, a willingness to substitute for people on vacation or sick leave or participation in further training measures proposed by the company (BAYER and AUDI). Some firms (BAYER, MBB, and AUDI) tie their commitment to reemployment to the condition that during the leave, the employee cannot enter an employment relationship with another employer for even casual, temporary, or part-time work. Besides the obligations to participate in training, some firms offer training on a voluntary basis.

Also significant is the extent to which and the conditions under which the length of service before the leave and periods of temporary work during the leave are credited to the length of employment in calculating pension benefits. The Wüstenrot group provides full credit for previous service. In other companies, credit for previous service depends on employment for a certain length of time after rejoining the work force. Limited employment during the period of leave is calculated only as part of the length of service in some companies. Only MBB includes the period of leave itself in the length of service and credits it as a period of eighteen months, regardless of the actual length of leave taken.

Wage Agreements. In a few cases, wage settlements that include family provisions have been negotiated, specifically by the Trade Union for Food, Catering and Restaurants. Wage agreements have a broader impact than do company agreements because they give the work councils the opportunity and the obligation to act on behalf of the company's employees by demanding that the promises made become reality through conversion into concrete regulations. The real value of these wage agreements can be assessed when put into practice.

Experiences with Claims. Because most of the company agreements and programs and wage agreements discussed have been in effect only for a short time, there are only limited data concerning employees' experiences in claiming benefits and returning to their jobs.

CONSEQUENCES OF THE PROVISIONS OF CHILD CARE BENEFITS AND LEAVE FOR FAMILY LIFE, FERTILITY, AND THE LABOR MARKET

Family Life

Child care leave and the payment of child care benefits have no obvious direct effects on the beneficaries' attitudes toward their children, response to their needs, or stimulation of their development. These benefits primarily affect the condition or framework of the child rearing task, and particularly the factors of money, time, and societal recognition of family work.[20]

For families in which the mother was not employed before the birth of her child, the benefits result in a clear financial improvement. The more meager are the family's financial resources, the greater is the effect of the benefits. What remains open is the question of whether child care benefits are in fact used to improve the family budget, because payment is not tied to proof of particular use of the funds.

With regard to the time factor, child care leave has the greatest effect in families where both parents previously worked full time. The leave provisions, however, cannot guarantee that the extra available time is devoted to the children. Child care leave and benefits therefore represent above all general assistance for families as a supportive environment for parents and small children. They also make a contribution, although a small one and only for a limited period, toward compensating for the previously low status of family tasks.

Fertility

Because the individual decision to have a child is dependent on a multitude of factors, the extent of the influence of the payment of childrens' allowances and the granting of child care leave on this decision can be determined only indirectly and approximately. One can only speculate about which obstacles that may deter people who want children from having them can be overcome by the variety of leaves and benefits described. One obstacle for working women could be the disadvantages arising from leaving their jobs. A maximum child care benefit of DM 600 certainly does not fully compensate for this loss of income. Additionally, the benefit is paid for only a very limited time—currently eighteen months. In the future, the availability and cost of child care after the child care leave is over will be important factors in determining how children will be cared for. Child care leave and benefits represent only temporary solutions, particularly in times of high unemployment when parents worry about whether they will be able to return to work eventually.[21]

Although the clear effects of these family policy measures on reproductive behavior cannot be determined, one can assume that the measures improve the social situation of families, that children's development is enhanced, and that at least a symbolic contribution has been made toward increasing the status of family responsibilities.

The Labor Market

Because of the relatively short span of the initial child care leave, there have not yet been any discernable consequences on the labor market; however, one can estimate the likely effects from the experiences of the Protection of Mothers Act and model projects with comparable provisions.

Because of the almost constant birthrate, approximate figures can be projected. At a 95 to 98 percent rate of claiming the child care benefit, not quite 272,000 persons would claim child care leave annually. Taking as a basis the likely number of working women in this group, 130,000 jobs thus would be vacant. Since only one job in two is temporarily filled by a replacement, there is a consequent labor market easing of about 65,000 jobs.[22]

The actual rate of return to work immediately after the end of child care leave is only slightly over 60 percent, as indicated by experiences with maternity leave and the developments in Austria.[23] Moreover, one can assume from the Austrian experience that only two-thirds of those women go back to work with their former employers. Consequently, only about 90,000, or less than 1 percent of all working women, actually need protection against dismissal from their jobs. Thus, protection against dismissal is relatively unimportant to the economic situation of firms. A higher than average rate of claiming of child care leave could occur in traditional women's jobs and have greater impact on those firms. However, a large number of those women who wish to return to work after a leave for family purposes look for part-time jobs.[24] Therefore, one can expect a growing demand for part-time jobs, particularly since the number of working women in the middle age groups could increase because of the provisions of child care leave. In comparison to earlier experience, one can expect an earlier reentry.

Companies' Personnel Needs

The introduction of FCCBA was strongly criticized by employers' groups because of the extra burdens placed upon them. One might assume that this attitude could affect their willingness to employ women who might use the provisions of the program. On closer observation, however, the burdens of FCCBA for employers are much smaller than those associated with maternity leave, which is still in effect. Moreover, maternity leave costs for firms have increased in the last few years because women's salaries rose and employers were required to make up the difference between the government benefit and the woman's wage. Together with a simultaneously increasing percentage of working women, this discrepancy has led to growing wage costs, particularly in companies with a large percentage of women. The reservations expressed about FCCBA often reflect these experiences.

A direct burden on the cost of wages for companies arises under the FCCBA only if a replacement worker must be hired at a higher wage or if the employment of the replacement entails particular expenses. At any rate, experience has shown that because of the large pool of unemployed people, replacements can usually be acquired for a lower wage.

The greatest burdens occur primarily in small and medium-size companies, as well as those with a high percentage of women workers. The problems of small companies with fewer than five employees have already been taken into consideration in FCCBA, which allows protection against dismissal to be suspended if it leads to unreasonable hardship for the company. For the burdens that remain for small firms or companies with a large percentage of women workers, these provisions could be met by creating a pool of temporary workers.

VIEWS ABOUT THE FURTHER DEVELOPMENT OF CHILD CARE LEAVE AND BENEFITS

A report by the Scientific Advisory Board to the Ministry for Family Affairs has advocated an extension of the length of child care benefit through the third year of the child's life.[25] This proposal is based on the results of research in developmental psychology, which regards the first three years of a child's life to be of central importance for personal development. Furthermore, the board refers to the fact that thus far child care facilities are available to any significant extent only beginning with the child's third year (kindergarten). The board rejects an extension of child care leave to more than three years because of the fact that an overly long leave from work adversely affects the chances of women (or men) to resume their previous employment.

In the view of the advisory board, the amount of the child care benefit is inadequate. A future increase is called for although for an amount less than the income from wages. Furthermore, the board has called for a standard child care benefit regardless of income. They oppose a means-tested benefit because its function is to compensate for the task of child care, not to correct a life situation that is difficult for other reasons. In any case, they propose that child care benefit should be increased in accordance with the general cost of living.

The Scientific Advisory Board asserts that child care leave should be extended to three years, complementary to a three-year child care benefit. It also suggests that during child care leave and while drawing benefits, the parents should have a joint time budget for gainful employment available to them—for example, one and a half times the normal working week. Half of this time budget could be established as the maximum working hours for single parents. The parents in a two-parent family could decide how to divide this time budget between them. This recommendation would also strengthen the partnership model of the family policy provisions because a sharing of child care and family responsibilities would be more likely if neither partner were required to restrict severely the amount of time worked.

The Scientific Advisory Board recommended suspending the restrictions on part-time work up to nineteen hours a week during child care leave because this amount of work did not require the payment of social insurance contributions. As of 1991 a full nineteen hours is permitted, creating benefit eligibility.

The question of child care benefits and leave is not a central theme in political discussion, particularly because most of the existing measures are supported by a broad spectrum of political parties, with differences of opinion confined to details. The CDU, which is represented in the federal government, advocates essentially preserving existing conditions while extending child care leave and benefits to three years; the FDP, also in the government, is more cautious, particularly with regard to child care leave and the protection against dismissal associated with it because of their concern that the burdens on companies could become too great and therefore deter them from hiring womem. The SPD also advocates in principle the extension of the child care benefit to three years, and it particularly calls for improved labor legislation. It is opposed to improving the benefits to women who were previously unemployed in comparison with those of working women.[26] It favors a higher child care benefit for single mothers.

The Greens go further than the other parties by calling for a three-year time allowance for child care leave during the first twelve years of the child's life, with a job guarantee and income compensation. They also propose that in two-parent families, the claim for parental leave and a reduction of working hours should be shared by both parents. Men and women on child care leave should have the same rights as those in full-time employment to training, retraining, and advancement.[27] In a report commissioned by the Greens, Geissler/Pfau suggested a model for temporary, subsidized part-time work as a legal right during the rearing of small children.[28]

CONCLUSIONS

German federal family policy has evolved considerably. In the postwar period, the emphasis was on providing support to large families to prevent financial hardship. In the 1970s family policy measures were extended to all families. During the term of office of the social-democratic-liberal government, tax relief for families was abolished in favor of a uniform children's allowance. Beginning in the 1980s the system again became a complex blend of tax relief and direct transfer payments. The changes in family policy over the last few years can be characterized mainly as reflecting an increasing emphasis on assisting families with very young children. This new direction is demonstrated primarily through the passage of the Federal Child Care Benefit Act in 1986, which along with other similar and supplementary provisions, is central to this discussion.

With a child caring (rearing) benefit and child care leave as the central points in a phase-specific family policy oriented toward assisting families with young children, the act primarily and formally pursued the following aims:

- Support for freedom of choice between family responsibilities and work for mothers or fathers when the children are very young.
- Support to enable parents to exercise their parental roles in the child's early years, considered crucial for personality development.
- Recognition of family responsibilities by the state and society at large.
- The easing of financial burdens on the family that stem from the expenses of child rearing.

Under the act, the child rearing benefit can be paid to only one parent. During the course of eligibility, a single change is possible but thus far has seldom occurred, probably because a shift in the caretaking parent would cause reorganization in both the workplace and the family. Moreover, this provision is intended only for critical situations.

In the short term, the child care benefit leads to a decline in the number of people employed. In the long term, it will tend to increase the employment rate because of the protection against dismissal and because it is expected to encourage more parents to return to work and to do so earlier than they otherwise would.

Allowing part-time work on a limited scale will lead to further pressure for part-time work from those eligible.

The experience and analysis suggest that despite various verbal formulations that evoke a feeling of partnership, the act is actually constructed in such a way that it will probably be used primarily by women. Moreover, one cannot ignore that it affects working women comparatively negatively. Even leaving aside the economic preconditions and consequences of such a law, the purported freedom of choice between gainful employment and family responsibilities is an illusion.

In discussing the sociopolitical, labor market, political, and family policy effects of the existing provisions, and particularly the FCCBA, concerning the compatibility of family responsibilities and gainful employment, one cannot fail to notice that the existing provisions primarily lead to a consolidation of both the existing division of work within the family and the difficult employment situation for women rather than encouraging equitable sharing of family and work responsibilities, organized on the basis of partnership.

On the one hand, compared to the Protection of Mothers Act, FCCBA represents not only an extension but also an improvement with regard to achieving equal rights because men as well as women are entitled to apply. The fact that FCCBA's provisions are used almost exclusively by women indicates, however, that reality is lagging far behind the legal possibility that they can also be utilized by men. This tendency cannot be exclusively or primarily explained by the fact that women are still confined to traditional roles. It is also substantially due to the fact that the objective conditions make it easier for women to apply.

In general, freedom of choice really exists only when a decision can be made between two equivalent options. Because the child care benefit is not, in fact, a wage replacement but more a symbolic recognition of family work, there is no equivalency for many families. Because of the different financial situations of different families, the benefit has different effects on their living situation. For example, a family dependent on the income of both parents could hardly get by on the reduced amount of DM 600. The situation of single parents is particularly precarious.

The financial burdens related to the birth of a child have clearly not been taken into consideration in setting the value of the child care benefit, and it is also not taken into account that these expenses also occur when both parents have been working full time. In contrast to the earlier provisions for working women, the aim of FCCBA was not to make a contribution in the form of wage replacement. The equivalence in treatment of different social situations and of both working women and housewives leads to social inequality.

The very high rate of claiming of the benefit among eligible women should not lead to the rash conclusion that this is the best possible provision for women. It is far more often the case that women are forced to accept what the act offers since they have no alternative because of lack of adequate child care facilities in West Germany.

Additionally, the other family policy benefits (in particular, the taxation provisions) are based on the same traditional image of the family. These benefits reinforce traditional family structure and do not accommodate recent changes in life-styles, particularly the increasing number of unmarried couples who live together, as well as the dramatic increase in the number of single parents.

Around the time the FCCBA became law, a lively policy discussion took place, with the critical points mentioned above playing a central role. Subsequently, however, the political and economic discussion has subsided. Even the main current political opposition, especially the SPD, has limited itself to demands for an extension of child care leave to three years, with a guarantee of a job and special regulations for small and middle-size companies, without advocating any basic change in existing provisions. The current debate centers around the need to coordinate labor, social, educational, wage, and company policies in the interests of improving the conditions of working women. A central point in the current discussion, supported by all political parties and group, is the need for improved child care, particularly in public child care facilities. Also stressed is the need to improve conditions for women returning to work after taking a leave for family reasons.

NOTES

As we go to press, the now-unified Germany has decided to increase the extended leave to three years, with the cash benefit provided for two. The states are asked to cover the benefit for the third year—and several may. There is considerable activity with regard to kindergarten (3-5s) coverage, especially better coverage for the work day, and infant/toddler care, but this will depend on what the individual states do.

1. Federal Ministry for Youth, Family, Women and Health, *Materialien zur Familienpolitik der Bundesregierung* (Bonn, 1989).
2. Federal Ministry for Youth, Family, Women, and Health, *Erziehungsgeld, Erziehungsurlaub und Anrechnung von Erziehungszeiten in der Rentenversicherung*, Schriftenreihe des Bundesministers für Jugend, Familie, Frauen, und Gesundheit, vol. 243 (Köln, 1989), p. 51.
3. Hans Hofbauer, "Zum Erwerbsverhalten verheirateter Frauen," *Mitteilungen aus der Arbeitsmarkt—und Berufsforschung*, no. 2 (1979): 217–40 and Gerhard Engelbrech, *Frauen und Arbeitsmarkt* (Nürnberg, 1984), p. 9.
4. Ibid.
5. Gerhard Engelbrech, "Erwerbsverhalten und Berufsverlauf von Frauen," in *Mitteilungen aus der Arbeitsmarkt und Berufsforschung*, no. 2 (1987).
6. Helga Krüger et al., "Privatsache Kind—Privatsache Beruf," in *Zur Lebenssituation von Frauen mit kleinen Kindern in unserer Gesellschaft* (Opladen, 1987).
7. Gerhard Engelbrech, "Erfahrungen von Frauen an der 'dritten Schwelle'. Schwierigkeiten bei der beruflichen Wiedereingliederung aus der Sicht der Frauen," *Mitteilungen aus der Arbeitsmarkt und Berufsforschung*, no. 1 (1990): 100–113.
8. Engelbrech, "Erwerbsverhalten und Berafsverlauf—".
9. Ingrid Langer-El Sayed, *Familienpolitik: Tendenzen, Chancen, Notwendigkeiten* (Reinbek, 1980), p. 97.
10. Vera Slupik, "Kinder kosten aber auch Geld. Die Diskriminierung von Frauen

im Kindergeldrecht,'' in Ute Gerhard et al., eds., *Auf Kosten der Frauen im Sozialstaat* (Weinheim, 1988), pp. 193–212.

11. Federal Ministry for Youth, Families, Women, and Health, *Erster Familienbericht, Bericht über die Lage der Familien in der Bundesrepublik Deutschland* (Bonn, 1968), pp. 109ff.

12. Langer-El Sayed, *Familienpolitik*, p. 100.

13. Federal Ministry, *Erziehungsgeld, Erziehungsurlaub*, p. 53.

14. Ute Rynarzweskie, ''Erziehungsgeld: Beitrag zur Emanzipation der Frauen oder Gebärprämie?'' *Streit* 4, no. 3 (1986): 94–99.

15. Federal Ministry, *Erziehungsgeld, Erziehungsurlaub*, p. 53.

16. Ibid., p. 66.

17. Ibid.

18. Ibid., p. 77.

19. Ingrid Ambos et al., ''Brufliche Wiedereingliederung von Frauen,'' *Schriftenreihe des Bundesministers für Jugend, Familie Frauen und Gesundheit*, vol. 248 (Stuttgart, 1990).

20. Federal Ministry, *Erziehungsgeld, Erziehungsurlaub*, pp. 147ff.

21. Ibid., p. 177.

22. Institut für Entwicklungsplanung und Strukturforschung, Erziehungsgeld, Erziehungsurlaub und Arbeitplatzdienung (1985), p. 27.

23. Ibid., p. 29. Also see chapter 2.

24. Engelbrech, ''Erfahrung von Frauen.''

25. Federal Ministry, *Erziehungsgeld, Erziehungsurlaub*.

26. *Records of the Plenary Session of the German Bundestag of November 14, 1989*.

27. Ibid.

28. Birgit Geissler and Birgit Pfau. ''Die Arbeitszeit als Ansatzpunkt der Frauenförderung—Einarbeitsmarktpolitisches Modell zur Vereinbarkeit von Eltenschaft und Erwerbsarbeit,'' *Frauenforschung* 7, no. 3 (1989): 43–65.

REFERENCES

Bundesminister Für Jugend, Familie, Frauen und Gesundheit. *Frauen in der Bundesrepublik*. Bonn, 1990.

Statistisches Bundesamt. *Bevölkerung und Erwerbstätigkeit*. Fachserie 1, Reihe 3, ''Haushalte und Familien 1987''; Reihe 4.1.1, ''Stand und Entwicklung der Erwerbstätigkeit 1987.'' Wiesbaden, 1989.

Zmarzlik, Johannes et al. *Mutterschutzgesetz, Mutterschaftshilfe, Erziehungsgeld, Erziehungsurlaub*. Vol. 5, neu bearbeitete u. ergänzte Auflage. Köln: 1986.

4

France: A Diversity of Policy Options

Marie-Gabrielle David and Christophe Starzec

Historical Overview

The origins of French family policy are best considered in the context of the development of the country's overall social security systems. These systems, which were created to address the effects of the nineteenth-century free-market economy, had the following basic objectives:

1. The introduction of a system of insurance benefits regarded as the counterpart of earnings from work.
2. The guarantee of minimum income, which is not always provided by the free play of market mechanisms.

The family policies inspired by these two main thrusts, already clearly defined by the end of the 1930s, have their own economic and demographic objectives. They are intended to provide families with income support through supplements or benefit payments so as to compensate for family expenses. They are also meant to halt the decline in the birthrate and ensure the renewal of the population.

In the last half-century, these two objectives have played an important role in French family policy, but their respective weightings in the system of assistance for families have frequently been modified in the light of the country's socio-economic changes. Incentives have been aimed at increasing the birthrate, as well as achieving income redistribution between families and single persons and between rich and poor. The enacted benefits have been part of a diversified strategy aimed at responding to economic and demographic developments. As a result, however, the system has become complex and cumbersome.

Its dual demographic and economic objectives have also sometimes introduced inconsistencies into French family policy. For example, support for the arrival of a family's first child has practically disappeared in recent years, and in the 1980s efforts were concentrated on encouraging a third child by increasing both direct and indirect help to *familles nombreuses*, with three or more children. This emphasis on encouraging additional rather than first children is based on the somewhat outdated theory that couples do not question the conception of their first child but only the later ones. In fact, many young couples now delay starting their families because of the changes in life-style that may result. Additionally, couples who experience economic and other difficulties with their first child may be reluctant to have more children.

The origins of French family policy actually date back to the end of the nineteenth century, when the first timid attempts were made to link remuneration for work with the expenses of raising a family.[1] These first family benefits, which were actually wage supplements paid by certain employers to ensure decent living conditions for workers and their families, were more charitable than institutional in character and distributed more for ideological than for economic or demographic reasons. After World War I, this practice became widespread and a standard component of trade union demands.

Unfortunately, these measures to benefit families had certain perverse effects, notably a tendency by employers not to hire heads of families because of the additional expense involved. This problem was eventually solved by the creation of compensation funds that took over responsibility for the payment of wage supplements for family expenses and were financed by proportional contributions, based on the total personnel costs of the firms involved. These funds were centralized on a nationwide basis in 1921, although they remained independent of the state. Additionally, government civil servants began to receive subsidies for family expenses in 1917.

During the 1920s, the state tried to incorporate the employers' contributions that were financing the family benefits into the federal tax system. However, this initiative was rejected because both the employers and the trade unions preferred to continue to administer what they regarded as a private matter between employers and workers.

Only in 1932 did affiliation to the family allowance funds (*caisses d'allocation familiales*) become theoretically compulsory for all industrial and commercial firms; all workers became eligible for benefits covering family expenses. However, a large number of firms (mainly small and medium-size ones) still did not enter the system even after it became mandatory.

Although the family allowance funds remained outside state control, the state began to play a key role in French family policy with the passage of the Family Code in 1938–1939. These laws were primarily the result of a strong national resolve to halt the increasing decline of the French population. The amounts involved in family benefits were now structured to increase with each child born (up to three) and to reflect the total number of children in the family.

This emphasis on and support for childbearing predominated for a long time.

The Vichy regime reinforced this aspect of family policy and indicated its clear preference for the model of the traditional family by introducing in 1941 a so-called *salaire unique* allowance for families in which only one parent was employed. Together with the already existing family allowances, the *salaire unique* allowance, which was paid automatically during the first two years of marriage and then stopped only if the young couple still had no child, clearly signaled the policy aim of encouraging large families in which the mother stayed at home to raise the children.

This system was not significantly altered after the liberation of France. In fact, the postwar social security system, which was enacted in 1946, integrated the family allowance funds into the new institutional framework of social welfare. Thus, the Law of 1946 adopted with virtually no change the 1941 scale of both family allowances and the *salaire unique*.

At the same time, however, the Law of 1946 extended the scope of family policy to such new fields as education, health, and housing. Now a certificate of school attendance and prenatal and postnatal examinations became required for eligibility for family allowances. Additionally, a housing allowance was created in 1948 as part of the family policy benefit system, conditional on the selection of housing that met certain standards. Along with improving the living conditions of families, this new benefit had a second objective, reactivating the building industry.

The Law of 1946 concerning family allowances was supported by a tax law that created the *quotient familial*, by which a family's taxable income is adjusted for the size, structure, and composition of the family. The level of family taxation then became indexed not only to the size of a family's income but also to its needs as indicated by the number of dependents. This new policy made the tax system a powerful instrument for redistribution of the tax burden. It is interesting to note that the *quotient familial* was originally more supportive of childbearing than it is today. From its creation in 1946 to 1959, the number of "adult" shares for couples (and thus the amount of their taxes) varied according to whether they had children. A childless couple was entitled to two shares (meaning that the taxable income was divided by two) during the first three years after marriage but only one and a half thereafter.

After these significant innovations, family policy basically marked time during the late 1950s. Although family allowances kept up with price increases, they did not match the growth in wages, and their share of family income consequently declined.

During the 1960s, family policy changed significantly with the gradual abandonment of the *salaire unique* allowance. It also became more neutral toward women's role in society and in the work force in particular. This shift, to the detriment of the emphasis on stimulating the birthrate, reflected popular sentiment in favor of increasing women's participation in a rapidly expanding economy. The decline of the *salaire unique* allowance, which encouraged wives to remain at home, went hand in hand with the introduction of a *frais de garde* allowance for child-minding expenses related to the mother's occupation. Furthermore, the need to limit overall expenditures and the resolve to strengthen the redistributive efforts of family policy encouraged the practice of relating the level of certain benefits to the family's other income. Both the gradual abolition of the *salaire unique* allowance and the broadening scope of income-related benefits were characteristic of a period when family policy was being adapted to the prevalent economic conditions, including industrial growth, full employment, and labor shortages, as well as to the growing (and increasingly accepted) occupational aspirations of women. The legislation of the time attempted to reconcile these new developments with the continuing desire to stimulate the birthrate.

In the 1970s the *salaire unique* allowance was replaced by measures to assist low-income families, whether or not the mother worked outside the home. This new emphasis strengthened the pronatalist nature of family policy, especially by increasing the measures intended to encourage families to have a third child, including a family supplement and a grant on the birth of the third child, as well as cheaper transport, access to museums, and other privileges for families with at least three children.

This policy in favor of the third child was reinforced in 1981 through increased family allowances, doubling of postnatal benefits, and an increased *quotient familial* for the third child, while at the same time neutrality in relation to the labor force activity of women was also preserved.

Following the major increase in the amounts of most of the benefits at the beginning of the decade, direct help for families remained stable throughout the 1980s because of the country's general budgetary austerity. New initiatives at the end of the decade were primarily in services rather than in income transfers to individuals, including assistance with child care both outside the public establishments and through expanding the number of public day care facilities. Thus, in recent years, family policy has moved toward helping mothers fulfill both their family and their work-related responsibilities, while at the same time favoring larger families. The primary objective seems to be to assist the mother in continuing or resuming activity in the labor market after the birth of a child, especially a second or third child.

SOCIOECONOMIC BACKGROUND

Demographic Evolution

Family policies have recently addressed demographic concerns more than economic redistribution. The fact is that the low birthrate now threatens the country's ability to maintain its current population. The aging of the population and its consequences for France are thus the motivating force for the country's family policy.[2] Fertility has been relatively stable in recent years but at a fairly low level (1.80–1.84) (table 4.1). A new factor has emerged, however, providing some room for optimism: an increase in fertility among somewhat older women (between 27 and 37 years of

Table 4.1
Fertility in France, 1975–1989 (Average Number of Live Births per Female)

Year	Rate
1975	1.93
1976	1.83
1977	1.86
1978	1.82
1979	1.86
1980	1.95
1981	1.95
1982	1.91
1983	1.79
1984	1.81
1985	1.82
1986	1.84
1987	1.82
1988	1.82
1989	1.81

Source: Institut National d'Etudes Démographiques.
Note: The most recent values may be subject to slight modification.

age), which indicates that while births have become rarer in the earlier part of the fertile period, they have become relatively more numerous at a more advanced age.[3]

This phenomenon of delayed marriages and delayed birth of the first child reflects a change in the behavior of couples, primarily due to the increased labor market activity of women. Additionally, women's desire to continue working is limiting the number of larger families. The development of new contraceptive techniques has enabled couples to space the birth of their children to accommodate their work schedules.

In recent years, the decline in the number of marriages has been accompanied by a steady rise in the proportion of births to unmarried couples (24 percent of the total in 1987, rising from 6.8 percent in 1970 and 11.4 percent in 1980). At the same time, the number and proportion of divorces has been increasing (although the increase leveled off in 1987 for the first time) while the number of remarriages is also falling. Although this phenomenon is quite complex, it is nevertheless highly significant. Considering only the remarriages of divorced

Table 4.2
Female Labor Force Participation Rates, Ages 25–49, by Household Status and Number of Children

Year	Single	Two Adults				Total (%)
		0 children	1 child	2 children	3 children or more	
1962	67.5	55.7	42.5	26.1	15.9	41.5
1970	80.4	58.3	54.3	34.6	20.2	49.3
1975	82.7	66.5	63.4	46.4	26.6	57.4
1980	84.9	71.1	69.6	54.3	31.3	63.8
1982	87.0	75.2	72.0	61.0	32.4	66.8
1987	88.3	78.5	76.1	66.2	36.4	71.6

Source: Les Collections de l'INSEE, série D. No. 123 (1987). (1962, Census; 1970–1987 *Enquête-Emploi*).

persons, the rate fell from 60 percent in the 1970s to 43.5 percent in 1986 (both sexes).

Abortion is another contemporary phenomenon with consequences for family policy. Although more difficult to measure and factor into demographic forecasting, the incidence of abortion seems to have declined since the early 1980s. These somewhat pessimistic observations concerning the demographic situation are by far the argument used most frequently to support an active family policy.[4]

Growth in Women's Labor Force Participation

The participation of women in the labor market has been continually increasing for several decades, with a sharp acceleration in the 1970s and 1980s, despite the increase in unemployment. Women's growing role in the labor market has been a long-term social trend that has tended to equalize the work situations of men and women. Family policy in France has always taken this evolution into account by trying to reconcile women's employment aspirations with the objective of maintaining demographic equilibrium.

Between 1975 and 1989, the female labor force participation rate rose from 42.3 percent to 45.8 percent. Although this rise is not particularly impressive overall, the increase among the 24 to 50 age group—from 57.4 percent in 1970 to 71.6 percent in 1987—is considerably more notable. The slow rate of increase in the participation rate among women both under 24 and over 50 is explained by the greater difficulty of finding a job and the growing danger of being forced into early retirement, respectively.[5] (See table 4.2.)

This evolution is even more spectacular for mothers of families. For the same age group during the same period (1970–1988), the participation rate rose 23 points in the case of women living with a companion with no children, 34 points

Table 4.3
Female Labor Force Participation Rates, by Number and Age of Children (Percentage in Labor Force)

Number and age of children	Type of Household: Couples	Type of Household: Single Parent	Total
1 child			
under 3	61.14	50.58	60.39
ages 3-5	68.74	65.21	68.26
age 6 and over	65.40	77.44	67.32
2 children			
youngest under 3	52.34	43.37	51.93
youngest 3-5	62.23	66.77	62.51
youngest 6 and over	64.61	71.58	65.21
3 and more children			
youngest under 3	22.16	17.78	21.97
youngest 3-5	30.38	31.09	30.42
youngest 6 and over	43.03	51.05	43.68
Total (rate)	57.33	67.56	58.35
Total Number	6,318,439	698,129	7,016,568

Source: *Enquêtes Emploi*, 1989, Institut National de la Statistique et des Études Enconomiques.

for those with one child, and 40 points for those with two (table 4.3). For those with three or more children, the increase was only 20 points. These figures, which indicate that the participation rate of mothers with three or more children has remained relatively low and has increased less rapidly than for mothers with fewer children, clearly explain the attention directed by family policy to the third child. The first and second children no longer present a serious obstacle to the mother's activity, but the third child is always a severe handicap to an employed mother.

In practice, the labor force activity of the mother depends on both the number and the ages of her children (table 4.3). The younger the child is, the more difficult it is to reconcile labor market activity and child care. Here again, this constraint seems to be much greater in families where there are three or more children.

Although adjusting working hours is one possible solution to this problem, it is not ideal.[6] The recent increase in the number of women working part time, which rose from 19 percent in 1982 to 24 percent in 1989, is linked mainly to the effect of unemployment and early retirement. The increase in part-time work is greatest among women under 24 and, to a smaller extent, over 50. Part-time work also increases appreciably with the number of children (tables 4.4 and 4.5). Nearly 40 percent of the women with large families who work do so part

Table 4.4
Part-Time and Full-Time Female Labor Force Participation by Family Status and Presence and Age of Children (Women Ages 15 and Over) (Percentages)

	Number	Not in Labor Force	In Labor Force Full Time	In Labor Force Part Time
All Women with Children	7,016,568	41.6	42.7	15.7
under Age 18	4,067,183	36.6	46.2	17.2
under Age 6	1,461,599	44.4	40.2	15.4
under Age 3	1,487,786	52.6	35.6	11.8
Married with Children				
under Age 18	3,420,707	38.3	43.4	18.3
under Age 6	1,227,108	45.0	39.0	16.0
under Age 3	1,210,109	52.4	35.3	12.3
Single, with Children				
under Age 18	76,854	27.2	60.0	12.8
under Age 6	52,728	42.4	48.2	9.4
under Age 3	50,942	59.3	34.1	6.6
Divorced/Sep., with Children				
under Age 18	333,258	22.3	66.9	10.8
under Age 6	56,569	36.8	54.3	8.9
under Age 3	28,075	57.4	30.2	12.5
Widows with Children				
under Age 18	84,759	41.8	44.2	14.0
under Age 6	9,784	43.5	35.9	20.6
under Age 3	3,462	46.1	49.5	4.4
Cohabiting, with Children				
under Age 18	150,252	32.8	55.6	11.6
under Age 6	115,065	42.8	43.0	14.2
under Age 3	195,198	51.9	37.8	10.3
All Men aged 16 to 64	20,674,390	39.3	58.6	2.1

Source: *Enquêtes Emploi*, 1989, Institut National de la Statistique et des Études Economiques.

time. Age, cohort, and marital status also have an impact on the incidence of part-time work.

Clearly women with large families who work part time generally do so because of the impossibility of finding a full-time job that is compatible with their family duties. It is worth noting that the percentages of women working part time is not higher but actually lower in public administration and similar kinds of work than among other groups of wage earners (table 4.5), despite special provisions favoring part-time work in the civil service, including a guaranteed return to full-time work at any time, as well as a salary loss less than proportional to the decline in hours worked. This suggests a preference for full-time work on the part of a majority of working women with dependent children, even those with large families. It should be remembered that French legislation on taxes on

Table 4.5
Part-Time Work among Working Women, Ages 25–49, by Number of Children and Marital Status (Percentages)

Number of dependent children	Working women		Employed in public administration	
	All working women	Women in 2 adult household	All working women	Women in 2 adult household
0	13.4	17.4	10.1	12.3
1	18.9	20.1	17.0	17.9
2	28.9	30.2	28.3	29.7
3 or more	38.7	40.9	34.1	35.7
Total	20.6	24.2	18.7	22.0

Source: *Enquête-Emploi*, March 1986, Institut National de la Statistique et des Études Economiques.

benefits is for the most part neutral in relation to part-time work and to working women in general.[7]

Impact of the Economic Situation

The economic crisis that has prevailed since the end of the 1970s and the rise of unemployment during the 1980s definitely had an effect on social policy as a whole but did not call into question its underlying principles and priorities, including those concerned with family policy.

The aging of the population and the lowering of the retirement age in 1981 have both demographic and economic effects. The equilibrium of the retirement pension system depends on the ratio between the number of retired beneficiaries and the working population who contribute to it. This ratio was 34.3 percent in 1985 and 37.8 percent in 1990, and it will be almost 54 percent in the year 2000.[8] Without additional funding or a revision of the rules governing retirement age, the pension system will have difficulty coping.

The rise in unemployment (to a peak of 11 percent of the labor force) and its continuation at a very high level (9–10 percent) are also imposing a burden on the social welfare system as a whole. The explosion of unemployment benefit payments, on the one hand, and the relative fall in the volume of contributions to the unemployment funds, on the other, have produced a chronic deficit requiring permanent intervention by the state.

Additionally, the increase in health care expenditures produced by a combination of a steeper rise in costs than in the growth in gross domestic product (GDP) and the aging of the population is producing a structural disequilibrium in social expenditures, necessitating budgetary transfers, increased compulsory contributions out of income, or reduced coverage of health care costs.

Families, and especially large ones, are always regarded as disadvantaged, and their material situation is often precarious, especially regarding housing (41 percent of households with three or more children live in overcrowded conditions and 15 percent in severely overcrowded conditions).[9] In addition to the financial insecurity caused by unemployment, the costs of education have substantially increased, both because of the longer time people now spend in school and the longer time children are continuing to live with their parents after reaching their majority.

At the same time, resources available to the various social benefit programs to address these problems are shrinking because of the prevailing economic constraints. Wages have been growing more slowly than national wealth as measured by GDP, with the share of wages in GDP falling from 40.6 percent over 1980–1985 to 37.2 percent in 1988.

These structural disequilibria have led to both fewer resources because of a decrease in the number of contributors and increased expenditures by the main social insurance systems, although the family benefit system had a surplus of 5 billion francs in 1989. The overall deterioration has continued for several years and is likely to persist beyond the year 2000.[10]

In view of the political determination to stabilize (and reduce if possible) both taxes and compulsory social contributions in France (45 percent of GDP in 1988), social welfare expenditures (including those related to family policy) are being subjected to ever-tighter restrictions. This economic constraint directly conflicts with the desire for a more active family policy. However, tension may finally be resolved in favor of family policy and, in particular, the incentive for population growth since the demographic changes this policy is intended to bring about could eventually help to resolve some of the economic problems, especially those related to the aging of the population.

Political Background

The likelihood that family policy will be spared cuts related to budgetary austerity is all the greater because of a broad political consensus on the principle of family protection. Although there are some differences of opinion at different points on the political spectrum, changes in government have never led to a questioning of the principle of family policy. Employers and trade unions are also generally in agreement on the need to maintain and even strengthen the system of benefits for families. These positions do diverge in certain respects, however.

Left-wing trade unions are attached to the principle of giving more help to poorer families and to developing child care facilities for looking after young children while their mothers are at work. Right-wing and center trade unions, on the other hand, are more inclined to favor a policy of reconciling women's labor market participation with their childbearing and child care through different forms of parental leave. The organizations representing families, which are large and influential in France, are concerned mainly with preserving family benefits and making their financing more independent of and consequently less exposed to the budgetary constraints of the government and other social welfare funds. They would like to upgrade family allowances and simplify the whole system.

French family policy must also face the challenge of finding its place in the European context in which the economic and social systems of the various member countries are to be aligned by January 1, 1994. To respond to this mandate, those responsible for social policies in France are advocating the convergence of family policies in Europe along the following lines:[11]

- Financial compensation adjusted to the family's responsibilities.
- Efforts to balance family life and the demands of the labor market.
- The creation of a more favorable environment for the family.

Most of these proposals are based on the established principles of French family policy and are considered both essential to families and capable of adaptation to the circumstances of other countries. They include the system of taxation and other contributions (especially the *quotient familial*), the development of various forms of child care, flexible working hours, and the maternity leave system—in other words, all the measures intended to facilitate the ability of parents to pursue both workplace and child rearing activities.

French family policy must be considered in the several contexts outlined, but reference must also be made to a fundamental question that underlies the concept of family policy: Is it aid to the family or aid to the child? There seems to be some doubt as to the target of the policy, although the family has traditionally been emphasized.

POLICIES FOR YOUNG CHILDREN

Family benefits linked to the presence of children have a very important place in social transfers in general. In 1988 they accounted for 13.4 percent of all social welfare expenditures.[12] These children-linked expenditures are equal to 3.2 percent of GDP, a substantial share and slightly up from the 1970s, when they were around 2.7 to 2.8 percent. It is difficult to separate out all the sums provided only for very young children because these are often indistinguishable from other benefits that depend not on the child's age but merely on the presence of children. It is possible, however, to put a figure on those age-specific expenditures paid out for very young children that have age as an eligibility requirement.

Table 4.6
Child-Related Social Benefits, 1988

Program	Number of recipients	Percent of expenditure
AJPE (Young children's allowance). .	1,629,150	13.9
APE (Parental education allowance) .	157,691	4.4
AGED (Allowance for child-minding . in the home) .	6,000	0.1
Family allowance	3,622,144	46.9
Complément familial (Large-family . supplement) .	723,000	6.8
(Single-parent allowance)	126,148	3.2
(Family support allowance)	399,593	2.7
Allocation de rentrée scolaire ("Back-to-school" Allowance)	1,990,250	1.3
AL (Housing allowance)	1,129,241	10.1
Other allowances (including invalids' allowance)	---	10.6
	6,969,150	100.0

Source: Caisse Nationale d'Allocation Familiales.
Note: The total is 160 billion francs.

Family allowances are by far the most important element in total expenditures on family benefits (47 percent) and cover the largest number of recipients (51 percent). *Allocation pour Jeune Enfant* (APJE) and *Allocation Parentale d'Education* (APE) account for 18.3 percent of the total (table 4.6). Roughly 50 percent of the total sum paid out in benefits is not related to the level of income. Therefore, some families who receive family benefits have high incomes. This is often true of two-earner households, which account for 32 percent of the recipients. (One-income households constitute 51 percent of recipients and single-parent households 17.1 percent.) Well-off households also enjoy the tax advantages stemming from the *quotient familial*, which represented a tax loss for the state (tax expenditure) on the order of 51 billion francs in 1988. This expenditure may be compared with the table 4.6 total for family benefits in 1988—160 billion francs. This easing of the tax burden clearly does not benefit the large number of families who pay no taxes because of low income.

In sum, combining direct outlays and tax expenditures, the provisions for aid for families with children come to over 4 percent of the GDP. This aid, which does not include expenditures for education, health care, or child care services, is fairly evenly distributed among families according to the number and age of the children.

The policy toward very young children that developed in France during the 1980s includes several kinds of measures that are intended to be neutral as to the choices made by the parents (and particularly mothers) concerning their labor market activity and how preschool children should be cared for:

- A strengthening of the legislation protecting women's employment in the case of maternity or adoption through maternity leave, parental education (child rearing) leave, and half-time work.
- The provision of cash benefits to give direct aid to families on the birth of a child (APJE) or to provide partial compensation for a reduction or cessation of activity on the part of one of the parents until the child reaches pre-school age (3) (APE).
- The development of child care facilities for very young children through investment in and equipment of child-minding services (the so-called *contrats-crèches*).
- A reduction in the cost of child care by such measures as special allocations (*Prestation Spéciale Assistante Maternelle [PSAM]* and *Allocation de Garde d'Enfant à Domicile [AGED])* and tax deductions.

Legislation Relating to Maternity and Adoption

Both maternity and adoption entitle employed mothers and, in certain cases, employed fathers to certain rights and benefits, including maternity leave, maternity insurance, protection of employment, parental education leave, and half-time work.

Maternity Leave. Maternity leave was created in May 1946 and then extended to include adoption in July 1976. This leave allows a woman to suspend her work activity for reasons of maternity for a legally defined period that varies according to the number of children already in the household (exhibit 4.1). Additionally, when the child's state of health necessitates its remaining in hospital until the end of the sixth week after birth, the mother can postpone the beginning of all or part of the leave due to her until the end of her child's hospitalization. In the case of the mother's death during childbirth, the father can suspend his work activity for the same amount of leave to which the mother would have been entitled. Moreover, mothers who breast-feed their children are entitled to an hour per day during working hours for this purpose for a year after the birth.

Maternity Insurance. Daily benefits for time off work are paid to working mothers for the period of maternity leave to which they are entitled by law. These benefits are also granted in the case of adoption. In addition, many collective agreements at the firm or industry level provide for continued payment of wages or salary beyond the statutory coverage. The basic benefit for time off work is equal to 84 percent of basic daily earnings, calculated on the basis of

Exhibit 4.1
Maternity Leave in France

	Length of maternity leave			Adoption leave
Family situation	Before childbirth (presumed date)	After childbirth	Total[a]	After arrival in family
Adoption of 1 child bringing the number of children to: - 1 or 2	6 weeks	10 weeks	16 weeks	10 weeks
- 3 or more[b] . . .	8 weeks[c]	18 weeks[c]	26 weeks	18 weeks
Births or multiple adoptions bringing the number children from: 0 to 2	6 weeks	12 weeks	18 weeks	12 weeks
0 or 1 to 3 or more	6 weeks	22 weeks	28 weeks	20 weeks
2 or more to 4 or more (2)	8 weeks	20 weeks		
Medical problems for the mother	+ 2 weeks	+ 2 weeks	--	--

[a] In the event of premature delivery, the postnatal leave is prolonged up to the stipulated limit—to the completion of the 16, 18, 20, or 26 weeks. In the event of delayed delivery, the postnatal leave is not reduced, since it is calculated from the actual date of childbirth (whether or not it corresponds to the presumed date). It has been specified that if the daily allowances from the social security fund have been paid for a period longer than the prenatal period off work, this will not reduce the period of postnatal coverage.

[b] The wage earner or the household takes on responsibility for at least two children or the wage earner has already given birth to two viable children.

[c] The 3-week period can be prolonged by a maximum of two weeks, the 18-week period then being correspondingly reduced.

the wages or salary received by the insured person during the three months before she stopped working.

Some of this insurance also covers women who are not in the labor force. Medical and hospitalization expenses related to pregnancy, childbirth, and postnatal care are reimbursed to mothers who are either members of the social security system themselves or are married to members of it.

Women must observe some formalities to benefit from this coverage:

- Declaring the pregnancy during the first fifteen weeks to the family allowances fund or the health insurance fund.

- Having a certain number of prenatal medical examinations (before the end of the fifteenth week, during the seventh month, in the first fifteen days of the eighth month, and in the first sixteen days of the ninth month) and postnatal examinations (submission of a certificate in the first three days, a gynecological and clinical examination of the mother in the first eight weeks after childbirth, nine examinations of the child during the first year, three examinations of the child during the second year, and two in each subsequent year up to the child's sixth birthday).

These various formalities and examinations are recorded in a *carnet de maternité* (maternity record booklet), which the mother receives at the start of her pregnancy.

To benefit from the coverage for time off work, the mother must establish that she will have been covered by the social security system for a period of ten months at the estimated time of delivery and have had a minimum of 1,200 hours paid employment in the preceding twelve months. If the mother dies as the result of childbirth, the father can benefit from the coverage for time off work.

Protection of the Mother's Employment. The mother's future employment is guaranteed by special regulations. At the time she is hired, she is not required to reveal her condition, and employers are forbidden to seek any information concerning it. Moreover, the employer cannot refuse to hire a woman or to terminate her contract during a probationary period because of pregnancy. An employer is also forbidden to terminate a woman's contract during pregnancy, maternity, or adoption leave or the four weeks following maternity or adoption leave. Moreover, renewal of a fixed-term contract cannot be refused because the employee is pregnant.

Parental Education (Child Rearing) Leave and Half-time Work. Parental education leave (also described as parenting, child caring, or child rearing leave) was instituted in 1977. Along with the Young Children's Allowance (APJE), the child rearing allowance (APE) is the main French program that corresponds to the family policy innovations in the other countries discussed in this book. All working parents who qualify have the right to a two-year, job-protected leave at the end of the maternity leave. Some also receive a cash benefit (APE).

Either parental education leave or half-time work can be claimed by any parent able to prove that he or she has been employed for at least one year at the time of the child's birth or adoption. Both mothers and fathers are eligible, including successively, at any time from the expiration of maternity leave to the child's third birthday. However, an employer of fewer than 100 people may refuse to grant leave if, after obtaining the opinion of the *comité d'entreprise* (a worker-management committee) or the staff labor representatives, he or she considers that it could detract from proper functioning of the firm.

During child rearing leave, employees continue to be entitled to work-related social benefits. Half the period of the leave is credited to length of service for various social benefit computations. The length of service counted for retirement benefits is increased by the length of the parental education leave taken by the mother (or by the father if the mother is unable to benefit from it).

Established along with the APJE in 1985 and modified in 1986, the APE is intended to provide partial compensation for the loss of income connected with an interruption of paid employment on the part of one of the two parents on the birth or adoption of a third or subsequent child. The APE is paid until the child (the youngest when the births follow closely after each other) reaches three years of age so long as a parent completely stops working. However, for one year preceding the child's third birthday, the APE can be paid at half-rate if the parent either returns to work part time or enters a course of paid vocational training. Payment of the APE is also subject to a condition of two years of prior work activity during the ten years preceding the birth or adoption of the third child.

The amount of the APE is equivalent to 142.57 percent of the monthly base for the calculation of family allowances. At the beginning of 1989, it was 2,578 francs, more than half the basic guaranteed minimum wage—compared with 831 francs for the APJE. Only one APE can be paid per family, and this allowance cannot be combined with the APJE, the daily maternity or sickness indemnities, or unemployment benefits. Recipients of the APE continue to be entitled to family allowances and can belong at no charge to the old age insurance system when the family's resources are below a certain ceiling. At the end of 1988, there were 157,691 recipients of the APE, accounting for 4.4 percent of the total family allowance expenditures (table 4.6).

Direct Financial Aid for Families with Young Children

Created in 1985 to replace the family supplement and the prenatal and postnatal allowances, the allowance to young children (AJE) in 1986 became the allowance for young children (APJE). It has a history of development and changes since 1932. The "short" APJE is paid regardless of family income, from the fourth month of pregnancy to the third month after childbirth (for a total of nine months), every time a child is born or expected. The "long" APJE, which is conditional on income level, is paid until the child reaches age 3. Only one APJE is payable per family until the last child becomes 3. The income ceiling for families eligible for the long APJE is raised by 25 percent for each dependent child. Starting with the third child the increase is 30 percent. The ceiling for eligibility is also increased when both spouses are employed or when one person is solely responsible for the children (table 4.7).

The monthly amount of the APJE is equivalent to 45.95 percent of the base used for calculating family allowances (table 4.7). On July 11, 1989, the monthly APJE amounted to 831 francs. This was 11.5 percent of the median wage and 13.0 percent of the median female wage at the time. The APJE is paid only if mother and child have undergone the medical examinations stipulated by law. At the end of 1988, there were 439,973 recipients of the short APJE and 1,190,108 of the long APJE. In 1988 the APJE accounted for 13.9 percent of

Table 4.7
Income Ceilings for APJE Program (in francs)

Household Type	1 child	2 children	3 children	4 children	Per additional child
Household with :					
. 1 income					
- gross taxable[a]	116,764	140,117	168,140	196,164	28,024
- net taxable[a]	84,070	100,884	121,061	141,238	20,177
2 incomes[b]					
- gross taxable[a]	154,308	177,661	205,685	233,708	28,024
- net taxable[a]	111,102	127,916	148,093	168,270	20,177

Notes: Single parents are treated the same as a two-income household.

[a] *Net taxable* income is the final sum appearing on the French income tax declaration after the various standard deductions. For purposes of illustration, we have calculated the gross taxable from the net taxable in the case of workers having no other source of income than their wages and salaries and unable to make any additional deductions for professional expenses, meaning that they enjoy only the normal 10 percent plus 20 percent deductions.

[b] There are deemed to be two incomes when each of the members has received during the year in question an income at least equal to twelve times the monthly basis for the calculation of family allowances in force on July 1 of the year. For 1988 this means: 12 × 1,770.18 = 21,242.16 francs.

total child-related social benefits paid in France as part of the family allowance system (table 4.6).

Child Care Facilities

In 1986 there were an estimated 2,205,000 under 3s, of whom 11 percent were already attending preschool, 43 percent had a mother with no outside job, and 46 percent had two working parents. In this last group, 24 percent were cared for by their mother who was self-employed and/or working at home. The remaining 770,000 children received the following kind of child care: public day nurseries, 12 percent; family day care, 6 percent; approved mother's helper, 26 percent; and other, 56 percent.

Thus, more than half of the young children with two working parents were not cared for in official facilities but were instead entrusted either to grandparents (between 21 and 25 percent of children) or to unauthorized family day care (between 19 and 25 percent).[13] To ease the serious shortage of child care facilities, a policy of investment in and equipment of child care services has been developed over several years, initially through the so-called *contrats-crèches* and, later, the *contrats-enfance*.

Official Child Care Facilities. Day nurseries (*crèches*) are partially financed by the municipal authorities, while approved mother's helpers are entirely paid for by the parents.

Alongside the traditional public day nurseries where child care is the responsibility of a public or private organization employing specialized staff in premises specially intended for the purpose, a number of other types of public or family day care facilities have sprung up:

Mini-crèches: Public day nurseries located in apartments, houses, or facilities used for social services and taking only twelve or fifteen children (compared with fifty-four in the traditional day nurseries).

Crèches parentales: Public day nurseries organized and run by a cooperative association of parents who take turns looking after the children in premises equipped for the purpose and in the presence of a professionally qualified person.

Crèches familiales: Developing since 1971 and at a faster rate than the public day nurseries because of their lesser cost, these services organize and monitor child care by mother's helpers, paid centrally and monitored by qualified state infant care personnel.

Haltes-garderies: Permanent establishments that provide occasional child care for children under 6. They were originally intended for children of nonworking mothers; now they are used by women who work part time, as well as by full-time workers who need to supplement another form of child care.

These types of day nurseries receive support for their operating expenses. This aid, known as *prestation de services* (provision of services), was created in 1970 and has become a form of family assistance since it reduces parental fees. To use American terminology, it subsidizes supply.

Since 1977 approved mother's helpers, the second kind of official child care arrangement, have enjoyed a special legal status that entitles them to a fixed minimum wage (two hours at the basic minimum wage, per child and per day), social insurance, and paid holidays. They must be approved by the maternal and child protection services on the advice of a board consisting of medical and social workers and are monitored after approval by visits from a doctor, a child care specialist, or a midwife who represents the board. The mother's helper is paid directly by the parents at an individually determined rate. The parents can be reimbursed for their share through a special allowance called the *Prestation Spéciale Assistante Maternelle* (PSAM). The average costs of these various forms of child care and their distribution at the beginning of 1987 are indicated in exhibit 4.2.

Contractual Assistance for the Development of Infant Care Facilities. Although the development of facilities for the benefit of very young children was included in the objectives of the sixth and seventh French National Plans, there

Exhibit 4.2
Costs of Various Forms of Child Minding (francs)

Distribution of Costs	Approved mothers's helps	Family day nurseries	Public day nurseries	Home child-minding
Monthly costs	1,448 (1,998 in Paris)	2,940	4,160	6,600
Contribution from the CNAF (child allowance fund)	264 [a] 18% (13% in the Paris region)	620 20%	830 20%	2,000[b] 30%
Contribution from municipalities	--	1,220 42%	2,250 54%	
Contribution from parents	1,160 82% (87% in the Paris region)	1,100 38%	1,080 26%	4,600 70%

Source: *Liaisons Sociales*, Documents, 109 (1986).

a PSAM.

b AGED.

was little progress in this direction during the 1970s. Legislation adopted in 1971 and 1974 to appropriate 100 million francs for this purpose to ease the investment costs of the developers of these facilities did not have the desired effect. In 1981, however, the provision of facilities for caring for young children became an institutional priority, spurring increased financial efforts and the introduction of contractual arrangements to serve as additional incentive to developers.

The *contrats-crèches*, created in June 1983, were an innovative arrangement designed to encourage a major increase in the number of day nurseries through a contractual mechanism involving the family allowance funds, local authorities, and the developers or managers. The last received substantial financial incentives to create or improve facilities. These incentives led to the signing of 215 contracts by the end of 1988 and the creation of 20,127 new places.[14]

The *contrats-enfance* were created in 1988 to complement or take the place of the *contrats-crèches*. This new type of contract was both more comprehensive and more flexible and covered not only ongoing care for children under 3 but also temporary care for all children under 6. These contracts are co-financed by the family allowance funds and the municipalities and last for three to five years.

The municipalities increase the financial contribution for every child under 6 by an amount ranging from 1,000 to 5,000 francs per child per year. Voluntary organizations, businesses, and other local groups can also be parties to the contract. In return, the Caisse d'Allocations Familiales (CAF) make a contribution calculated solely on the basis of the new net expenditure of the contracting parties. The rate of this contribution varies according to the previous effort and can range between 30 and 50 percent of net new expenditures. This allowance is in addition to the normal contributions. It represents 30 percent of a ceiling price set by the CNAF (national family allowance fund) and is paid to all day nurseries.

At the beginning of 1989, about a hundred *contrats-enfance* had already been signed and, according to CNAF, resulted in an increase in crèche places from fewer than 35,000 in 1970 to about 150,000 in 1988, of which about 40,000 were in *crèches familiales* and the remainder in *crèches collectives*.

Measures Aimed at Reducing the Cost of Infant Care for Families

Allocation de Garde d'Enfant à Domicile (AGED) (Allowance for Child Care in the Home). This allowance, introduced at the end of 1986, is paid to households that employ a person in the home to look after at least one child under 3 years when both of the parents (or the single parent) have outside employment. The AGED is paid without regard to family income until the child's third birthday. Only one allowance is payable if there is more than one child under 3. The amount of the AGED is equal to the social insurance contributions of the employee and employer paid for the employment of one (or more) child care worker, up to a maximum of 2,000 francs a month. The AGED can be combined with a half-rate APE when a parent returns to part-time work between the child's second and third birthdays.

It was initially forecast in 1986 that there were 150,000 potential recipients of this allowance. These estimates were later substantially reduced. In 1988 there were, in fact, 6,000 recipients, and only 7,500 were expected in 1989. This allowance accounts for only 0.1 percent of the allowances paid.

Prestation Spéciale Assistante Maternelle (PSAM) (Special Mother's Helper Allowance). This allowance, created in June 1980 and revised in July 1987 following the creation of the AGED, is intended for parents who employ an approved mother's helper—in other words, one who is a member of the social insurance system. Like the AGED, this measure eliminates the financial cost to the family of the employer's social security contributions, payable by the family, to employ a mother's helper. The PSAM was also created to legitimize the previously clandestine mother's helper. As recently as 1977, 90 percent of the mother's helpers were not affiliated with the social security system.

In 1980 the likely number of recipients of the PSAM was estimated at 275,000, at a medium-term cost of 600 million francs. In fact, the real numbers have fallen far short of this forecast. In 1987 there were 45,000 recipients at a cost of 144 million francs, although 128,000 under 3s were being cared for by approved mother's helpers. Consequently the resources allotted to the PSAM have been scaled back.

Most mothers are poorly informed about this allowance. According to a survey, four out of five do not even know it exists. Another factor leading to low utilization is that the mother's helpers themselves are not interested in social insurance coverage that they obtain in any case and are worried about a possible tax disadvantage from the inclusion of their salary in the household's income. Only 14 percent of the independent mother's helpers pay their social insurance contributions. Finally, the PSAM, which comes to 22 francs a day, is a much smaller benefit for families with small children than the assistance available to those who use family day nurseries (34 francs) and public day nurseries (49 francs).

Tax Deductibility of the Costs of Looking after Young Children. Until 1987 the costs of care for young children were deductible from employment income up to a limit of 10,000 francs per child. In 1988 this deduction was replaced by a reduction in the amount of tax equal to 25 percent of the actual cost of care, up to a limit (1990) of 15,000 francs per child, with a maximum reduction of 3,750 francs. The child care expenditure involved must be for children who are under 6 at the beginning of the tax year and are cared for either at home or elsewhere by qualified caregivers or in a day nursery. Married taxpayers must prove either that both are working full time or that one is working full time and the other half time. The names and addresses of those providing the care must be supplied.

OTHER CASH BENEFITS AND ALLOWANCES FOR FAMILIES

Calculation of Benefits

Most family benefits are calculated using a monthly base (BMAF), which is fixed by government decree.

In 1946 an effort was made to arrive at an evaluation of the "objective" cost of a child by reference to the estimated cost for a typical family—that of a manual worker in the metal industry in the Seine department (Paris). Each family benefit, according to this initial approach, would be calculated as a percentage of the wages earned by the head of this typical family. Family benefits were therefore indexed to the manual worker's wages and were, accordingly, bound to increase with wages. But financial difficulties soon led to the abandonment of this association with wages. A law passed in June 1949 stipulated that the reference wage would be fixed by decree, meaning that family benefits were no longer indexed.

What happened next was to be expected. Because the social insurance branch almost inevitably shows a deficit (health care expenditures rise much faster than wages and salaries and therefore faster than contributions), successive governments have taken pains to achieve surpluses in the family branch in order to meet the health care deficits. Instead of increasing the reference wage in the light of the increase in wages in general, they increased it only to keep up approximately with price increases. The result has been that the purchasing power of benefits has been roughly maintained, but the gap between their increase and the much faster increase in wages and salaries has not allowed families to improve their standard of living significantly. Compared to single persons, therefore, their situation has considerably deteriorated.

Allocations Familiales (AF) (Family Allowances)

Family allowances are paid to families with two or more children. The AF is the major family benefit, accounting for 46.9 percent of the total allowances paid in France in 1988 (table 4.6).

The monthly amounts as of July 1, 1989, when there were over 3.6 million recipients, were:

Two children, 579 francs.
Three children, 1,320 francs.
Four children, 2,061 francs.
Five children, 2,802 francs.
Six children, 3,543 francs.
Each additional child, 746 francs.
Increase for each child age 10–15,* 163 francs.
Increase for each child over 15,* 289 francs.
*Only in families with three or more children

Allocation de Parents Isoles (API) (Single-Parent Allowance)

This allowance, created in 1976, is aimed at ensuring a minimum income for everyone who is rearing one or more children alone. The minimum income is set at 150 percent of the monthly base for calculating family allowances (BMAF), plus 50 percent of this base for each dependent child. On July 1, 1988, the allowance came to 2,712 francs for a single expectant mother; 3,616 francs for a single parent with one child; 4,520 francs for a single parent with two children; 5,424 francs for a single parent with three children; and 904 francs for each additional child. As a point of reference, in 1989, the median monthly wage was 7,075 francs and the median female wage was 6,375 francs.

The single-parent allowance, which is means tested, is paid for twelve months or until the youngest child reaches 3 years of age. It is meant to supplement personal income and the family allowances already being paid up to a certain ceiling. At the end of 1988, there were 126,148 recipients, practically all of them women (98.8 percent) and more than half of them unmarried (55 percent). The API accounted for more than 3.2 percent of the total allowance expenditures in 1988.

Allocation de Rentrée Scolaire (Back-to-School Allowance)

This allowance, created in 1974 and intended to cover the clothing, stationery, and other expenses incurred at the start of the French school year, is paid to families receiving a family allowance with net taxable income in 1988 of less than 79,637 francs for families with one child, plus 18,378 francs for each additional child. The amount is equal to 20 percent of the BMAF, meaning 362 francs per child at the start of the 1989–1990 school year. More than 2 million families received the allowance in 1988. The sums involved accounted for 1.3 percent of the total family allowance expenditures.

Allocation Logement (AL) (Housing Allowance)

The housing allowance, created in September 1948, is calculated by a formula that takes into account a family's income, the proportion of income spent on rent, and the number of dependent persons. At the end of 1988, 1,129,241 households (over 30 percent of all family allowance recipients) were receiving this allowance, accounting for 10.1 percent of total family benefit expenditures.

Allocation de Soutien Familiale (ASF) (Family Support Allowance)

Originally created in 1970 as the "orphan allowance," this allowance was paid without any income ceiling from 1973 on and was renamed ASF in 1985. It is paid for young orphans or children abandoned by one or both parents and for children with a parent who is not meeting support obligations.

The amount of the allowance is 22.5 percent of the BMAF if the child has been abandoned by one parent and 30 percent if he or she has been abandoned or both, coming to 407 francs in the first case and 542 in the second as of July 1, 1989.

Complément Familial Versé aux Familles Nombreuses (Large-Family Supplement)

Since the beginning of 1985, this benefit has been reserved for families with at least three children who are 3 years of age or older and meet an income test. The amount of the supplement is equal to 41.65 percent of the BMAF or 753 francs as of July 1, 1989.

Prime de Déménagement (Moving Grant)

Since June 1, 1987, this grant has been paid to families having or expecting a third or subsequent child who move between the fourth month of pregnancy and the child's second birthday. The actual moving expenses are reimbursed up to a limit expressed as a percentage of the BMAF and are increased for each dependent child.

Quotient Familial

This is the provision of the French personal tax system for adjusting the amount of taxation to the size of the household. Total taxable income is divided by a number of "shares," representing the number of adults and children in the household. The result of this division is the basis for determining the amount that a household owes. The larger the number of "shares," the lower is the tax bill.

The *quotient familial* was created by a Finance Act in 1946. At that time, a couple represented two shares during the first three years of marriage; later it was reduced to one and a half plus a half-share per child. In 1959 all couples became two shares, and in 1981, an extra half-share was allotted to the third child. In 1982 a ceiling was placed on the tax benefit due to the *quotient familial*. Finally, in 1986, an additional half-share was provided to each child, starting with the fourth.

The present scale is as follows: one share for each adult; one-half share for the first child; one-half share for the second child; one share for the third child and each later child; and one-half share in addition for a single person with dependent children.

The tax reduction resulting from the application of the *quotient familial* had a ceiling (11,420 francs in 1988) for each of the half shares beyond the two shares for the parental couple. In the case of single, divorced parents or couples who have opted to be taxed separately, the ceiling in 1988 was 14,600 francs. (These expenditures do not appear in table 4.6.)

Retirement

The pensions of mothers with a history of paid employment are calculated to compensate them for child rearing. The length of service considered in determining old age insurance benefits is increased by two years for each child brought up for at least nine of his or her first sixteen years. The pensions of parents who have reared three or more children are, typically, increased by about 10 percent, the supplement not being taxable.

A TENTATIVE ASSESSMENT OF THE FAMILY POLICY MEASURES

Economic assistance for families can be intended to redistribute income in their favor or to protect them against impoverishment because of child rearing expenses. It can also have the objective of encouraging procreation, which is often postponed or decided against because of a couple's fear that their living standard will fall substantially as a result of the related costs. Whether the family policy has the objective of encouraging additional births or bolstering inadequate incomes, any tentative assessment of its effects may take into account the cost of the child and the extent to which this cost is covered by the relevant allowances. It must also consider whether the recipient families are satisfied by the nature and extent of the assistance.

Before comparing the family allowance package to the actual child rearing costs experienced by families, it is useful to consider the not insignificant worth of the package of benefits available to average French families with two children, ages 9 months and 4 years. The benefits combined for the estimate include the various special allowances for very young children, the allowances for all families with children, the income tax credits, and child care tax credits, all involving several estimations and approximations. The yearly value of these benefits based on a median wage of 86,500 francs yields the following approximate comparisons:

Husband/wife family, mother at home: 28.5 percent.

Husband/wife family, mother in labor force: 22.4 percent.

Single mother at home: 64 percent.

Single mother in the labor force: 35.5 percent.

Cost of the Child in Relation to the Family Allowances

Several statistical and quantitative approaches have been applied by various experts in attempts to assess the cost of a child according to various criteria and especially with reference to ordinal position in the family. Estimating this cost is far from simple, and the results obtained are strongly influenced by the assumptions underlying the approaches. It is in fact difficult to imagine how an "objective" cost can be attributed to a child. How does one isolate from all the expenditures those items that are specifically linked to that particular child, especially when there are others in the family, and also assess the consequences of these expenditures for the family's standard of living? Putting aside the methodological problems for the moment, however, estimates that have been developed do provide a good account of the cost variations among first, second, and third children.[15] The additional resources a couple needs to cover the additional expenditure of the first child are about 19 percent. When a second child is born, an economy-of-scale effect comes into play, and the additional cost is only 16 percent. The effect disappears for families with three children. New expenditures associated with the increase in family size then enter the calculus (moving to larger quarters, for example), and the additional cost is substantially greater (21 percent).

Estimating how costs change with the age of the child raises somewhat greater methodological problems, but calculations indicate the increase in resources needed to compensate a household for children-linked expenses is 14 percent for a child under 5, 17 percent for children between 5 and 9, and 23 percent for children in the 10 to 15 age group.[16]

The same approach can be extended to extrapolate the cost of the child over the family life cycle. Over the long term, economies of scale emerge as a stronger factor in all cases compared to a point-in-time analysis. The relative fall in the cost increases between the first and second children is 19 percent and 14 percent, respectively. The cost of the third child over the whole life cycle is appreciably lower than when recorded at a given moment (16 percent compared with 21 percent). Thus the cost of children measured over the whole of the life cycle is less than the cost when measured at a given moment, with the additional cost of the third child, in particular, coming out much lower.

To what extent do the family allowances and tax benefits associated with the presence of children compensate for these costs? An estimate of the increase in net income resulting from social transfers compared with the average cost of children for each size family shows shortfalls ranging from 15 to 30 percentage points, depending on the number of children and the income level. In only one case (families at the very bottom of the income range with three dependent children) is the cost of the children almost entirely offset by the transfers. In all other cases, there is a shortfall that remains practically unaffected by either the level of income or the labor force status of the woman (table 4.8). Indeed, the results are even less impressive if one takes into account life cycle variations in female labor force participation, taxes, and benefits.[17]

In other words, despite the fact that the family allowances and the tax benefits are quite substantial, they cover only a small part of the cost of a child. It is primarily the absence of any specific benefit for the first child that produces this result; the transfers always seeming to be one child behind, regardless of the number of children.[18] The relative insensitivity of this transfer effect to income level (and to its corollary, the labor market activity of the woman) is due to the fact that the allowances with income ceilings that are provided to poorer families are balanced by the tax advantages granted to families with relatively high incomes. In fact, the question can be asked whether family policy has always been centrally concerned with reimbursing the cost of the child. Despite all the statements and the repeated appeals for providing economic aid to families, family allowances have gradually lost their role as financial compensation, whether this compensation is linked to the presence of children or to the mother's work. Since 1946 wages and salaries have actually risen much faster than family

Table 4.8
Increase in Net Resources as the Result of Cash Benefits and Tax Allowances by Number of Children and Labor Force Status of the Mother (after taxes and benefits)

Net earned income of head of household in 1986 (classified by deciles)	Couple/ 1 child		Couple/2 children		Couple/ 3 children	
	1 working	2 working	1 working	2 working	1 working	2 working
D1 [a]	103.1	104.0	117.3	113.9	142.6	128.3
D3	102.4	103.3	113.2	110.8	132.6	125.0
D6	104.7	103.1	114.5	109.8	129.4	120.7
D8	102.2	103.0	110.1	108.4	123.6	118.0
D9	102.6	104.2	108.3	109.4	115.8	115.6
D9 X 1,2	103.7	103.1	108.9	108.2	115.1	114.3
Average cost of child	119		132		146	

Source: Gérard Lattes, ''Aide à la famille et le coût de l'enfant,'' *Économie et Statistique*, no. 203 (1987).

Note: Index numbers, 100 = resources of a childless couple.

[a] First decile, meaning that 10 percent of male wage earners earn less than D 1.

allowances, although the latter were originally indexed to the typical wage of metal workers in the Paris region. If family allowances therefore provide less and less compensation for the cost of the child, what about the objective of stimulating the birthrate and the need to bolster the precarious financial situation of poorer families?

Family Policies and Fertility

There is no available statistical model capable of explaining the relationship between fertility and aid for families, given the complexity of motivations involved in procreation. Birthrates everywhere follow similar evolutions linked to changes in life-styles and in society. It is nevertheless possible to establish correlations with certain factors that can influence fertility. This kind of analysis indicates that the correlations between the family policy indicators and fertility are significant and provide an explanation for differences in fertility rates in countries that are socially and economically similar. For example, the differences between the family policies of the United Kingdom and France are largely responsible for the fact that France's fertility rate is considerably higher, with

French women bearing 0.17 more children per female than those in the United Kingdom.[19]

Using the same kind of model, one can estimate the increase in fertility that would result from increasing financial aid to families to the level of the costs associated with the presence of children. In that event, the fertility indicator would rise by 0.3 children per female.[20] These results explain the interest in family policy and demonstrate its limitations. On the one hand, family policy appears necessary at least to maintain the birthrate, but on the other, the financial effort needed to increase the birthrate seems disproportionate to the results.

Family Policies and Family Income

A different aspect of family policy—the redistribution of income in favor of families and their economic protection—is as important as the emphasis on stimulating the birthrate. Families in general, and especially large and single-parent families, are very often poor or at least in precarious economic circumstances. This is particularly true of households where the wife is not in the labor force.[21]

Analysis of the structure of those households with the lowest incomes confirms that regardless of the poverty threshold chosen, a high proportion of poorer households are found to include dependent children (table 4.9). In particular, there is a marked overrepresentation among the poorer families of family units where the mother either does not work or is a single parent.

The first assessments made since the introduction of *revenue minimum d'insertion* (RMI) (a recently instituted form of guaranteed minimum income conditional on demonstrable attempts to enter or return to active work) have confirmed the substantial number of families with children among those households with incomes below a minimal standard (in 1989, 2,025 francs a month for a single person, 3,038 francs for a couple, and 608 francs for each additional household member). Almost 37 percent of the household recipients of this allowance have at least one dependent child, and 19.5 percent have two children. The other recipients are single individuals (57 percent) and couples without children (6.5 percent). The proportion for families with a dependent child is only slightly larger than for the population in general (35 percent), but it is still very high and indicates that in certain cases the various family allowances and other assistance to families are not in fact sufficient to prevent poverty.

Satisfying Family Needs and Aspirations

It should be remembered that 50 percent of very young children need child care because their mothers work. Among these children in care, 25 percent are looked after by their mothers (farmers' wives, shopkeepers, self-employed, or those otherwise able to do so). The other 75 percent are cared for either in official day nurseries or by qualified caregivers or through private arrangements with

Table 4.9
Labor Force Participation of Women as a Poverty Factor (Disposable Income, Family Benefits Included)

Family type	All households	Poorest household, with income per CU[a] of less than 2nd decile (31,600 F/Y)	1st decile (25,000 F/Y)	40% of average income (21,100 F/Y)
Man working, woman not				
- no children	5.4	5.9	7.3	8.2
- 1 or 2 children	10.9	18.4	19.0	17.3
- 3 or more children	5.7	15.6	13.9	10.2
Man working, woman working				
- no children	7.6	2.7	2.7	2.8
- 1 or 2 children	18.4	7.6	6.4	5.8
- 3 or more children	3.3	3.4	2.9	2.0
Woman not working, with children	0.9	3.3	5.4	6.5
Other single-parent famiies	3.8	4.7	4.9	4.8
Man not working, woman working	2.6	3.0	3.3	3.3
Couple, neither working	15.1	15.4	13.8	13.7
Working person, living alone	10.2	6.3	9.2	10.8
Inactive person, living alone	16.1	13.5	11.2	14.5

Source: Institut National de la Statistique et des Études Economiques, *Enquête Revenus Fiscaux 1984* (Paris).

[a] CU = consumption unit: The first adult in a household counts as 1 consumption unit, the second as 0.7 unit and each child as 0.5 unit.

nonapproved nurses or grandparents. These private arrangements predominate, covering 56 percent of very young children. In other words, the vast majority of very young children who need child care are not cared for in official day nurseries or by authorized caretakers.

To what extent do the families concerned regard these arrangements as satisfactory? The degree of satisfaction was measured in a CREDOC (Centre de Recherche pour L'Etude et L'Observation des Condition de Vie) study on the aspirations of the French people in 1987 and 1988. A satisfaction index (constructed by comparing desired behavior and actual behavior) shows that families were most satisfied with the public day nurseries (77 percent) and least satisfied with nonapproved caretakers (44 percent).[22] The satisfaction scores were 67 percent for those using official family day care, 62 percent for those relying on grandparents, and 46 percent for those with official home helpers.[23]

Another indicator of family satisfaction is the number of families who report an inability to find a place in the child care facility of their choice and are therefore required to fall back on a different arrangement. For example, 57 percent of families who would have preferred a public day nursery were unable to find a place. Also disappointed were 54 percent of those who would have preferred at-home child care, 49 percent of those who would have preferred an approved family care arrangement, and 25 percent of those who would have preferred an informal family day care arrangement. In other words, the greatest disappointment stems from the lack of sufficient space in public day nurseries and the next greatest from the difficulties of obtaining home child care.

The degree of disappointment due to a scarcity of slots in public day nurseries is much less (41 percent) if one considers only those parents with children under 3 at the time of the survey. This difference probably reflects the increased availability of day nursery slots in recent years.[24]

A temporary leave from work, however, actually seems to be the solution most frequently preferred by mothers (table 4.10). Respondents seem to regard as inadequate the current policies concerning this option, especially the guarantees of a return to the same job after the leave. The problem of finding alternative income seems relatively less important than the job protection.

Current Orientations of Family Policy

The urgency of family policy derives from concerns about fertility, the need to be responsive to the increase in female labor force participation, and the aging of the population. General economic circumstances will make it necessary to manage new family policy initiatives through better management of all social insurance rather than new budgetary allocation. In fact, the family fund was in surplus in 1989 and was used to meet deficits in the health care and retirement pension systems.

In any case, this is the thrust of the social welfare board, which noted that major changes could not be expected at present.[25] Nonetheless, the special concern for the most disadvantaged families and for larger families would not be put aside. Emphasis is placed upon measures to increase equity in reimbursement of child expenses because current tax-related measures are most responsive to the needs of families with higher incomes, to increase the family allowances for one or two children, and to continue to expand and diversify child care facilities for very young children.

None of these points was addressed by the government's "Plan for the

Table 4.10
Parenting Solutions Preferred by Working Women, 1988 (Percentages)

Solutions	Whole French population	All those with a child under 16	All those with a child under 3	All working women
Be allowed to continue working through the provision of increased services and facilities	28.2	30.3	26.8	36.8
Receive financial support to enable them to stop working temporarily	70.8	69.2	72.9	62.9
No opinion	1.0	0.5	0.3	0.3
TOTAL	100.0	100.0	100.0	100.0

Source: Centre de Recherche pour l'Etude et l'Observation des Condition de Vie, *Enquête "Aspirations"* (Autumn 1988).

Family," presented on January 20, 1990. Although designed as a comprehensive program to renew family policy, the plan's actual impact is likely to be considerably more modest. The new measures proposed, costing 1.5 billion francs, would include the payment of family allowances and personalized housing assistance up to the age of 18 (previously 17) when the child is neither attending school nor working; paying the back-to-school grant up to the age of 18 and extending it to low-income families with only one child; and extending the mother's helper allowance (PSAM) to children between 3 and 6 and calculating it on the basis of actual expenses rather than continuing to pay a flat rate.

CONCLUSION

An overall assessment of the results of family policy indicates that the initial objective of stimulating the birthrate and redistributing income in favor of families cannot be obtained by simply paying out benefits. In contrast, it seems that the economic situation of certain families can be more effectively made secure by providing incentives for mothers to become employed rather than by adding specific benefits. The *revenue minimum d'insertion*, which is based on a strong incentive to work (*contrat d'insertion professionnel*), is a good example. However, if the mother has an incentive to become employed, the objective of encouraging additional births can be achieved only by measures that relieve mothers of part of their family responsibilities, especially by providing child care during working hours.

This is precisely the direction taken by recent measures, mostly concerned with very young children, which expand the specific benefits or tax advantages for child caring. The assistance to large families has also been reinforced but by means of tax cuts that do not benefit low-income families who do not pay taxes. Additionally, the first child is still entirely ignored by family policy.

NOTES

1. J. J. Dupeyroux, *Droit de la Sécurité Sociale* (Paris: Dalloz, 1984).
2. Pierre Laroque, *Rapport sur les Politiques Familiales en Europe* (Paris, Secretary General's Report to Council on Europe, 1988).
3. Institut National d'Etudes Démographiques (INED), *Dix-huitième Rapport sur la Situation Démographique de la France* (Paris, 1989).
4. Laroque, *Rapport*.
5. Institut National de la Statistique et des Etudes Economiques (INSEE), *Population Active, Emploi et Chômage Depuis 30 ans*, Les Collections de l'INSEE, Série D, No. 123 (Paris, 1987).
6. B. Belloc, ''De Plus en Plus de Salariés à Temps Partiel,'' *Economie et Statistiques*, no. 193–94 (1986).
7. M. G. David and C. Starzec, ''The Redistribution Effect of the Socio-economic Environment on Family Income and Wives Earnings in France and United Kingdom'' (paper presented at the IARIW [International Association for Research in Income and Welfare] Conference, Lahnstein, Germany, 1989).
8. *Protection Sociale*, Rapport de la Commission Présidée par René Teulade, Commissariat Général du Plan (Paris, 1989).
9. Ibid.
10. Ibid.
11. Laroque, *Rapport*.
12. National Accounts (France, 1989).
13. G. Hatchuel, ''Accueil de la Petite Enfance et Activité Féminine,'' in Centre de Recherche pour l'Etude et l'Observation des Condition de Vie (CREDOC), *Collection des Rapports*, no. 61 (Paris, 1989).
14. Caisse Nationale de l'Allocation Familiales, *Report* (Paris, April 1989).
15. L. Bloch and M. Glaude, ''Un Approche du Cöut de l'enfant,'' *Economie et Statistiques*, no. 155 (1983); also see G. Lattes, ''L'Evaluation de la Politique Familiale, Les Prestations Familiales,'' in *Donnés Sociales 1987* (Paris: INSEE, 1987).
16. Bloch and Glaude, ''Un Approche.''
17. Ph. Madinier, C. Sahut d'Izarn, ''Familles Nombreuses: les Aides sont Loin de Compenser les Charges,'' *Notes et Graphiques*, no. 11 (Paris: Centre d'Étude des Revenues et des Coûts (CERC), 1990).
18. Lattes, ''L'Evaluation''; see also G. Lattes, ''Aide à la Famille et Côut des Enfants,'' *Economie et Statistiques*, no. 203 (1987).

19. Olivia Ekert-Jaffe, "Effets et Limites des Aides Financières aux Familles: Une Expérience et un Modèle," *Population*, no. 2 (1986): 327–48.

20. Ibid.

21. "Mères de Famille, Côuts et Revenus de l'Activité Professionnelle," Documents du CERC, no. 75 (Paris, 1985).

22. Hatchuel, "Accueil de al Petite Enfance et Activité Féminie." The *école maternelle*, here described as the public day nursery, is an entitlement for the 3-5s and practically all attend. When there is space the 2s are admitted and 40 percent in fact now attend.

23. CREDOC, *Enquête "Aspirations"* (Paris, 1988).

24. Ibid.

25. Teulade, "Protection Sociale."

REFERENCES

Atkinson, A. B., and J. Hills. "Social Security in Developed Countries: Are There Lessons for Developing Countries?" Discussion Paper WSP/38. London: London School of Economics, 1989.

Barbier, J. C. "La Protection Sociale de la Famille dans les Pays de la Communauté. *Revue Française des Affaires Sociales* (November 1989).

Baroin, D. "Le Travail à Temps Partiel en France." in J. P. Jellade, ed., *L'Europe à Temps Partiel*. Paris: Economica, 1982.

Centre d'Etude des Revenus et des Coûts. "Familles Nombreuses, Mères Isolèes, Situation Economique et Vulnérabilité." *Documents du CERC*, no. 85. Paris, 1987.

Centre d'Etude des Revenus et des Coûts–Institut National de la Statistique et des Etudes Economiques (CERC-INSEE). *Les Familles Nombreuses, Contours et Caractères*. Paris, 1989.

Collert, Y. *Rapport sur les Structures d'Accueil de la Petite Enfance*. Paris: Institut de l'Enfance et de la Famille, 1987.

Commissariat Général du Plan. *L'Avenir de la Protection Sociale*. Paris, 1983.

Les Comptes de la Sécurité Sociale. Rapport de la Commission des Comptes de la Sécurité Sociale, *Documentation Française*. Paris, 1989.

Fournier, J., and N. Questiaux, *Le Traité du Social*. Paris: Dalloz, 1984.

Gokalp, C., and M. G. David. "La Garde des Jeunes Enfants." *Population et Sociétés*, no. 161 (1982).

Roland, R. *Le Coût de l'Enfant, Approches Théoriques, Méthodologiques, Empiriques*." Ministère de la Communaté Française. Brussels, 1985).

Villeneuve-Gokalp, C. "Garder son Emploi, Gardes ses Enfants: Une Analyse par Catégorie Sociale." *Cahiers Québéçois de Démographie* 18, no. 1 (1989).

"Work and Family, The Child Care Challenge." *Conditions of Work Digest*, Vol. 17, 2/1988. Geneva: International Labor Organization.

5

Hungary—Supporting Parenting and Child Rearing: Policy Innovation in Eastern Europe

Maria Adamik

Hungary has a parenting policy that provides financial support for mothers (and to some extent fathers) who have had some prior attachment to the labor force and who may remain at home until their child is 3 years old. The policy is linked to prior labor force attachment in that benefits are more generous if the parent has been in the labor force and still more generous for parents with relatively good jobs and higher wages. This link between family benefits and employment was strengthened in the mid-1980s.

The total policy package includes maternity benefits and leave, a family allowance, two types of child care (or child rearing) grants (one a flat-rate benefit and one a wage-related benefit), and a period of job-protected child care (parenting) leave from work. The child rearing grants and leave are the most significant aspects of the Hungarian parenting policy and thus receive the major attention in this chapter.

The child care–parenting policy emerged out of a combination of factors, including concern with fertility rates and a desire to increase birthrates, interest in shaping female labor force patterns to respond to changing labor market needs, and some ideology about the roles of women and the needs of children. Since its establishment in 1967, the policy has been modified several times in response to social and economic changes.

Given the current economic dislocation in Hungary, a number of concerns about the policy and its effects have emerged. One is that rising unemployment will affect women more than men. As a result, the link between employment

Table 5.1
Birth and Fertility Rates, 1949–1988

Year	No.of live births in thousands	Crude birth rate per 1,000 pop.	Total fertility rate
1949	1,903	20.6	2.59 (1948)
1962	1,300	12.9	2.02
1967	1,488	14.6	-
1970	1,518	14.7	1.97
1980	1,486	13.9	1.92
1985	1,302	12.2	1.83
1988	1,242	11.7	1.79

Source: Hungarian Statistical Yearbook.

and support for parenting will have negative consequences for low-income women and children, who may then fail to qualify for the benefit. Moreover, given high unemployment rates, women will increasingly be accepting the full child care grant not out of real choice but because they have no employment option.

A second concern is that since the child caring–child rearing benefit is not adequately indexed (linked to the cost of living), the real value of the benefit(s) will not keep up with Hungary's rampant inflation. [In what follows, *child-rearing benefit, child-caring benefit* and *child-care benefit* are synonymous—*Ed.*] Families depending on this benefit for income will find themselves more and more economically deprived over time.

A third concern is that Hungarian social and family policy, as well as wage policy, has been predicated on a traditional family structure with two working parents in the family and therefore a family income consisting of two wages. With the increase in single-parent, female-headed families in recent years, the benefits will not be sufficient to support these nontraditional families adequately.

CONTEXT: DEMOGRAPHY AND LABOR MARKET

Hungary's parenting policy, introduced in 1967, has been influenced by different, and often contradictory, interests: the demographic situation of the country, the economic situation (mainly the demand for female labor), the role of women, and the welfare of children.

In respect to demographic trends—except for mortality—Hungary has followed a European pattern. The decline in birth and fertility rates is similar to the pattern throughout developed Europe, but in Hungary it took place within a very short period (table 5.1). In 1962 the crude birthrate reached its lowest point (12.9); it then increased briefly, but since 1983, it has been below the 1962 level and is still falling (11.7 in 1988). Throughout the 1980s the average number of children per woman stabilized at 1.89 or 1.88.

After 1962 the downward trend in fertility basically was not affected by the temporary increase in the number of births. The total fertility rate in 1988 was 70 percent of what it was after World War II (1948) and less than half of what it was in 1921. From the 1970s to the mid-1980s, almost 95 percent of births were to women under 35 (80 percent to women under 30). Since 1985 the proportion of women bearing children between the ages of 30 and 39 has grown. Since the 1960s the proportion of children born out of wedlock has doubled (from 5.5 per 100 live births in 1960 to 11.9 in 1988).

The number of marriages stabilized at 8 or 9 per thousand population after the war. This number has decreased since 1968 (refined figures) or since 1976 (crude figures). By 1988 it had reached the lowest rate since the war: 10.7 in 1948 and 6.2 in 1987–1988. The continuous decrease in marriages (and remarriages) has been accompanied by an increase in divorces (2.8 per thousand within the population over 15, or 11.3 percent of marriages in 1987). This trend in divorce came to a halt in 1988, when the rate fell back to that of the 1960s (2.3 and 9.1). Since 1960 the number of children affected by divorces per year has tripled.

These developments, in conjunction with Hungary's high mortality rates, have produced the following results:

- The proportion of the population living in families is decreasing (86.4 percent in 1960, 83.8 percent in 1984).
- The number of families with children is decreasing (60.3 percent in 1949, 51.4 percent in 1984).
- The number of one-parent families is increasing (in comparison with the 1970s, it has grown by 30 percent and is currently 12.6 percent of all families) and has reached the rate of the postwar period; 13.4 percent of children under 15 are living in one-parent families, 80 percent of them headed by women. On average, these families raise more children per family than two-parent families do.
- The crude mortality rate in Hungary has increased steadily and in 1978 reached the level 13.1 per 1000 population, higher than in 1941, a year of terrible social and economic deprivation. In the 1950s and 1960s it ranged from 9.6 to 11.7. Between 1978 and 1985 it increased from 13.1 to 13.9. In 1988 it was still 13.2. There was progress on infant mortality in the late 1980s.

The rising mortality rate and the declining birthrate led to an overall decrease in population, and by 1988 the rate of natural decrease became -1.5 per 1000 population (table 5.2).

The data on longevity are unfavorable even in comparison to other East European countries. In 1980 life expectancy was 65.5 for men and 72.1 for women. In 1987 it was 65.7 for men and 73.7 for women. The summarized mortality data conceal certain facts—for example, that from 1960 to 1987, the mortality rate of men aged 40 to 44 tripled and that the previously favorable mortality rate of women has also become unfavorable. The factors underlying mortality and morbidity in Hungary resemble what is seen in both developed and underdeveloped countries.

Table 5.2
Birthrates, Mortality, and Population Impacts, 1980–1988

Year	Crude birth rate (per 1,000 pop.)	Mortality rate (per 1,000 pop.)	Infant Mortality Rate (per 1000 live births)	Natural growth/ decrease
1980	13.9	13.6		0.3
1982	12.5	13.5	20.0	- 1.0
1984	11.8	13.8	20.4	- 2.0
1986	12.1	13.8	19.0	- 1.8
1988	11.7	13.2	15.8	- 1.5

Source: Hungarian Statistical Yearbook.

Table 5.3
Active Labor Force, 1949–1989

Year	Proportion of active earners				
	Totals		women		men
	% of total popula-tion	% of popula-tion of working age	% of women aged 15-54	% of all active earner women	% of men aged 15-59
1949	44.4	62.6	34.6 (-)	29.0	91.0
1960	47.8	71.3	49.9 (51.7)[a]	37.3	92.1
1970	48.3	76.3	63.7 (68.7)	41.8	87.3
1980	47.3	79.5	70.7 (75.2)	44.8	87.4
1989	45.5	77.3	73.9 (80.8)	46.0	80.5

Source: *Hungarian Statistical Yearbook.*

[a] Numbers in parentheses correct the rate for those in regular education. To this one should add those on child rearing leave (8 percent in 1988).

The facts described and the rates of morbidity have had a fundamental influence on the labor market activity of the potential Hungarian work force and on changes in women's roles and an indirect influence on the desire to have children.

After World War II, a so-called planned economy was developed in Hungary by means of massive industrial development and the collectivization of agriculture, with the goal of putting an end to the poverty that had existed before the war. The mechanism used was full employment. Wages were set at a low level because the central budget established nonmarket prices, subsidized child care centers, a free health service, low-cost housing, pensions, and so forth. In accordance with its underdeveloped infrastructure, this economy employed thousands of unskilled people, most of them women.

The data in table 5.3 indicate the increasing levels and rates of women's employment over the years. This is in the context of the decreasing trend in overall employment, especially in the rate of male employment. By 1989 employment rates within both the total and the working-age population had decreased from their levels at the beginning of the 1980s—from 47.3 percent to 45.5 percent and from 79.5 percent to 77.3 percent.

Women's employment increased most dramatically in the 1950s. In 1960 there were nearly a half-million more women working than in 1949 (a growth of more than 10 percent). Between 1960 and 1980 the number rose by the same amount. In the 1980s this rate of growth was not maintained, but it is remarkable that the trend for women was the only one that continued upward while all the others began to decrease; male employment reached its lowest rate since the war, compared to the number of men of working age.

At the beginning of 1987, the total number of people in the work force (4,885,000) exceeded the number in 1949 by 800,000; this was due solely to the increase in female employment, since the 1,055,000 increase in the number of working women was accompanied by a 255,000 decrease in the number of working men.

In 1988, of all women aged 15 to 54, about 80 percent were active in the labor force, while an average of 8 percent were on child care leave. Looking at this 89 percent total component by age, the highest levels of labor force participation were for women under 30 and between 30 and 39—both around 92 percent. These data signify almost full employment for women under 40, who are also the cohort of all women of childbearing age. The number of employed women over 40 is gradually decreasing. This age group increasingly includes full-time housewives, disabled persons, pensioners, and, in the last five years, pensioners still of working age but entitled to take early retirement. Although the general educational level of women is higher than that of men, they have fewer opportunities to acquire formal qualifications and employment and receive lower pay. In 1982 average female earnings were equal to 72.4 percent of male earnings. Of female workers, 50.2 percent are in the unskilled category as contrasted with 69.7 percent of males; 37.8 percent are white collar and intelligentsia compared to 16.6 percent of males.

There have been some attempts to introduce part-time jobs for women, but most of these have failed. Thus, there is only the possibility of full-time employment (eight or more hours of work a day, 40 to 48 hours a week). The retirement age is 55 for women and 60 for men.

The number of nonworking mothers has decreased. Before the introduction of the child care grant, the rate of nonworking mothers was about 50 percent. The proportion of children born to nonworking mothers was about 20 percent in 1973; later this number was reduced to 11 or 12 percent (1979–1986). It has not been possible to identify specific relationships between the marital and work status of mothers and the number and ages of their children.

HISTORY OF THE POLICY

After 1948 the new government enacted several laws intended to create a new society through a planned economy, nationalization and collectivization, full employment, centralization and redistribution of gross domestic product (GDP), and low wages. Of particular importance is the fact that the emancipation of women was guaranteed by the constitution; women had the right to work, there were legal concessions for working mothers, and there was pressure on factories to establish day care centers for their employees. To increase the number of births, a strict law against abortion was enacted in 1952 (although it was slightly relaxed two years later). The birthrate decreased markedly after 1954.

The period up to 1967 was the time when the most women—including mothers—entered the labor force. It soon became apparent that, on average, mothers worked only 50 percent of the standard working hours due to the legal concessions and absence due to children's illnesses. The female labor force was therefore said to be unreliable and inefficient; in view of the costs of child care and the compensation that had to be paid to employees for absenteeism, it simply increased costs.

Further, the capacity of children's institutions (day care centers and kindergartens) did not meet the demand. In 1960 only 7 percent of children of child care or day care center age (under 3) and 33 percent of those of kindergarten age (3–6) could be placed in these institutions.

The child care grant (GYES) was instituted in 1967. This flat-rate benefit accompanied by job protection is provided to mothers who withdraw from the labor market to care for their children at home, originally up to the age of 2 ½ and now to 3 years.

The provision of a wage-related benefit rather than a flat-rate benefit was considered in 1967, but the idea was abandoned due to insufficient financial resources. A child whose mother received the child care grant was not entitled to a place in a child care center. Moreover, any elder siblings of kindergarten age or school age in a GYES family were unlikely to be accepted into kindergarten or after-school day care, primarily in view of a shortage of capacity in these institutions until the early 1980s. In 1970 58 percent of the kindergarten cohort attended kindergarten; this rate increased to more than 80 percent at the beginning of the 1980s.

At the close of the expansionary period, the economy as a whole had no interest in increasing the participation of women in the labor force; in fact, the opposite was the case. However, this basic tendency was counteracted by a new central wage ruling that made it worthwhile for a number of firms to take on unskilled—and therefore low-waged—labor. These employers were more prepared to tolerate mothers-to-be as employees, even if only temporarily. In conjunction with the rising cost of living and the real decline in the value of the child care grant, it became possible, despite various restrictive conditions, for mothers receiving the grant to increase their income by doing some kinds of work.

These mothers had two basic options: interrupt their child care grant to return to work and then return to the child or continue to receive the grant and work a maximum of four hours a day. Neither of these two options proved to provide sufficient income, and from 1974 onward, the flat child care grant, which was not indexed, was supplemented by various benefits. In 1982 the grant was made a parental right (as opposed to a maternal one) but only after the child was 1 year old.

The changing number of women of childbearing age and the falling birthrate meant that more women wanted to give up the child care grant and return to work than wanted to leave work and receive the grant. Consequently there was a lot of tension around these mothers' returning to work—in other words, resentment of the job protection provided along with the parental leave. Many women experienced the resentment individually, although there was no widespread awareness of this problem.

There were many reasons for the introduction of the child care allowance in 1985, including the following:

- The decline in demand for labor.
- The absence of the hoped-for fertility increase.
- The inadequate standards of child care centers and the consequent interest in their abolition.
- The worsening mortality statistics.
- The government's wish to increase its generally declining legitimacy at a time of worsening economic and social conditions by redeeming a long-standing promise.

The child care allowance (GYED) required the mother (or father) to have been employed longer than did the child care grant and was wage related, as well as featuring job protection. The history of this allowance passed through stages similar to those affecting the earlier child-care grant. GYES and GYED developed in parallel from 1985 on, partly because, to a certain extent, they had become alternative options.

The length of time for which the child care allowance, GYED, could be claimed was increased from one and a half to two years in 1986, and when the child reached the age of 1, the father was entitled to claim the allowance as well. From the child's third year, either the mother or father was automatically entitled to the child care grant (GYES).

Both the allowance and the grant covered an increasingly wide circle of women employed outside the state sector. The grant increased slightly but did not keep pace with inflation, while the allowance rose in step with wages.

These developments and the policies set for GYES and GYED were not the subjects of debate by competing political parties. (Hungary was establishing a multiparty system only as this chapter was being drafted). In the previous period, public debates went on despite the absence of competing parties or organizations. Writers, economists, sociologists, and other experts argued about these matters in papers.[1] Studying their articles, we can identify two groups with different values. One group considered it important to encourage the qualified reproduction of society—that is, to exclude disadvantaged groups from receiving social benefits (GYED). The other group would have preferred a higher-level universal family allowance and a more generous GYES to promote social justice. In 1985 the first idea could make progress, but after the events of April 1990, the family allowance is likely to become a universal right. There is a similar plan with regard to GYES, although new social legislation has not yet been passed.

GYES AND GYED

The child care grant (GYES) and the child care allowance (GYED) are the most important programs supporting care for children at home. They have always been closely connected, both complementary and interdependent. The benefits are in the form of cash, the earnings-related benefits are taxable; the flat-rate lump sum is not.

Both programs start from the same point: two short programs covering the six months after birth. The first, a maternity grant, is a flat-rate lump sum to which every female citizen is entitled (and for which the only eligibility criterion is that the mother have at least one medical examination during pregnancy). The sum (6,000 forint [Ft]) is paid once and is about 90 percent of an average monthly wage. All working mothers are also entitled to the second program, a paid maternity leave, which allows them to take leave from work for twenty-four weeks (four weeks before and twenty weeks after childbirth). The sum they receive is related to the length of the time they were employed. The mother's entitlement to maternity leave determines her eligibility for the child care allowance and the amount of the benefit.

Common features of the child care grant and the child care allowance are the following:

- Both are intended to enable mothers (or fathers) to raise children at home without using an outside facility, with some money to replace their lost earnings.
- Parents can leave work for this purpose without losing their jobs and pension benefits.
- Parents have job protection, which is included in the labor legislation.
- Parents are entitled to the family allowance if participating in either of these programs.
- Both benefits are available to women when their maternity leave expires.

Child Care Grant (GYES)

This is a flat-rate grant for mothers (or fathers after the child is 1 year old) if they have been insured for a certain period of employment. The benefit can be taken up serially if additional children are born. It is available until the child reaches his or her third birthday or enters kindergarten, whichever happens first. Parents of sick children are entitled to use the grant until the child is 10.

Parents on the grant may interrupt it at their convenience and go back to full-time work, or, without interrupting the grant, they may work for a limited number of hours or have a supplementary job at home. Depending on eligibility, they can also choose the child care allowance, if this is to their advantage, and after it expires, they are entitled automatically to continue with the child care grant (for the third year).

Child Care Allowance (GYED)

This wage-related (and taxable) benefit is available for mothers (and fathers after the child is 1 year old) if they have been insured for a certain time of employment, but the eligibility criteria are stricter than they are for the child care grant. The allowance can be chosen instead of the grant and used after maternity leave until the child is 2 and can then be continued serially with the child care grant if the mother or father chooses. The upper and lower limits of this benefit are determined on the basis of the official minimum pension at any one time. Within these limits, the benefit is equal to sick pay and is generally 65 to 75 percent of previous earnings.

Value of Benefits

The value of the child care grant two years after its introduction was about 40 percent of the average wage of a young working woman (Ft 1,506) and about 31 percent of the overall average wage. Continuous price indexing began in 1974, but the real value of the benefit was not preserved. In 1980 it was 30 percent of the average national wage; in 1987 it was only 24 percent.

If the mother has additional children while she is receiving the child care grant, she is entitled to further sum(s). The sums granted for the second and third child are slightly higher than for the first child but do not increase for any subsequent children. If the births closely follow each other, the mother could in some instances receive more money from the grant than by choosing the child care allowance, especially if her previous wages were low.

The average value of the grant is about 55 percent of the earnings-related child care allowance (table 5.4). The family allowance, which in the late 1970s represented significant income, even in comparison with the rest of Europe, now covers a gradually diminishing proportion of the increasing costs of a child. It has, however, increased more quickly than has the child care grant.

Official reports show that the average ''costs'' of children have increased at a quicker pace than the real value of the child benefits. We should bear in mind that these benefits—in contrast to the family allowance, a form of wage supplementation—are intended to replace only the wages of the mother (or father) for the period covered.

Table 5.4
Value of Benefits and Costs of a Child (Ft per Month)

Year	Child care grant with one child (GYES)	Child care allowance average [a] (GYED)	Costs of a child	Family allowance average with one child
1986	1,540	2,790	3,190	739
1987	1,640	2,970	3,710	853
1988	1,870	3,660	4,670	1,263
1990	2,420	4,170[b]	5,700[c]	-----

Source: *Hungarian Statistical Yearbook*.

[a] For 1988, average earnings were Ft 8,817. The 1987 average was Ft 6,808.

[b] Minimum value: It is officially defined and guaranteed by the government, which means that the value of the minimum pension is the same and social security must pay these sums. (It does not mean that it is indexed.) As there is no definition of the minimum child care grant, its real value may decrease more than that of child care allowance and pensions. (One U.S. dollar was worth Ft 60 in April 1990).

[c] Estimated data: The validity of the data of the Central Statistical Office (KSH) has been questioned recently. Since a black market has been operating, the KSH has not been able to follow real incomes. The measure of inflation included in reports and calculations represents an official declaration of the government and not necessarily empirically unified facts.

Duration

Normally, eligible mothers (or fathers) can raise children at home for a period beginning four weeks before birth and ending when the child is 3 years old. In the case of a healthy child, there are two possible scenarios:

1. The earnings-related child care allowance (GYED) between the ages of 6 months and 2 years, followed by the flat-rate child care grant (GYES) between ages 2 and 3 years.
2. The flat-rate child care grant (GYES) between the ages of 6 months and 3 years.

In both cases the father is also entitled to claim the benefits after the child is 1 year old. In the case of a dependent, chronically ill, or severely handicapped child, the mother is entitled to the allowance until the child is 10. All of these time periods have gradually increased since their introduction.

Eligibility Criteria

Because of recent developments, it has become quite possible that a worker's job can become very unstable very quickly. Nevertheless, the eligibility criteria for benefits have remained the same:

- For the child care grant, at least 180 days spent in employment within the two years before childbirth (in which case the maternity allowance is 65 percent of wages).

Table 5.5
Statistics on Beneficiaries

Year	Child care grant (GYES)	Child care allowance (GYED)
1985	155,550	67,000
1986	117,100	104,800
1987	113,860	117,350
1988	79,000	158,000

Source: Hungarian Statistical Yearbook.

- For the child care allowance, at least 270 days spent in employment within the two years before childbirth (in which case the maternity allowance is 100 percent of wages).

The gradual improvements made over the years were always related to the recognition of more and more forms of employment as legitimate eligibility criteria. Thus, students, part-time workers, home workers, and, later, self-employed artisans, self-employed artists, lawyers, and partners within firms have become eligible for benefits. People employed in agriculture were accepted later and have received less generous allocations than have other eligible persons. During pregnancy, the following conditions must be met: the mother must be insured at the time of childbirth or the birth must have taken place within forty-two days after her insurance expired, or more than forty-two days after the expiration of her insurance but during a period when she was receiving sick pay, or within twenty-eight days from the expiration of the sick pay.

Before the child care allowance (GYED) was introduced on March 1, 1985, the number of mothers using the child care grant (GYES) was over 200,000. Previously, the greatest use of the grant (by 295,000 families) was in 1975, due to a demographic peak. From 1977, utilization of the grant gradually declined, parallel with a decline in the birthrate. Use of the grant decreased to 222,000 in the year before the child care allowance was introduced. Once the allowance became available, the number of families using the grant decreased to 155,000, while 67,000 families received the allowance (table 5.5). However, the total number of families receiving either the grant or the allowance is not significantly greater than the number receiving child care benefits in 1984 (though it should be kept in mind that the number of births continued to decrease over the period in question).

Between 1985 and 1988 most eligible mothers (96 to 97 percent) used the child care grant for rearing one child, 2.5 to 3.6 percent used it for two children, and only 0.2 to 0.3 percent for three or more children. During this time, two changes were made with the goal of increasing the number of families using the child care benefits: the extension of the child care allowance by half a year in 1987, which increases the number of users even without an increase in childbirth, and the extension of eligibility to other forms of employment, which in principle

Table 5.6
GYES and GYED Users as a Percentage of All Childbearing Women in the Labor Force

Year	Participants
1967	72
1973	78
1979	83
1986	89

Source: Hungarian Statistical Yearbook.

should have the same effect. Parallel with the increase in utilization, the most important changes that took place in 1987–1988 were in the duration of utilization and the overall social composition of child care benefit users. However, this process had in fact begun before the child care allowance was introduced.

The grant encouraged women to work, at least for a short time, in order to become eligible for benefits. It is thus clear that the mothers who did not enter the labor market to qualify for the grant were also unlikely to work to qualify for the allowance, which requires longer employment, and they were thus even more likely to remain ineligible.

In short, the same mothers have been excluded from both receiving benefits and entering the labor market. They are often women with a low level of education and/or an above-average number of children, which means they cannot take a job. Alternatively, they may live in underdeveloped rural areas where there are no possibilities of employment. It is not surprising that we have no precise data about this group. Economically nonactive mothers exist neither for social security nor for the statistics.

While more and more of those entitled to benefits were utilizing them (table 5.6), labor market statistics indicate this actually led to a decrease in the number of mothers leaving work. In 1980 11 percent of the female population of working age left the labor force. Due to the decreasing number of births, the rate has since decreased to 9 percent, which represents 4.7 percent of the entire active work force. It must certainly be cheaper to pay these benefits than to pay unemployment benefits to the same proportion of the population.

CHILD CARE SERVICES

Services for children under school age provide additional forms of support for families with children. One system of services is child care and day care centers for the under 3s, the age group for which the child care grant and the child care allowance are also provided. Twelve percent of this group makes use of the centers, while nearly 90 percent of children aged 3–6 go to kindergarten (covering kindergarten, pre-kindergarten, nursery schools, and pre-schools in the U.S. sense).[2]

At this point, it should be noted that political and economic interests have influenced the operation and development of the day care centers and kindergartens. Parallel with the gradual weakening of these interests came the growing perception that these programs do not in fact promote the well-being of children at all.

However, a distinction must be made between day care centers and kindergartens, not only on the basis of their different functions (the centers being under the jurisdiction of the Ministry of Health and Social Affairs, kindergartens under the Ministry of Education) but also because their functions, especially those of the kindergarten, have also changed over time, leading to a change in the social composition of the families using them.

The development and growth of these institutions did not keep pace with demand. Overcrowding and lack of resources had extremely detrimental effects on the level of services and created socially unjust systems that benefited families with "good connections." Although the decreasing number of children has reduced the demand (some centers have been closed), the care has steadily deteriorated, just as in other fields financed by public funds.

However, parents cannot give up kindergarten since its new preschool function is perceived as being important for the child. They have therefore resorted to other solutions, including using their influence and that of their employer to improve the quality of the kindergartens. Alternatively, they have begun to use expensive private kindergartens, which have expanded simultaneously with the deterioration of conditions in public kindergartens. Consequently, despite the appearance of an equitable distribution of facilities, there is enormous variance in quality, not only among regions but even among neighborhoods in a single town.

With respect to both accessibility and quality, socially selective processes have been in operation that contrast with the original political aim of these programs to reduce the role of the family in the socialization of the child. The essence of community education was that it would enable every child to receive a centrally determined and controlled education rather than rely on unreliable family values. In this way adults would grow up malleable and loyal to socialist society. Another function of the institutions was to reduce social inequalities to counteract the differences in families' circumstances, which reproduced advantage and disadvantage.

The deficiencies of the system were such that it did not provide opportunities to the people who most needed them. The criterion for admission was the working status of the mother, and even this qualification entailed many discriminatory conditions. When the economy needed women to work, the institutions had to enable them to do so by accepting more children even though these institutions were substandard in several respects, especially with regard to care for the under 3s. There has been very little research on the possible effects of the system on children.

Table 5.7
Child Care Centers

	1970	1980	1985	1987	1988
Child Care Centers (total)	1,044	1,305	1,292	1,204	1,159
Capacity	40,010	64,502	68,274	63,902	60,947
Skilled, assigned personnel	4,998	10,713	10,981	10,225	9,878
Children enrolled	41,771	69,768	53,970	51,788	44,362
Children enrolled as % of children under age 3	9.5	14.8	14.4	13.7	11.9
Average daily number of children attending as % of capacity	84.5	81.6	64.9	62.0	60.6
Capacity per skilled child care worker (child/room)	8	6	6	6	6

Source: Hungarian Statistical Yearbook.

Child Care Centers

This institution provides day care and health care for children from 6 months to 3 years and in 1960 had enough places for 68 children per 1,000 of this age. In 1984 the child care centers accommodated 15.4 percent of the cohort, with that proportion declining to 14.4 percent in 1985, 13.7 percent in 1987, and 11.9 percent in 1988 (table 5.7), largely as a result of the impact of the introduction of the child care allowance in 1985.

Factories, companies, and others employing large numbers of women were obligated to maintain day care facilities, with the consequences that infants had to adapt to the working hours of factories; for example, they had to travel with their mothers for one to two hours early every morning. In industrially underdeveloped regions, centers were not established.

In 1970 almost 30 percent of all day care centers were maintained by factories and other workplaces; by 1988 this proportion had fallen to 12 percent. The decrease occurred because of the generally reduced demand for female labor. The number of centers maintained by factories decreased faster than the number financed by the state. Because the costs of maintenance were high, it was cheaper for employers to pay contributions to other centers.

Data up to 1980 indicate extreme overcrowding. In 1980, with use running at 120 percent of capacity, slightly more than 80 percent of the under 3s attended child care centers at any one time, with two unfavorable effects. First, the spread of infections among children became unavoidable and increased the number of illnesses. Second, overcrowding led the tired and sometimes unskilled staff to introduce a strict, regimented routine. One skilled child care worker was responsible for from six to eight children.

In spite of the low prestige and wages of female labor, the development and maintenance of day care centers is expensive. These expenses amount to twice the child care grant per child, and each new place cost three to four times as much as in the 1980s as it did in the 1960s (Ft 200,000–250,000). The decreasing number of children therefore does not mean an increasing level of supply. In fact, more and more institutions are being closed in response to the preference for other methods of child care, such as the child care grant or the child care allowance, which involve the mother's giving up work for a time.

Depending on their wages, parents pay a fee, which does not completely cover the costs of center care. Consequently, families having access to centers and kindergartens receive a subsidy that is the equivalent of a Ft 1,000–2,000 social benefit per month in comparison with the families who cannot make use of this kind of institution because of their circumstances (having a large number of children, being unemployed, being on child care leave, being gypsies, or living in poor conditions). On the other hand, parents who do use the centers also do not always do so as a matter of choice; they may, for example, be single parents without other options.

Kindergartens

These centrally financed, universal institutions provide care and education for children between 2 1/2 or 3 and 6 years of age. Kindergartens are used eight times as much as are centers. Although there are no rules actually excluding anyone, there is no legal right to this service.

Kindergartens have a long history, both in theory and in practice, particularly in comparison with centers. This tradition may be the reason that the system has always been able to protect itself rather better than have other child care institutions. For example, while the number of educated middle-class parents using centers had declined between 1972 and 1982, the number using kindergartens had grown.

The shortage of kindergarten places brought selective mechanisms into operation. For example, a second or third child was not accepted if the mother was at home on child care leave with the youngest child. The situation was especially difficult for mothers living in small villages, two-thirds of which had no kindergarten.

Kindergartens were relatively free of negative effects on children as long as there were still high-quality teachers who regarded the development of the child's personality as important or as long as their ideas had some influence. After a while, however, despite increasing overcrowding, kindergartens were ordered

Table 5.8
Kindergarten Use, 1938–1988

Year	Number of children in kindergarten (000)	Year	Number of children in kindergarten (000)
1938	112		
1950	106	1980	478
1960	184	1985	425
1970	227	1988	395

Source: Hungarian Statistical Yearbook.

to serve the school system, and games and other play were given low priority in favor of activities more like the disciplined, drill-like lessons given to children at school.

This association with the school system had two major consequences: competition was introduced in the kindergartens, and acceptance in school was made dependent on a recommendation from a kindergarten.

Again parents did not revolt. Instead, they tried to prepare their children for competition, formed pressure groups, or, if they had more money than influence, paid to send their children to expensive private kindergartens, which provided not only better education but also excursions, sports, and other services. These changes in the kindergarten system have both caused it to become a more selective mechanism and predestined the children who do not attend to failure.

In 1950 fewer children attended kindergarten than did in 1938, but the number grew steadily until 1980 despite fluctuations in live births (table 5.8). Since 1980 a decrease in attendance has paralleled the decreasing numbers of children and parents' growing preference for alternative means of child care.

Combining Benefits and Facilities

There are about 65,000 children in the age group birth to 6 months. The benefits aimed at them are the maternity grant and the maternity allowance. Because utilization is practically 100 percent, all the children belonging to this age group are looked after by their mothers. But after this first half-year, care may continue in several ways.

The total number of children in the age group 6 months to 3 years is about 310,000. There are several possible patterns of care:

- The mother or father continues to care for the child at home (with the child care allowance and/or child care grant). About 240,000 children (77 percent of this cohort) are cared for in this way.
- About 44,000 children (14 percent of the cohort) are cared for by their mother at home without cash benefits because she lacks eligibility.
- The third group consists of 30,000 children (9 percent of the cohort) who are cared for

in centers while their mothers work. These families either do not want to use the child care allowance and/or grant or cannot afford to do so.

From the child's perspective, independent of cohort or year, the child care arrangements are the following, listing by order of frequency:

1. The child is at home until the age of 3, when he or she goes to kindergarten and the mother goes back to work. Some children begin kindergarten at the age of 2 1/2, the lowest age permitted.
2. The child is looked after at home until the age of 6 months; then he or she enters a day care center, after which he or she enters kindergarten. The mother is at work after the child is 6 months old.
3. The child is at home between birth and age 3. The child is also looked after at home between ages 3 and 6 because the mother does not go back to work or because she has another child and utilizes the child care allowance or a child care grant once again.
4. The child is at home between birth and age 3 (the mother is ineligible for any benefit), and the child continues to be at home until the age of 6.

The last two cases are often modified by the child's going to kindergarten at the age of 5, because kindergarten has a special function of preparing children for school. In fact, 80 to 90 percent of children attend kindergarten at some point between the ages of 3 and 6.

COSTS AND FINANCING OF PROGRAMS

Social security is under state control but until 1988 did not have formal status. Its only function was to administer payments determined by the state. It had no influence over its income and could not adjust income to expected expenditures. Its budget was part of the state budget, and the balancing of its income and expenditure was subordinated to the need to balance the overall budget.

In 1988 a parliamentary decision separated the social security budget from the central budget, but since social security still had no independent statutory authority, the situation did not essentially change. Even today, the state decides which new costs will fall to social security. In 1989 social security could not use the surplus of its increased income as a result of increased payments by both employers and employees in accordance with its own interests, but, rather, with relation to those of the central budget.

From 1984 to 1987 the state suspended contributions while continuing to waste large sums of money subsidizing companies that lost money. The costs of the child care allowance, for example, were covered only by reducing the level of sick pay.

The rate of contributions paid by employees, which prior to 1988 had been set at 3 percent of the monthly wage up to Ft 2,100 (rising to 15 percent of a monthly wage exceeding Ft 14,300), was changed when the personal income

Table 5.9
Distribution of Social Security Expenditures, 1988 (Percentages)

Program	Expenditures	
Sickness benefits		8.8
Drugs and Medical Equipment		8.3
Benefits for Children and Maternity		22.8
- family allowances, approximately[a]	(17.0)	
- child care grant[b]	(0.81)	
- child care allowance[b]	(3.23)	
- maternity allowance[c]	(0.89)	
- maternity grant[c]	(0.31)	
Pensions		59.5
TOTAL		99.4

Source: Hungarian Statistical Yearbook.

[a] 2.5 million children.

[b] 240,000 parents (mostly women) withdraw from work.

[c] 120,000 births annually.

tax was introduced. Since January 1, 1988, the rate has been set at 10 percent of the gross salary or wages earned by the employee for work in his or her insured principal occupation. (Enterprises contributed 43 percent of contributions in 1988).

As a result of these new contributions, the total revenue of social security rose to almost five times its income between 1977 and 1988. Contributions paid by the state rose 200 percent while those of employers and employees rose 600 percent.

The two cash programs here in focus (GYES and GYED) cover 4.04 percent of total social security expenditures (table 5.9). Between 1975 and 1988, total social security expenditures rose 480 percent, with a similar rise in pensions. The benefits for children and maternity rose 440 percent in that same period.

In 1988, social security expenditures came to 19 percent of GNP and 15.6 percent of GDP (table 5.10). The child care allowance, a component of these expenditures, amounted to 0.6 percent of GNP and 0.5 percent of GDP and the child care grant to 0.16 percent of GNP and 0.13 percent of GDP.

USERS AND NONUSERS AMONG THOSE ELIGIBLE

Before the introduction of the child care allowance, the use of the child care grant had changed with respect to both the length of use and the social composition of users (table 5.11). In 1970 about 30 percent of all users stayed at home with the child for the whole period of the benefit (until the child was 3). This 30 percent consisted of 44 percent of all blue-collar mothers and 23 percent of all white-collar mothers. By 1986 the number of mothers staying home for

Table 5.10
Social Security Expenditure as a Percentage of GNP and GDP

Year	Social Security expenditure (Ft million)	Proportion (%) of GNP	of GDP
1975	44,898	11.4	
1980	83,808	14.4	11.6
1981	90,465	14.2	11.6
1982	98,690	14.2	11.6
1983	107,842	14.6	12.0
1984	120,801	15.0	12.3
1985	132,342	15.8	12.8
1986	142,939	16.2	13.1
1987	155,524	15.6	12.7
1988	218,473	19.0	15.6

Source: *Yearbook of Social Security Administration* (1986, 1987, 1988).

Table 5.11
Users Among the Entitled by Employment Category

Year	Blue-collar (manual workers except in agriculture)	White-collar	Workers employed in agriculture	Total
1967	78	63	68	72
1969	72	55	71	66
1973	83	73	55	78
1979	88	79	69	83
1986	93	85	84	89

Source: Hungarian Statistical Yearbook.

the whole period had grown remarkably to over 50 percent of all eligible (60 percent of all blue-collar mothers and 43 percent of white-collar mothers).

The high utilization in 1986, a year after the introduction of the child care allowance, reflected the fact that utilization of the child care grant was approaching the maximum, and this tendency was being reinforced by the attractiveness of the child care allowance (thus increasing the average number of users).

At the same time, there was a decrease in the number of mothers going back to work before the child was 1 1/2 years old. About 40 percent of mothers, including 33 percent of blue-collar mothers and 50 percent of white-collar mothers, went back to work before their benefits expired.

Along with the change in length of the use of benefits, there was also a shift in the social backgrounds of the users. There is a tendency toward a more even social distribution of users (table 5.12); nonetheless, analysis of the data on utilization does reveal some differentiation by occupation, education, and payment level since the allowance, as contrasted with the grant, is wage related.

Table 5.12
Users of Child Care Grant and Child Care Allowance among the Eligible by Educational Level

Educational level	1969	1973	1979	1986	1986 in % 1979 = 100
Primary school	71.6	81.1	85.9	88.6	103.1
Secondary school	59.9	76.4	82.9	91.0	109.8
University	32.6	56.2	68.7	81.8	119.1

Source: Hungarian Statistical Yearbook.

The evidence of a more even social distribution of users was already apparent in 1979, mainly in comparison with the disproportion in 1969 and 1973. By 1986, one year after the introduction of the child care allowance, the highest number of users was among manual workers (93 percent), a great deal higher than the national average and an increase of 5 percent over 1979. The comparable proportion of white-collar mothers was 85 percent, which is lower than the national average but represents a growth of 6 percent over 1979. The highest growth (15 percent) was shown by agricultural workers.

There is abundant evidence, not here repeated, of the importance of education in determining women's employment. A certain level of education is not only a condition of entry into the labor market but also a condition of remaining in it.

There is an increase in the utilization of child care benefits in every group in every period, but the rate of growth is faster (university) or slower (primary school), affected, of course, by the initial level of labor market participation. The remarkable increased use among university graduates (119 percent) in the last period (1979–1986) can be ascribed not so much to the increase in births as to the fact that the child care allowance, which is wage related, is particularly attractive to well-educated women earning higher salaries.

Examining the proportion of blue-collar and white-collar users in terms of the amount of their child care allowance (generally 75 percent of previous wages), we note that low-wage users are heavily represented in both groups (table 5.13). Blue-collar mothers are heavily concentrated among users receiving benefits of less than Ft 3,000. White-collar users predominate (proportionately) only at benefits over Ft 3,500; at the highest level of benefits, there are numerically twice as many white-collar users as blue-collar ones.

While data on the use of the child care grant and the child care allowance indicate that the proportions of different groups in the female population are gradually evening out, this fact may actually conceal some differences in the use of the allowance. For example, the introduction of the allowance may be the reason that the number of users among mothers over 30 grew faster than the average—even faster than among women between 20 and 24. In Hungary, one of the closest correlations has been between wages and years spent working. In reality, however, the relation is with wages, not with age. The increase in use

Table 5.13
Number of Child Care Allowance Users by Amount of Benefit

allowance monthly (Ft)	1986		
	White-collar	Blue-collar	Total
2001-2500	11,522	22,673	34,195
2501-3000	11,927	17,097	29,024
3001-3500	8,299	8,644	9,305
3501-4000	5,030	4,275	16,943
4001-4500	2,953	1,931	4,884
4501 and more	3,336	1,275	4,611
unknown	445	2,154	2,599
Total	43,512	58,049	101,561

Source: Hungarian Statistical Yearbook.

was most spectacular with women over 30, but women under 30 bear 80 percent of all children.

In 1988 over 90 percent of women under 39 worked. Almost 22 percent of women under 29 and 7 percent of women between 30 and 39 were not at work but at home on leave, with their child. A large majority (93.2 percent) of these users were married; 4.2 percent were single, 2.3 percent were divorced, and 0.4 percent were widowed.

By 1986 the utilization rates for married (89 percent) and unmarried women (82 percent) had become similar in contrast to 1979, when only 63 percent of unmarried eligible women were users.

Comparing utilization by location in 1986, the growth was the highest in big cities—except for the capital, which remained under the national average—and the lowest in small towns; in villages the growth was higher than in small towns but still substantially lower than the national average.

POLICY IMPACTS

Benefits and Birthrates

The parenting benefits were the instruments of a so-called pronatalist population policy in Hungary with the declared aim of encouraging three, and subsequently two, children in each family. (In 1973 there was also a ''planned'' crude birthrate of 16.)

Many factors affect the desire to have children, so the failure of this parenting policy package to achieve its aims of increasing the population and establishing the three-child family should not be attributed to a flaw in the package. Although it failed to produce either a lasting increase in the birthrate or an increase in the fertility rate, it probably did slow the rate of population decrease.

The benefits introduced a new factor to those already influencing a family's planning. If a mother had more than one child, she could space the births so that she could stay at home with her children for six, nine, or more years without returning to work in between. This kind of family planning led to a reduction in female fertility.

Whenever the introduction of improvements in benefits coincided with years when large numbers of women reached the childbearing age, there was a temporary increase in the number of births, causing an imbalance in the age structure. This in turn caused serious problems of bulging in all institutions, from kindergartens to schools to universities, and even the labor market.

Since the child care grant allocates additional sums for a second and each subsequent child, certain groupings that are concerned about the qualitative reproduction of the Hungarian nation hold the grant responsible for the above-average number of children born to unskilled poor families. To attribute this imbalance to the child care grant rather than to a difference in cultural values is, however, a dubious and somewhat prejudiced argument. It is similarly contentious to claim that the child care allowance was intended to benefit only highly qualified employed women. Nevertheless, we must acknowledge that the allowance has not turned out to be accessible to all women (mothers) in economically and socially disadvantaged circumstances.

Benefits and Children's Welfare

In conjunction with the traditionally efficient network of social workers and the health service, benefits can be shown to have had a positive effect on infant mortality (the proportion of deaths below the age of 1) (see table 5.2). A parent's presence and proximity is beneficial to both the physical and psychological development of the child. At the same time, research comparing the effects of good child care facilities and upbringing at home has been able to establish differences only in the socialization process rather than any clear ultimate advantages or disadvantages. However, the still relatively unfavorable although declining rate of infant mortality indicates that there are situations where the parental environment and family circumstances may not be able to offer as much to the child as can a child care facility with minimum standards of nutrition and hygiene. (Parents in these circumstances, however, are often unable to make use of such a facility).

Benefits and the Labor Market

We have noted the connection between eligibility for benefits and participation in the labor market. As long as the employer and the state responsible for social benefits are one and the same—in other words, have the same centralized interest—the economic system (or subsystem) and social policy (as another subsystem) will be significantly interdependent, according to the relative dominance of various political goals. Thus, the benefits interact with the demands of the labor market to create a flexible labor force of 4 to 5 percent.

This labor force of women on the child care grant or allowance is included in the statistics as employed, which helps to maintain an appearance of (or belief in) full employment. The grant and the allowance cost less than an acceptable level of unemployment benefits for an equal number of people. The fact that this peculiarly hidden form of unemployment exists indicates that the legally guaranteed return to the workplace is becoming more and more problematic. A woman cannot be dismissed while she is receiving the child care grant or the allowance, but she can be let go on the first day she returns to work. Moreover, during the mother's absence from work—when there is rarely any contact, no pay raises, and no bonuses—problems may arise or changes may occur at her workplace that she cannot accept. She may have become unsuitable for her previous job simply because she now has a child, but if she gives it up, she cannot be certain she will be able to find another.

Child Care Centers

Besides the already cited problems affecting day care (child care) centers, including high costs, overcrowding, and a declining number of children, the existence and accessibility of benefits have provided a rationale for gradually closing them down rather than expanding supply. This policy was not a direct consequence of the benefits, however, but a decision of principle.

Because the centers provided inadequate service, mothers would use them only out of real necessity or with a guilty conscience. If they were not forced to use centers and cared about their children's well-being, they had the option of using the child care grant or the allowance.

Benefits and Social Security

Benefits and social security have an indirect and mutual influence on each other. The child care grant and the allowance are responses to identical situations but have nevertheless been the first widely available benefits to be put on a double track—that is, to provide different levels of support with different criteria of eligibility. This double-track system is becoming a model for other benefits, and both pensions and health care are likely to be structured in the near future to provide two, or several, quite separate levels of support.

Benefits for Men and Women

The declaration of women's emancipation in 1949 and women's right to work (with all that entailed) was a government gesture toward women rather than a personal agreement between men and women. In a country where five or ten years previously everything, including gender roles, had been completely different, men from the outset resented the rights that women had been given by the government. Men and women did not arrive at a consensus about the new situation but adjusted to it individually—and unwillingly.

That women also had feelings of guilt about this process is demonstrated by the fact that years later and even up to the present day, they have not been able to bring about any changes in the domestic division of labor (housework). This division of labor is an important factor because the promised service sector has not developed in Hungary, and what there is is far beyond the financial means of the average Hungarian family.

It was in this context that first the child care grant and then the child care allowance were introduced. The cost of living had risen so steeply by that time that people were forced to take on more and more jobs in the second (black market) economy and a thirteen- or fourteen-hour workday had become the norm.

The increase in the mortality of middle-aged men sparked the first loud and public argument between the sexes. This debate neither cleared the air nor increased understanding; rather it reinforced women's feelings of guilt that their emancipation was responsible for men's mortality and the rising number of divorces.

Overworked fathers could—and can—hardly take part in family life. It was also shown that the household of a woman bringing up a child or children at home was not as well equipped as a working woman's, although even the latter had few modern conveniences.

If we also consider that men's wages are always higher than women's, it becomes clear why the fathers' right to claim the child care grant and allowance remains largely unused. The occasional father who claims them is considered a curiosity, and the number doing so nationwide has remained in the hundreds.

Research has shown that if a woman stays at home with her child for a year, this is enough time for traditional roles to become established even if they were not characteristic of the couple before. These roles are extremely difficult to change when the mother goes back to work. Fathers are also extremely reluctant to take over the parental leave after the first year.

For this reason, rather than because they are looking after children, women's experience during the three years of the benefit is largely negative. There is such widespread awareness of the phenomenon that is called child care grant neurosis, a consequence of the isolation of mothers who stay at home. The significant connection, however, is not between neurosis and the child-care grant but between neurosis and the unsatisfactory nature of social and family relationships.

Even the best parenting policy cannot avoid reflecting the contradictions of the society that created it, used it, operated it, and shaped its character. In the recent situation in Hungary, the only reasonable course for experts assessing the parenting policy and its effects is to insist that the parenting policy neither be withdrawn nor that it be turned into a benefit system that links support to the existence or reinforcement of a particular family model rather than to previous employment.

A CHANGING SOCIETAL CONTEXT

The current political transformation has been the third attempt in this century to bring about a basic change in Hungarian social structure (1918–1919, 1945, 1989). All have been imposed solutions. Without a democratic tradition, there has been no chance to achieve a well-balanced development that is accepted and supported by the majority of society. This fact has always been a source of new dangers and artificial solutions.

Joining Europe, building a market economy, creating political democracy—all this is now happening in a process that has shaken societal security to its foundations. The state is withdrawing from providing social services, and there are no responsible managers and no guarantees.

One-quarter of the population lives under or at the poverty line. Social allocations—including the child care grant and the child care allowance—cannot prevent growing poverty since wages themselves do not fulfill their function; they do not even cover the reproduction of the labor force. Nor can the social welfare system—including child care benefits—fulfill its original functions as long as wage levels are so low. It serves more as an indirect support of the economy than as a support for the raising of children. With the changes in socioeconomic conditions, one of the most important devices of social policy has thus become distorted in spite of its pronatalist aims and its increasing tendency toward universality.

Along with the increase in poverty, social inequalities are growing to an unprecedented extent. The average person is shocked by all of this, and the enormous incomes being earned by some citizens, unregistered and untaxed, offend his or her sense of justice.

These events are causing a huge amount of stress. For some generations, this may be the second crisis of adaptation they have had to experience since the war. Meanwhile the successful development of a new order on the basis of a democratically achieved consensus requires the maximum possible effort from the Hungarian people.

Not only have financial and employment security been impaired (which, of course, affects women or men trying to return to work after the child care grant and the child care allowance are over), but other factors affecting security are also under threat, including the maintenance of health and medical care. The entire health service, like all other services financed by public funds and considered free, has not actually been free for a long time and has also been of appallingly low quality. The government intends to hand over this health service now functioning with state guarantees to a social security system lacking financial resources and any experience in self-direction. The consequences of this action cannot be foreseen. It is likely not only to produce "first-class" and "second-class" citizens but due to local inequalities in health services may even diminish people's chances of survival. Local self-administering bodies, nonprofit organizations, voluntary associations, and health networks are either not ready to fill the vacuum or do not even exist.

At the end of the 1980s, the number of families with children was overrepresented in the lowest wage decile (exceeding pensioners, also in an extremely bad situation). There will be a new poverty in Hungary, child poverty, which was previously unknown. However, it should be emphasized that this poverty cannot be regarded as a consequence of the benefit system. The problems of all income-transfer programs in Hungary are related to the downward pressure on wages and the inflation imposed by the government. Since January 1, 1990, the official minimum wage has been Ft 4,200, which is also the lower limit of the child care allowance and the official poverty line. However, the cost of one child (as officially calculated) had already reached this figure in 1988. Thus, even in a two-parent, and consequently economically optimal, family, the minimum wages of two parents combined may not cover the costs of one child.

The official minimum wage of a single parent rearing one child covers less than half the costs of a child. We do not even dare to examine the relationship between the minimum wage (Ft 4,200) and the estimated costs (Ft 5,700) or the case when wages slightly exceed the minimum, not to mention the rare but not unknown situation when earnings are below the minimum wage, primarily in rural areas.

The new tax system introduced in 1988 requires mention. Although it is a progressive tax program, contrary to the illusions of the government, certain incomes have remained beyond effective control so that the system favors people with higher incomes. Legal concessions in the form of tax allowances and tax credits cannot be used even by the people who need them most because their incomes are too low. There is no refundable tax credit, and compulsory insurance cannot be deducted from the basis of assessment.

Public housing (financed by the state) has been abolished, and the cost of private construction increased 238 percent between 1980 and 1988. Buying a flat costs even more. In a good district, the price of 1 square meter of space amounts to five or six times the average monthly wage. Rents rose 35 percent in February 1990, and the costs of maintaining an apartment are increasing continuously.

Expenditures on social assistance are growing. Means tests, as in the case of all nonstatutory subsidies, require an extensive bureaucracy. Single parents receive no financial support except for the increased family allowance (Ft 300–400, or about $5–6, with a little more for orphans). They also have a slight advantage in gaining admission to child care centers and kindergartens.

As far as it can be judged in mid-1991, two decisive factors will determine the future of parenting policy in Hungary. The first is political will. The new government, strongly supported by the Catholic Church, has been attempting to influence public opinion by spreading the idea that the upbringing of children is no longer a collective, public responsibility, but the duty of the families. At the same time the importance of a higher fertility rate is emphasized.

The second factor, which is partly independent of party politics, is the deep economic crisis, limiting the state's resources that can be allocated to welfare policy.

Future changes also depend on the operation of the political forces. The Parliament is legislating relatively slowly, and in a politically contested way. Thus basic issues—privatization, the compensation for past wrongs, the relationship between central and local government, the future of social security—are still pending. A new factor of considerable influence on social policy is the tension between the central government and local authorities. The elections in March 1990 brought into Parliament a majority of conservative/right of center parties. Because of mounting general discontent with the government, the local elections in October 1990 ended with the victory of the opposition parties.

In the field of welfare politics, the only major legislation passed by this point was the ratification of the Employment Act (February 1991), which created two separate funds: an insurance fund for "passive" labor market measures (unemployment benefits and the like); and the other, a government fund for "active" measures (job-creation, training, and so on). It should be noted that while unemployment is increasing rapidly, it does not yet affect women disproportionately. Registered unemployment was 150,000, or 3 percent, in May 1991. According to forecasts, it may reach 10 percent or more by the end of 1991.

Currently, the main proposals concerning social security that seem to be gaining the support of the parliamentary majority are the following:

- The "purification" of the system from its non-insurance based elements. This means the tightening of eligibility criteria and the separation of universal benefits from social insurance. The family allowance has already become state financed (April 1990), and the same may happen to the flat-rate child care grant.
- The switch to the insurance principle in the cases of former tax-funded universal systems, unemployment, and the Health Service initially.
- The strengthening of selectivity, and the introduction of means-tested benefits on an increasing scale.

Parenting policy may be closely affected by some of these proposals, and some of the political trends. To name just a few:

- The local authorities are financially hard up. Therefore the child care institutions—crèches, kindergartens, day care centers in the schools—are threatened. One of the envisaged solutions is privatization, the other is the increase of fees. In both cases, the situation of poor families and the consequences for their families is unclear but worrisome.

- There are strong proposals to abandon the universal child care allowance, and to introduce a means-tested benefit instead.
- Social assistance has remained discretionary. The parliament will not be able to deal with the Social Act before the end of the year, and even then it is not sure whether it will adopt a normative approach to social assistance. The shortage of funds and the lack of rights mean that poverty, especially child poverty, is on the increase.
- The three-year job-protected paid child care leave is in jeopardy. It is unlikely that private firms will accept the current conditions of the grant.
- The pro-life movement is strengthening, asking for the prohibition of abortion.

In short, the change of the system, inevitable and salutary in itself, is accompanied by increasing social problems. One may only hope that the tensions will be solved before they lead to open conflicts.

NOTES

1. Maria Heller and Dénes Nemedi, "Debates on Population Issues in Hungary," unpublished manuscript (1988).

2. Data in this section are only approximations, for many reasons: (1) The cohorts 0 to 3 and 3 to 6 do not exactly cover center age and kindergarten age. (2) The upper limit of center age has been reduced to 2 1/2. (3) In certain cases children over 6 are found in kindergarten. (4) The number of children enrolled is not the same as the number of children attending.

REFERENCES

Bné Tóth, Matild. *A Magyar nôk Jogainak Fejlôdése* (Development of Hungarian women's rights). Budapest: Táncsics Könyvkiadó, 1975.

Burgerné Gimes, Anna. *A Háztartaś és a Szolgáltatások* (Household and services). Budapest: Kossuth Könyvkiadó, 1975.

Demographic Yearbook. Budapest: Government Printing Office, various years.

Documents of the Ministry of Social Affairs and Health, and the Directorate of Social Insurance, with Proposals for the Reform of the System of Social Insurance. Budapest: 1988, 1989.

Erdész, Tiborné. "A Dolgozó Nôk Iskolázottsági és Szakképzettségi Szinvonala, Kulturális Aktivitása" (The level of schooling and training and cultural activity of working women). In Egon Szabady, ed., *Nôk, Gazdaság, Társadalom* (Women, economy, society). Budapest: Kossuth Könyvkiadó, 1976.

Evaluation of Family Policy with Respect to Sickness and Maternity Schemes. Budapest: National Social Insurance Administration, 1989.

Fekete, Gyula. "A Gyermeknevelés Költségei és Várható Változások az Adóreform Után" (Cost of children and its probable changes after tax reform). *SZEKI Tájékoztató* (1988/2).

Ferge, Zsuzsa. *A Society in the Making: Hungarian Social and Societal Policy, 1945–1975* London: Penguin, 1979, Sharpey, 1980.

———. "Gyermekes Családok és a Szociálpolitika" (Families with children and social policy). In *Gyerekek a Társadalomban* (Children in society) vol. 2. Budapest: Magyar Uttörôk Országos Tanácsa, 1986.

———. "Once Again on the Socio-Economic Basis of Intersex Equality." In *Nôk, Gazdaság, Társadalom* (Women, economy, society). Budapest: Kossuth Könyvkiadó, 1976.

———. *Társadalmi újratermelés és Társadalompolitika* (Social reproduction and social policy). Budapest: KJK, 1982.

———. "The Changing Hungarian Social Policy." In Else Oyen, ed., *Comparing Welfare States and Their Future*. London: Gover, 1986.

———. "The Impact of the Present Economic Crisis on Hungarian Social Policy" *Eurosocial* (1983).

———. "The Trends and Functions of Social Policy in Hungary." In Jean-Pierre Jallade, ed., *The Crisis of Redistribution in European Welfare States*. London: Trentham Books, 1987.

Gömöri, Edit. "Special Protective Legislation and Equality of Employment Opportunity for Women." *Hungary International Labor Review* 119, no. 1 (January–February 1980): 67–77.

Horváth, Erika, and Keszei, Pálné, eds. *Hivatásom a Munka* (Work is my calling). Budapest: Szakszervezetek Országos Tanácsának Nôbizottsága, 1977.

Hungarian Statistical Yearbook. Budapest: KSH (Central Statistical Office), various years.

International Labor Office (ILO). *Conditions of Work Digest*. Geneva: ILO, various years.

Kahn, Alfred J., and Sheila B. Kamerman, eds. *Child Support: From Debt Collection to Social Policy*. Newbury Park, Calif.: Sage Publications, 1988.

Kardos, Andor. *A Bölcsôdék Túlzott Feltöltésének Problémái* (Problems of overcrowded crèches). Budapest: Népegészségügy, 1977.

Klinger, András. "Társadalmunk Gazdasági Szerkezete, az Ország Munkaerôforrásai" (The economic structure of our society, the country's sources of labor power). In Egon Szabady, ed., *Nôk, Gazdaság, Társadalom* (Women, economy, society), Budapest: Kossuth Könyvkiadó, 1976.

Kulcsár, Rózsa. "The Socioeconomic Conditions of Women in Hungary." In Sharon L. Wolchik and Alfred G. Meyer, *Women, State and Party in Eastern Europe*. Durham: Duke University Press.

Lampland, Martha. "Unthinkable Subjects: Women and Labor." *Socialist Hungary East European Quarterly* 23, no. 4 (January 1990).

———. "Working through History: Ideologies of Work and Agriculture Production in a Hungarian Village, 1918–1983." Ph.D. dissertation, University of Chicago, 1987.

Miltényi-Jobb-Kiss. *A Gyermekgondozási Dij Igénybevétele és Hatásai* (Take-up and impacts of child care allowance). Budapest: KSH, 1988.

Molnárné Venyige, Júlia. "Nôk a Változó Társadalmi Munkamegosztásban" (Women in the changing division of labor). *Társadalmi Szemle* nos. 8–9 (1986): 43–52.

Munkácsy, Ferenc. "A Nôk Gazdasági Aktivitása és a Termelékenység" (Women's economic activity and productivity). *Közgazdasági Szemle* 32, no. 12 (1986).

Neményi, Mária. "Válás-Ideológiák" (Ideologies of divorce). *Szociológia* nos. 3–4 (1984–1985).

Ratkóczi, Eva. "Gondolatok az ún. Gyes-Neurózis Kérdéshez" (On so-called child care grant neurosis). *TBZ Bulletin* 14 (1989).

Sándorné Horváth, Erika. *A Gyestôl a Gyedig* (From child care grant to child care allowance). Budapest: Kossuth Könyvkiadó, Magyar Nôk Országos Tanácsa, 1986.

Social Security Administration. *Yearbooks*. Budapest: SSA. 1986, 1987, 1988.

Statistical Yearbook. Budapest: Government Printing Office, various years.

Sugár Kádár, Júlia. ''The Effects of Choice between Mothering and Work of Hungarian Women in the Infant Care Period.'' Unpublished manuscript, 1989.

Szalai, Júlia. ''Mire Kell az óvoda és Kinek?'' (What kindergarten needs for and whom?). In *Nôk és Férfiak* (Women and men) Budapest: Kossuth Könyvkiadó, Magyar Nôk Országos Tanácsa, 1985.

———. ''Hiány és Szelekció'' (Shortage and selection, kindergarten). *Valóság*. (1981/1).

6

Finland: Supporting Parental Choice

Matti Mikkola

Parenting policies for families with young children in Finland consist of the following: special protection of maternity from environmental risks; prenatal and postnatal care, as well as maternity care; maternity, paternity, and parental leaves (with job security) and related benefit systems; and parental choice of either publicly subsidized child care or a home care (child rearing) allowance. As in other European countries, the rearing of young children is also affected by many other measures related to social and tax policy, as well as recent legislation aimed at preventing the impact of environmental hazards on the fetus and the child.

Following the Continental tradition, the level of cash benefits provided through the maternity, paternity, and parenting policies is determined by the prior earnings of the individual recipient. In contrast to the Central European plans, however, no earlier work history is required of either parent to qualify for the parental or home care allowance. Rather, this allowance is paid to all parents who are Finnish residents as a form of basic security for families with very young children.

The vigorous growth of the Finnish economy during the 1980s made it possible to develop the system of benefits and services encompassed by the Finnish parenting policy. Recently child care services have been offered to parents of very young children as an alternative to the cash allowances, thus increasing parents' freedom of choice. Strong societal support of the parenting policies has also been expressed in the acceptance of some combination of part-time child care, shorter working hours, and cash benefits (for the remainder of the standard working time), a policy specifically designed to facilitate better meshing of work and family life. Review of how this plan has been developed and an assessment requires a more detailed description.

From an international point of view, a child born in Finland has a relatively good start. The impressive statistics for infant mortality show that the rate has been reduced from 200 per thousand live births in 1870 to fewer than 5 per thousand, placing Finland among the international leaders along with Japan, Iceland, and Sweden, according to United Nations statistics.

This positive development has been obscured recently, however, by reports (due in part to improved diagnostics) of increasing numbers of babies affected by parental substance abuse or disabled in other ways and difficulties related to fertility. It is estimated, for example, that every tenth married couple remains childless in spite of improved treatment for infertility.

Nonetheless, if despite a benign environment the healthy development of Finnish children is endangered by environmental factors or conditions at home, the health or child welfare system can intervene. In a child welfare crisis, the family has the right to adequate housing and income before further intervention takes place. Yet in spite of the increase in the use of such supportive measures, 1,700 children and youth are placed outside their homes annually and about 300 children are relinquished for adoption in Helsinki, which has 500,000 inhabitants. Infants and young children in need of care are generally placed in foster families; young persons in need of care are placed in special group homes or institutions. There is little poverty in Finland in the traditional sense, but the term *the new poor* has recently emerged to describe families with multiple problems.

BACKGROUND OF FINNISH PARENTING POLICIES

Political Background

Finland's social security system was not established as the result of industrialization, as occurred in many Central European countries. Rather, the Finnish social protection system was initiated by a radical labor movement and conflicts in the labor market. However, this political conflict was diverted by the massive threat of the Red Army in the Winter War (spring 1940). Thus, the Finnish social security system was created after World War II. Even then, it developed slowly at first, for several reasons. To begin, Finland belonged to the losing side in the war, and although it was never occupied, it was required to pay extensive reparations to the Soviet Union. Second, Finnish industry was not included in the Marshall Plan and did not receive aid at all comparable to that received by other countries. Finally, as a consequence of the peace treaty, the country had to resettle 10 percent of its population from the regions annexed by the Soviet Union.

After the war, four parties dominated the domestic policy of the country. From the left to the right, they were the Communists, the Social Democrats, the Center (within which the strongest party was the Agrarian party), and the right-wing parties.

Finnish social security developed from conflicting political interests and objectives. As far as economic security and income transfer policies are concerned, the Communists and the Agrarian party have advocated the development of a policy of basic security (providing universal flat-rate grants), while the Social Democrats and the right-wing parties have favored earnings-related benefits. The reforms began with the creation of the child allowance system in 1948, and the 1950s and 1960s were decades in which social insurance was stressed—first the flat-rate so-called basic security and then the earnings-related aspects.

In contrast, the 1970s and 1980s were characterized by a shift in priority toward the development of adequate treatment and care services. While the left wing (Communists and Social Democrats) has strongly advocated the development of public services, the center and the right have stressed home care and private services through the payment of cash benefits to parents. These cash benefits are designed to provide financial support for at-home care for very young children or to permit parents to purchase child care in the private market.

The form of government in Finland has largely determined the outcome of policy. For the government to operate effectively, it must be a majority government. Furthermore, a two-thirds majority is required in Parliament for the annual budget to be accepted. As a result, there have usually been two central parties in an effective government, the Social Democrats and the center, and often one of the large parties of the left or right wing as well. From the point of view of social policy, this means that the government always includes at least one party advocating universal flat-rate benefits and one advocating earnings-related benefits, as well as at least one party advocating public services and another advocating home care through cash benefits. As a result, the opposition party can never make a truly distinctive contribution to the political agenda of the party in control of the government.

The country's geographic position, between the Scandinavian countries and the Soviet Union, may also be seen as an external factor affecting Finnish social policy. Because Finland is the only European market economy country bordering on the Soviet Union, it has been an integral part of national politics to include the communists in the government from time to time. Popular front governments have been center-left governments. Given the positions of the members of this coalition, a policy of basic security to all citizens, as well as the development of public services, has been emphasized in Finnish social security more than in some other European countries. Nordic cooperation and the drafting of joint Nordic legislation have also strengthened certain features of Finland's social policy.

Thus, no major decision concerning social security has been made without considering advantages of both flat-rate benefits and earnings-related benefits. In fact, the development of Finnish social security has been characterized by the parallel development of alternative systems through political compromise. If one side of the political spectrum achieves its demands, then the other does too. If the reasons for the creation of alternative policies are basically political, the opportunities for their implementation have resulted from economic growth, which has been more rapid in recent years than in the other West European countries.

Economic Development

As measured by gross national product (GNP), Finland's position after World War II ranked it as twentieth to twenty-fifth among countries, rising gradually to fifteenth to eighteenth, and to the eighth position in 1989. The transformation from a deprived Nordic country to a welfare society occurred simultaneously with industrial development, especially in the wood-processing industry, and with the growth of a skilled labor force. In addition to the expansion of the wood-processing industry, including lumber, wood processing, and paper, the development of the Finnish economy has been decisively influenced by a number of other factors:

- The development of agriculture and the shift to animal husbandry.
- The development of the metal industry, in connection with providing reparations to the Soviet Union.
- The development of new industries in the 1960s, including the chemical, textile, clothing, and leather industries.
- The development of the service sector.
- The emergence and growth of information technology.
- Investments in human resources through education and improved care and treatment services.

The special feature of Finnish foreign trade has been that three-quarters of the country's products have been sold to the West and one-quarter to the East, mainly to the Soviet Union, from which Finland has imported mainly raw materials, while reciprocally exporting products from the labor-intensive industries. The trade with the East has been active during a recession in the West and vice versa. Finland has been especially successful in recent decades in taking advantage of its geopolitical and economic position between East and West.

Because of the great demands on the national economy in recent years, including periodic unemployment in the postwar period and inadequate investment in housing, the country has increasingly learned to cope with crises. Thus, for example, Finland may have been the first European industrial country to emerge from the depression of 1976–1978. On the other hand, constant pressures have taken a toll on the national standard of living. In spite of increasing affluence, living conditions have become more difficult. Earlier provincial activities, community integration, the traditional Finnish neighborhood spirit, and the stability of family life have all been affected. Now, for example, every third household in Helsinki consists of a single person.

For a long time, the primary social policy debate concerned efforts to achieve a more balanced distribution of income. As a result of this struggle, income disparities were reduced by the late 1970s, due mainly to the development of pensions and other systems providing basic economic security. Since that time, however, there have been no significant new initiatives, partly because of achievements of the earlier years when purchasing power and consumption increased for virtually all segments of the population and partly because other problems, such as family break-up, loneliness, mental disturbances, and the need for social services, have become more urgent. Increasing production and consumption have clashed with the realities concerning the regeneration of the nation and the care of young children. People's primary concern has shifted from just coping with daily life to consumption. The population is declining.

A Changing Labor Market and the Female Labor Force

Women were primarily responsible for maintaining the country's productive capacity during World War II and did not become passive after peace was restored. Despite the general expectation that they would return to the home, they remained active in the labor market in large numbers. Nonetheless, the size of the labor force (2.1 million workers) remained fairly stable between 1940 and 1960. Although the number of people of working age increased from the early 1960s as the baby boom population matured, the increased numbers completing formal education and specialized training programs and the lengthening of the period of formal education led to a reduction in the number of people actually entering the labor force. Moreover, considerable migration to Sweden also contributed to keeping the size of the work force unchanged.

In the 1960s structural change began to transform Finland from an agricultural society to an industrial and postindustrial information society; this transformation took place at record-breaking speed—twice as quickly as in neighboring Sweden. It has been said that the change was too rapid, since once on the move, manpower would not remain inside the borders of the country. Between 1960 and the mid-1970s, almost 10 percent of the labor force migrated to Sweden, attracted by higher wages and better living standards. This out-migration produced the country's first labor force shortage in 1974.

Finland now has a labor force of about 2.5 million. The number of unemployed persons is about 100,000 (4 percent unemployment). Unemployment is mainly structural. Women constitute 48 percent of the Finnish labor force. In contrast to other West European countries, Finnish women did not enter the labor market in recent times but have always performed full-time work. While female labor force participation rates are lower than male rates, mainly the older age groups show the lower rates. Almost 90 percent of women ages 20 to 40 participate in the labor force, just slightly below male rates.

Table 6.1
Female Labor Force Participation by Family Status and Presence and Age of Children, 1987

	Numbers in 100s			Percentages	
	Total	Not in Labor Force	In Labor Force	Not in Labor Force	In Labor Force
All Women with Children					
under Age 18	659	97	562	14.7	85.3
under Age 7	318	67	251	21.0	79.4
under Age 4	207	51	156	24.6	75.4
Married and Living with Children					
under Age 18	589	91	498	15.4	84.6
under Age 7	297	64	233	21.5	78.5
under Age 4	195	50	145	25.6	74.4
Single and Living with Children					
under Age 18	70	6	64	8.6	91.4
under Age 7	21	3	18	14.3	85.7
under Age 4	12	1	11	8.3	91.7
All Women	1,665	486	1,129	29.2	67.8
All Men aged 16 to 64	1,683	371	1,312	22.0	78.0
with Children under age 18	603	20	583	3.3	96.7

Source: National Board of Social Welfare, 1989.

Note: All tables and exhibits in this chapter produced from the files and by the staff of the National Board of Social Welfare.

Seventy percent of women with children under the age of 7 are employed, as are 85 percent of those with children under 18. The presence of one or two children has no noticeable impact on their mother's presence in the work force, but mothers of three children work somewhat less, though at a much higher rate than in other Western countries (tables 6.1 and 6.2). In Finland, most of these women work more than thirty-five hours a week. Part-time work is still comparatively rare, involving 20 percent of women workers and 7 percent of the men. It is expected, however, that part-time work will increase gradually in coming years for many different reasons.

Finnish time-use studies (table 6.3) have found that parents with children under the age of 18 average sixty-one working hours a week. Men in these families work forty-two hours a week in paid employment and fifteen hours a week in domestic work, for a total of fifty-seven hours per week. In contrast, the women in these families work on average twenty-six hours a week in paid

Table 6.2
Female Labor Force Participation Rates by Number of Children under Age 6, 1987

	Number in Thousands	Mothers in Labor Force No.	%
No. of mothers with Children under Age 18	659	562	85%
1 Child	318	278	82%
2 Children	246	211	85%
3 or more Children	96	74	77%

Table 6.3
Family Work and Labor Market Work

	Paid Employment Hours per week	Domestic Work Hours per week	Total Hours per week
Woman and 1 child under 7	33	34	67
Women and 2 children under 7	28	40	68
Man and 1 child under 7	46	17	63
Man and 2 children under 7	44	17	61

Source: Työakak (hours committee), Helsinki 1981, 1985, 1989.

employment and thirty-seven hours in domestic work, for a total of sixty-three hours per week. The total working hours of childless married couples average fifty-one per week—about ten hours less than the working hours of parents with children. The longest working hours are those of employed mothers of very young children.

In Finnish families with one child under the age of 7 (the age at which compulsory school begins), the father works relatively long hours outside the home (forty-six hours per week). Total working hours for men (inside and outside the home) amount to sixty-three, four hours less than for mothers (table 6.3). When there are two children in the family, the fathers' working hours outside the home are two hours shorter, on average, but their participation in domestic work is no greater than in a family with one child. Thus, having two children does not increase the total working hours of the father, as it does for the mother, but rather leads to a decrease.

Women with one child under the age of 7 work an average of sixty-seven total working hours. Mothers of two children participate an average of five hours less in employment but devote six hours more to housework, for a total of sixty-eight working hours a week.[1]

Women earn about 72 percent of male wages. The lower level of women's wages in comparison to men's continues to contribute to the perpetuation of traditional gender roles and the traditional division of labor within the family. The position of women in the labor market will improve in the future, however, as their level of education rises. For some years now, girls have constituted the majority of the young people taking their matriculation examination. Also, for a very long time in Finland, girls have outstripped boys as students of medicine, law, behavioral and social sciences, and business administration. Finland is a small country in which university education is free, enabling the most successful and talented students to pursue advanced studies. Since girls tend to be better students than boys, they progress further in their studies. Moreover, this trend is continuing. Males are distinctly dominant only in the technical sciences.

Perhaps because of the lengthening period of studies or the availability of the child home care allowance—or a combination of both—the rate of labor force participation among women 20 to 25 years old has not risen during recent years. Instead it seems to have declined slightly. Since the labor force activity of older women also has declined slightly, largely because of the availability of an early disability pension, Finland has rapidly developed a shortage of female labor.

Demographic Factors

The Finnish demographic structure is often compared to playing cards. Twenty years ago it looked like the shape of the ace of spades. Today it resembles the ace of diamonds; after the year 2030, it is likely to look like the ace of hearts, and in the year 3000 perhaps the ace of clubs.

Finland is an aging country. About 100,000 children were born annually after World War II; however, by 1986, annual births had declined to 60,000. In the long term, this demographic change will affect the size of the population and the number of workers unless external factors such as immigration, emigration, or changes caused by wars or ecology have an impact in another direction.

There are approximately 1.7 children per family. According to forecasts, the Finnish population will begin to decline around the year 2000. Still, the average number of children in a family did not decrease significantly during the 1980s. Birthrate statistics indicate that the proportion of third and fourth children has increased slightly over the 1970s. However, only one-quarter of the children born in 1985 were third or subsequent children. The birthrate would have to increase by one-third to maintain the present Finnish population.

Almost every child born in Finland is a wanted child. In fact, infertility is becoming a growing problem. Out of a total population of 5 million, 60,000 couples are involuntarily childless, and the number is increasing by 3,000 annually. For every thirteen couples with a child, there is one childless couple. The problem of infertility is expected to grow in the future, at least partially because prolonged education and housing problems have led couples to postpone having children until an age when fertility decreases. At present, the average age of primaparas in Finland is 26.

Nevertheless, an estimated 90 percent of all women do become mothers at some stage of their lives. Eighty-five percent of the children are born to married couples, and 15 percent are born out-of-wedlock. Among children born out-of-wedlock, 7 percent are born to common-law couples and 7 percent to single parents.

According to estimates, every seventh child remains an only child. Families with one child are less common than they would appear to be on the basis of certain cross-sectional data. The typical family has two children; most children have siblings even when they are quite young. Among all children under school age (age 7), 93 percent live in families with two parents. Among divorced families, one-fourth are childless; as a rule, divorce affects families with largely grown children. Approximately 16 percent of all children under the age of 16 experience the divorce of their parents. Divorces are most common in cities. In the Helsinki area, there are approximately 50 percent more divorces than in the country as a whole.

Background Factors in Family Policy

Postwar Finnish family policy was based on the development of maternal and child health centers and the related maternity allowance system, as well as the equalization of family expenses by means of child allowances. The interest of the largest group of taxpayers, the wage earners, was protected by tax deductions favoring families, the value of which in Finnmarks is still as large as that of the child allowances. The growing value of the child allowance is also a good indicator of trends and changes in family policy, which have usually been initiated with an increase in the purchasing power of the child allowance. In 1990 the real value of the family allowance was three times what it had been in 1951, almost twice what it was in 1976, and 30 percent above its 1982–1987 level.

In 1974 Finland experienced its first absolute labor shortage; there were more unfilled jobs than unemployed persons in the country. Both employers and unions agreed, in connection with a comprehensive incomes policy agreement, on substantial investments in the development of child care facilities. These initiatives were intended to encourage women still remaining at home to enter the labor market. At the same time, a heated discussion developed regarding the relative superiority of home care and center-based care. In order not to ignore home care, it was agreed that the period of maternity leave and allowance would be lengthened. The expansion of this maternity leave policy was also influenced by the fact that for the first time, the birthrate had fallen below 60,000 in the early 1970s, despite an increase in number of women in the prime childbearing years.

Since the mid-1970s, the supply of child care places has increased at record speed, by as much as 10 percent per year. The maternity leave and allowance were gradually lengthened, from one month before and three months after the birth of a child, to the present policy of five weeks before and nine and a half months after birth. In spite of these decisions, the public continued to be divided on the issue of family policy between those supporting home care and those supporting day care. In addition to full-time mothers, the former included farmers and most men. Politically, home care was supported by the center and the right. Center-based day care was supported by employed mothers and the left. An overall settlement was not reached until the mid-1980s, when both positions were incorporated in a compromise approach.

A new phase of family policy activity occurred during the early 1980s. It was still characterized by continued growth in the supply of day care places, but now other elements were added: the creation of a support system for home care (child home care or child rearing allowance) as an extension of the period of maternity and parental leave allowance; the extension of leave up to the child's third birthday; and the provision of either public day care or a home care allowance to parents as alternative options beginning in 1990. Moreover, the parents of children under the age of 4 were permitted to shorten their daily workday from eight to six hours and to receive 25 percent of the basic amount of the home care allowance as compensation.

Encouraging fathers to take care of their young children is also a feature of the family policy. Fathers are granted a two-week paternity leave and a paternity allowance immediately after the child is born. Moreover, the parental leave-allowance has been lengthened from 100 days to 158 days (weeks are computed as having 6 days).

The demographic and policy developments of recent years have been similar to those of the early 1970s. The birthrate has fallen to near 60,000, and the labor shortage, now characterized especially by a shortage of female labor, has increased. The family policy developments of the 1980s also followed the earlier pattern. First, the actual value of the child allowance was raised. Second, the problem of a still inadequate supply of child care services was faced. As part of the comprehensive incomes policy agreement of 1990, labor, management, and government decided to extend a legal entitlement to day care to cover all children under school age by the year 1995, and this was enacted late in 1990. Decisions on extending the home care allowance have not yet been made.

Family policy expenditures as a percentage of GNP and of total social expenditures declined steadily from the time of the postwar expansion until the early 1970s (table 6.4). Since 1974, however, the investments in family policy have followed the general pattern of growth for social policy as a whole.

Table 6.4
Family Policy Expenditures as Percentages of GNP and Social Expenditures

	GNP	Social Expenditures
1950	3.7	41.3
1952	3.7	39.3
1954	3.5	34.5
1956	3.1	30.9
1958	2.7	23.3
1960	2.4	23.6
1962	2.6	23.4
1964	2.5	22.5
1966	2.4	15.6
1968	2.3	13.7
1970	2.5	15.5
1972	2.4	12.6
1974	2.2	11.8
1976	3.4	12.5
1978	4.0	13.2
1980	3.8	13.8
1982	4.3	14.1
1984	4.4	13.5
1986	4.8	13.0

PARENTING POLICIES: CORE PROGRAMS

The core programs targeted at families with very young children include those providing job-protected leaves, those providing financial support, and various in-kind (service) benefits, including health care and day care. One cluster is linked to pregnancy and childbirth and the other to child care.

Maternity, Paternity, and Parental Leaves and Benefits

The Finnish Collective Agreements Act includes provisions defining as maternity, paternity, and parental leave that period during which the wage earner receives maternity, paternity, or parental benefits payable under the Sickness Insurance Act. All mothers are eligible for maternity and parent's benefits for a period of forty-four weeks, provided that they have lived in Finland during the

Exhibit 6.1
Maternity, Paternity, and Homecare Allowances

	Maternity & Parental	Home-care
Duration	105 days (mother only) + 158 days. If the insured person returns to work during the parental leave, the allowance will be paid to the employer.	Follows parental allowance. Until child is 3 years old or until the family chooses day care instead of home care.
Period	Up to 5 weeks before birth; 9.5 months after birth.	Any time until child is 3 years old.
Financing	Social Insurance Institution (federal)	State and municipalities
Benefit value	Minimum FMk 1,388 per month or 80% of income	Minimum FMk 1,388. Maximum (with local addition) FMk 5,000 per month.

Note: Six work days per week.

six months immediately preceding the expected time of confinement. Mothers become entitled to the maternity allowance five weeks before the expected time of confinement and for 75 workdays (computed on a 6-day week) after the child's birth. For the following 158 workdays, a parent's allowance may be paid to the mother—or to the father if he is the child's primary caretaker. In the event of multiple births, the parent's allowance period is extended by ten weeks.

Subject to the approval of the mother, a paternity allowance is payable to fathers who stay at home to help care for the baby (or an older child) for one to two weeks following confinement. Some 33 percent of the fathers take advantage of this provision.

The eligibility criteria for the parental leave are similar to those for maternity and paternity cash benefits. The leave is available to only one parent at a time, and at the beginning of this period, the mother is always eligible. If a mother returns to work in the middle of the parents' leave period, a minimum benefit is paid until the end of the period. Approximately 6 percent of all mothers receive their cash benefit at a lowered rate because of having returned to work before the end of the leave period. This represents some 3 percent of all parental leave days. The parents' benefit and leave are also available to fathers in the case of parents who live together, provided that the father stays home to look after the child and the mother agrees. Fathers, however, take only 2 percent of all parental leave days.

The amount of the maternity, paternity, and parental benefits is determined primarily by annual earned income. For most wage earners, the allowance is 80 percent of their earnings. The minimum allowance for persons without any earnings is FMk 1,387 a month (17 percent of the median wage or 19 percent of the median female wage). (As reported by OECD, the average exchange rate for 1989 was FMk 4.288 = U.S. $1.00.) There is no ceiling, but for high wage earners, the allowance is less than 80 percent of earnings. An increase is added to the allowance of the spouse with a larger income, in the amount of FMk 176 a month for one child under 16 and FMk 353 a month for two or more children. The allowances are taxable income.

A considerable number of maternity allowance recipients receive full pay for at least part of the maternity allowance period (an average of six weeks but up to three months), depending on the collective agreement covering them at work. In these cases and for this period, the government allowance is paid to the recipient's employer.

A parent's benefit is also payable to working parents who adopt a child under the age of 2. An adoptive parent (the father or the mother) is expected to take maternity leave when the child is placed in his or her new home. The child's age at the time of adoption determines the duration of the leave. The leave is never for fewer than 100 working days and never extends beyond 234 working days after the child's adoption.

The maternity and parental benefit and leave system has existed since 1966, growing from a modest start to the present scale. Almost all of those eligible utilize it. To a large extent, the corresponding Swedish system has been the model. An important characteristic is that the system encompasses both an earnings-related and a flat-rate national insurance-type benefit. Nonworking mothers and/or fathers are entitled to basic security.

A political tug of war concerning the development of the system has taken place between the Agrarian and the Social Democratic parties. The former has wanted to raise the level of the minimum allowance, whereas the latter has wanted to increase the proportion of wages replaced. At first, both the basic daily allowance and fixed ceiling for the wage-related component were quite low. Given this unimpressive starting point, both ruling parties have succeeded in reaching their objectives.

Maternity Benefit

Every expectant mother receives a special maternity benefit prior to childbirth in the form of either a package of child care necessities (a layette) or a cash benefit. About 20 percent of the mothers, mainly those who have received a maternity packet in the past, opt for the FMk 640 cash benefit. As a postwar development, this benefit was intended to create an incentive for early prenatal care. Almost all the mothers (95 percent) receive the benefit through maternal and child health centers. It is also granted on application to some mothers who have not come to the health center in time.

Maternal and Child Health Centers

Maternal and child health clinics, operating in connection with local public health centers, are responsible for providing health examinations to expectant mothers and young children and for referring them for further examinations or treatment if necessary. Regular physical examinations start after four months of pregnancy. To qualify for the maternity benefit, expectant mothers must undergo regular prenatal care, and, to receive the parent's allowance, mothers must have a certificate issued by a physician or a public health nurse attesting that they have had a final examination, conducted five to twelve weeks after childbirth. The average number of prenatal visits per pregnancy is a little under four to a physician and fourteen to a public health nurse. Most children are delivered at hospitals, increasingly at the maternity ward of municipal hospitals or special maternity hospitals. As a rule, municipal hospitals charge FMk 65 per day, but in many local districts, there is no charge for childbirth-related expenses.

The average number of visits made to a maternal and child health clinic during the child's first year of life is thirteen. From 1 to 6 years, the average number of visits is two and a half a year. The clinics provide an extensive vaccination program during these visits.

Homemakers

Families with dependent children are also entitled to temporary domestic (home) help, financed by local authorities, during childbirth or if the parent who normally looks after the children becomes ill. Income-based fees are charged for these services. On average, families pay 10 percent of the total cost of these services. Finland has about 10,000 homemakers and home helpers.

Substitute Help

So that self-employed persons, and especially farmers, can benefit in full from their entitlement to maternity and parental leave, a substitute help system has been developed. As of January 1, 1989, female farmers were entitled to substitute help financed by local government in connection with childbirth for thirty-three weeks (previously twenty-six weeks). In the agricultural collective agreement negotiations conducted in 1990, it was agreed to lengthen the entitlement period for substitute help to forty-four weeks (the length of full maternity and parental leave).

Child Rearing Support: Leaves and Home Care Cash Benefits

After the parental (maternity, paternity) leave and its forty-four-week post-childbirth duration, parents are entitled to a child rearing (child caring or child care) leave until their child is 3. This leave was introduced in order to guarantee very young children the possibility of at-home parental care without parents' losing their jobs. Both parents are eligible for the leave, but only one at a time can take the leave.

In addition, a cash allowance is paid to the parent or guardian on child care leave. The allowance consists of a basic flat amount, a sibling increase, and an income-related addition. The basic amount is payable at the same rate as the minimum maternity-paternity-parental allowances: FMk 1,387 a month (17 percent of an average wage, 19 percent of an average female wage). The sibling increase is paid when two or more children in the family are under age 7 and not in public day care. This benefit is payable at the rate of 20 percent of the basic amount for each child. For parents to be entitled to the income-related addition, one of them must stay at home to care for the child. The full addition is payable at the rate of FMk 1,110 per month. To qualify for the full addition, a family's total net income must be under FMk 3,144 a month. Any additional income reduces the addition by 25 percent of its value until, at the income level of FMk 7,500 a month (slightly above the median female wage of FMk 7,300 but below the FMk 8,300 median wage), the addition is no longer paid. The basic amount is not paid if the family starts to receive the maternity-paternity-parental allowance again. The sibling increase and the income-related addition, on the other hand, remain payable. The child home care allowance is taxable income. About 83 percent of those eligible use it at the beginning of the period but only 20 percent at the end.

In addition to this statutory, nationwide, child home care allowance system, supplementary allowances are provided by local governments. The need for such additional programs has been greatest in the Greater Helsinki region and in some other larger cities. In these cities, there is an inadequate supply of public day care because of a personnel shortage and the high costs of day care. The supplementary allowance in Helsinki as of January 1, 1990 was FMk 2,612 a month when the total amount of the allowance was a maximum of FMk 5,000 (U.S. $1,166) to a family with a child aged 9 1/2–18 months and FMk 1,612 a month when the total amount of the allowance for that period was a maximum of FMk 4,000 (about $930) to the family with a child aged 18 to 36 months.

In the past when families did not have a choice between day care and a home care allowance, only 60 percent of the parents used the allowance for staying home themselves; 10 percent used it to purchase private care, and the rest of the families arranged for care by domestic servants, relatives, and neighbors or in another unofficial way. Today when the families can choose either assured public day care or the allowance, unofficial alternatives are considerably fewer. In general, children are cared for either by their own parents or by day care. At the beginning of the period when the child is 9 1/2 months old, 83 percent of the mothers extend their parental leave and take the home care allowance for an average of fourteen months (until the child is 2 years old).

The average earnings in families that chose the home care allowance was FMk 7,200 per month for the father and FMk 4,200 for the mother in 1988–1989, when the average earnings among all men ages 25 to 34 years was also FMk 7,200 per month and among the women ages 25 to 34 years, FMk 5,300. One significant difference between families that chose the allowance and families that chose day care was the lower earnings of the mothers.

Partial Child Care Leaves and Partial Child Home Care Allowances

If both parents are working, one is entitled to partial child care leave until the child is 4 years old, as well as during the child's first school term (compulsory school entry is usually at age 7). According to the agreement between the parent and employer, the partial leave can take the form of either a shorter workday (a six-hour day) or a shorter work week (a thirty-hour week).

A partial child home care allowance became effective on March 1, 1989 (see exhibit 6.1). The allowance is payable until the child's third birthday at the rate of 25 percent of the basic amount of the allowance. When introducing the bill, the government estimated that about 35,000 parents of children under the age of 4 would use the partial child care leave and that the number would grow to 39,000 users if a cash benefit were attached. It was also estimated that 3,500 parents of children starting compulsory school would use the leave. These preliminary estimates were based on a nationwide survey of parents by the Central Statistical Office. In reality, considerably fewer parents have taken advantage of the option of shorter working hours than was expected. About 7,000 to 8,000 parents used partial child care leave during the first year it was available. During the 1989 autumn term, about 5,500 parents of children who had just begun primary school shortened their working hours.

There are many reasons for this limited use, including the newness of the system, insufficient information concerning it, a strong tradition of full-time work, high interest rates on home mortgages, and other financial incentives for working full time.

CHILD CARE SERVICE SYSTEM

Finland was the first Nordic country to offer day care for children. The first day care or child care centers were founded more than 100 years ago in 1888 for poor working-class children in the Helsinki area. Gradually more centers were established, and their functions expanded. Although Finland now has an extensive system of child care centers and family day care, a large number of children whose parents want them enrolled are on waiting lists.

The Children's Day Care Act, passed in 1973, was revised in 1985 to increase the availability of care for very young children. Beginning in 1990, the new law guaranteed parents the right to choose the form of care they prefer for a child under age 3—either at-home care (by means of a home care allowance) or public day care. The availability of these options is leading to an adequate number of

Table 6.5
Use of Child Care Facilities

	Child Age Categories					
	Children 0-1		Children 1-3		Children 3-7	
	No.	% in care	No.	% in care	No.	% in care
Cohort Size	63,000		122,000		247,000	
Parent care only (with parental benefits +/or child home-care allowance)	62,400	99	37,000	30	54,000	22
Relative care, Child home care allowances up to 3 years old + sister's children under 3 years			27,000	22	18,000	6
Family day care	315	0.5	33,000	27	63,100	26
Center or preschool	315	0.5	25,000	21	82,400	34
Other[a]					30,000	12

[a] private day care; combined care (private plus open day care centers; play activities; playgrounds); special day care for children with delayed development or disturbance; and mission day care clubs (run by religious groups).

public or publicly funded day care places for children under age 3 whose parents want them to have this kind of care. For children ages 3 to 6, however, there is still a shortage of public day care, a reversal of the usual pattern seen in other countries. As noted, legislation enacted late in 1990 guarantees by 1995 a child care place to all children ages 3 to 7 as well. (See table 6.5.)

Day Care Center System

Finland has over 3,000 publicly subsidized municipal day care centers or preschools. About one-fourth (107,000 in 1989) of the 432,000 children under age 7 attend these centers—two-thirds of them full time and one-third part time. There are also private day care centers that receive government subsidies and function to a great extent in the same way as their public counterparts do. Exhibit 6.2 lists the varieties of Finnish child care.

Each group of children in a public or private day care center or preschool must have at least one preschool teacher and two trained staff, as well as support personnel. The Day Care Act prescribes the number of the staff members and the child-to-staff ratios. The latter vary according to the age and the needs of the children but meet the standards of child development specialists.

A preschool teacher training course takes three years, and the actual training

Exhibit 6.2
Types of Child (Day) Care Facilities

1. STANDARD DAY-CARE CENTERS

   Part- and full-time day-care:
   —1–2 year old age groups (12 children/group)
   —3–6 year old age groups (20 children/group)
   —6 year old groups (25 children/group)
   —sibling groups for ages 1–6 (15 children/group)

2. DAY CARE CENTERS FOR SCHOOL-AGED CHILDREN

   After school activity for first and second grade students (ages 7–8).

3. SPECIAL DAY CARE CENTERS

   Special care for children with special needs (because of delays or disturbances in physical, cognitive, psychological, or social development).

4. OPEN DAY CARE CENTERS

   For children of different ages as well as adults. These are geared toward child rearing and parent/caretaker education, in particular for at-home mothers babysitters and their children.

5. ROVING DAY CARE CENTERS

   For sparsely populated areas, mainly preschool activity for 5–6 year olds (maximum 25 children)

6. TWENTY-FOUR HOUR DAY CARE CENTERS AND DAY CARE CENTERS OPEN FOR EXTENDED HOURS

   For children whose parents work irregular working hours.

7. FAMILY DAY CARE

   There are several patterns.

takes place in special preschool teacher-training institutes or in teacher-training units at universities. The training curriculum is currently under reform and in the process of becoming more standardized. After basic training and at least two years of practical experience, a preschool teacher can take a year-long training course to become a specialized preschool teacher for children with special educational needs. Training to become a staff member in a day care center takes two and a half years.

Despite the fact that teaching in a day care center has been a profession since the 1800s, the majority of preschool teachers are young, with 70 percent under the age of 32. Most preschool teachers are women; only 4 percent are male.

Family Day Care System

Day care centers are at the heart of the Finnish child care system, but families are offered other options too. Approximately 22 percent (96,000) of all 432,000

Finnish children under school age are cared for in the public family day care system. The family day care providers in this system (87 percent of them full time and 13 percent part time) are permitted to care for a maximum of four children at a time. Family day care can be provided at the family day care provider's home, the typical way; in so-called three-family day care, where children from two to four different families share a common provider who cares for all the children in each family's home alternately; or in group family day care, where the local government provides a place for two to three caregivers who together care for the children in their charge in one small group.

The staff for family day care are the caregivers and their supervisors. The Day Care Act requires that a person working as a public provider be qualified for this work by attending a basic 250-hour course. They also receive ongoing guidance, support, and advice from their supervisors, who make regular visits to the day care homes, and they can attend local training sessions. The supervisors, each of whom works with at least thirty caregivers, are mostly preschool teachers or have appropriate academic qualifications for the job. They also supervise the activities of the staff of private day care centers.

Compared with day care center personnel or family day care supervisors, the family day care providers are usually older women. Most begin working when their own children are young. As their children grow up and start school, they continue the training required for the job while caring for other children.

A good deal of family day care is privately operated but is supervised by the local authorities. In addition, there is supervised playground activity, which is also part of the day care system. This type of activity can go on both year round as well as only in the summer, and approximately 10 percent of all children under school age participate in this program. The Finnish Lutheran church also arranges play groups that meet two or three times a week for three hours at a time. About 20 percent of children under school age participate in these groups. These latter activities are most common in sparsely populated areas, where other kinds of child care are less available.

Child Care Supply and Demand

Although the Finnish child care system is relatively standardized and well developed compared with child care in many other countries, problems do exist. One is the lack of sufficient supply. The Day Care Act requires local authorities to arrange day care for all children who require it, but this goal is not yet fully achieved, especially in larger cities. In addition, as many of the quantitative goals are reached, there has been concern about maintaining the quality of care.

Currently public day care centers and family day care homes are estimated to provide about 80 percent of the places needed. Centers, the largest component of the system, provide about 51 percent of the total places. About 60 percent of the center places and 88 percent of the family day care places are full day.

The need for day care varies from family to family. The length of the child's

Table 6.6
Public Care Only, Children under 2

	Number	%
Total	185,000	100%
Parental benefits	53,000	29% (parents' care)
Child home care allowances	77,000	42% (parents' care or private care, or relative care)
Day care	55,000	29% (municipal care)

day in care is dependent on the parents' working hours. Since most Finnish parents work full time, the children are in care for a long time—often for eight to ten hours a day. The fees for public day care are income related and cover, on average, 14 percent of the total expenses of these services.

Parents seem to prefer at-home care or "homelike" family day care for the under 3s. On average, parents take care of their children at home during the first nine months with the aid of the maternity-paternity-parental allowance; then, with the aid of the home care allowance, they continue to care for their young children at home until their child is 2 years old (table 6.6). Most of the 1- to 3-year-olds who are taken care of outside their own homes are in family day care. Beginning at age 3, center care becomes the preferred kind of care, and the role of family day care declines. Twenty-five percent of all 5-year-olds and 50 percent of 6-year-olds are in center care. In many cities, almost all children are in center care the year before they start primary school.

PARENTING POLICIES: CONTEXTUAL PROGRAMS

In addition to its contributions to the care of very young children, the social infrastructure supporting parenting policy includes subsidies or allowances to help meet family expenses, protection of mothers from the hazards of pregnancy, child health services, support of physically and mentally handicapped children, emotional and social support of the family, as well as child welfare services. Many of these services are not particularly focused on the under 3s.

Family Benefits

As in many other European countries, there has been a long discussion in Finland about the various combinations of child allowances, tax relief, and housing allowances for families with children that would lead to a more equal distribution of the burden of family expenditures. The discussion about the integration of the European community has now slowed these efforts. Nonetheless, it is generally expected that further equalization of family expenses will occur in the future in the form of an adjusted system of child allowances, tax relief, housing allowances, and special benefits for single parents.

Child allowances are now payable for children under 17, primarily to the mother. The total amount of the child allowance depends on the number of children under age 17 in the family. The allowance for a particular child varies by ordinal position: first child, FMk 218; second, FMk 253; third, FMk 326; fourth, FMk 425; and fifth, FMk 512. For under 3s a special supplement of FMk 108 a month is payable. It is tax-free income. The government plans to increase the child allowance more rapidly than other social security benefits in the coming years.

The various child benefits are complemented by tax relief provisions. Health and maternity care expenses are tax deductible. Furthermore, an income tax deduction is available to parents of children under 16. The parents of children under the age of 7 are entitled to a larger tax deduction. Single parents are also entitled to a special tax benefit. The totality of expenditures for deductions available to the family through the tax system is equal in amount to expenditures for the child allowance.

Advanced Maintenance (Child Support) Allowances

The purpose of the advanced maintenance allowance is to ensure financial support to a child of divorced or unmarried parents in cases where the noncustodial parent has failed to pay court-ordered support or where paternity cannot be established. A partial allowance is paid if the support ordered is less than the full allowance (owing to the wage or reduced circumstances of the liable person or because he is already supporting another child).

The full allowance in 1990 was FMk 514 per month. The total number of children receiving the full or partial allowance was 75,000.

Sickness Benefits for the Care of an Ill Child

If a child becomes ill suddenly, a working parent is entitled to temporary child care leave for a maximum of four work days in order to look after his or her own child or a child under 10 permanently living with the family or to arrange outside help. To qualify for this leave, both parents (or a single parent) must be employed outside the home except in cases in which the parent who normally looks after the child cannot do so because of illness. About 75 percent of working parents are covered by collective bargaining agreements that ensure them of their full pay while out on leave; for the others, only partial wage replacement is statutorily available.

Treatment Allowance for Disabled Children

The treatment allowance for the care of disabled children is payable in the case of an ill child under 7 or a child between 7 and 16 suffering from a severe illness or disability. The allowance is paid to a parent who, because of this illness, treatment, or rehabilitation, is unable to be at work and is thus not receiving pay. The allowance is generally paid to only one of the parents unless a doctor considers it necessary for the treatment and rehabilitation of the child that both parents stay at home.

The allowance is payable for a maximum of ten weeks each year for hospital treatment or rehabilitation, as well as for ten weeks of treatment at home. In special cases, these maximum periods can be exceeded; in the case of home treatment, however, extensions are granted only up to fifteen weeks. The allowance is payable at the same rate as the sickness and maternity allowances under National Sickness Insurance (NSI) but with a ceiling of FMk 5,700 a month. The treatment allowance is taxable.

Special Child Care Allowance

A special child care allowance is payable for a child under 16 who because of an illness or injury needs special treatment and rehabilitation for at least six months, provided that the treatment entails a special financial or other strain for the family. A child who is in public inpatient care does not qualify for the allowance. The child care allowance is a graduated payment with three levels (FMk 339, FMk 792, and FMk 1,470 a month) according to the financial or other burdens resulting from the care of the child. Further, local authorities may grant a special means-tested care allowance to families with children suffering from severe disability. The child care allowance is tax-free income.

Health Care Services for Children

Public health centers provide largely free health care for children. In- and outpatient hospital care carries a modest fee. NSI partially reimburses private health care services for children, including the cost of transportation.

Psychological and Social Welfare

The Finnish social services system features a system of child guidance centers for the promotion of the mental health of children, as well as a system of social services for the mentally retarded. Except for the severely retarded, these children are guaranteed the right to basic education and are taught within the public school system. Social services of various sorts are also available as needed to all children attending school.

Every Finnish child who spends his or her days in some kind of child-oriented services (day care, outdoor play, school), receives one free hot meal a day, which, according to standards, should cover one-third of the daily food requirements. In addition to its nutritional value, this meal is intended to encourage good eating habits among children and youth.

There is also a last-resort child welfare system for children having difficulties at home. Eight thousand children are taken care of outside their homes, 5,000 in foster families, and 3,000 in institutions.

Measures of Occupational Safety and Health for Expectant Mothers

A reform of the Occupational Safety Act in 1988 enlarged the scope of occupational safety to include men. In addition to the potential dangers to the fetus, dangers to the genotype were also included within the sphere of the act. With the lifting of the ban on night work for women in 1989, women gained an equal footing with men in the labor market. Consequently, the occupational safety measures for mothers will increasingly feature individualized care provided by maternity clinics and occupational health units.

Currently under review is the need for a special maternity allowance program that would enable expectant mothers to stop working earlier than under the regular maternity allowance program if their work is judged to be potentially harmful to the fetus. The primary aim, however, is to bring about changes in expectant mothers' duties that will reduce the danger to the fetus.

As part of child welfare, efforts have been made to wean expectant mothers from alcohol and to protect children from fetal alcohol syndrome. About 600 mothers with alcohol problems annually give birth to 300 children with the syndrome, whose need for special treatment and care often continues throughout their lives.

CONCLUSIONS

An Expenditures Overview

Family policy expends 4.8 percent of GNP and 13 percent of the social budget. Social security expended almost 27 percent of gross domestic product in 1987 (including user fees).

Finnish family policy measures concerning families with children can be divided into income transfers and child care services. Table 6.7 indicates the more detailed distribution of these social expenditures. Clearly the income transfer costs are larger, as they tend to be in most places.

Results and Consequences

Finland's family policy package has been the outcome of many factors, each having its own impact. It has been said that the idea of strong Finnish societal

Table 6.7
Social Expenditures, Children and Families, 1987 (FMk Billions)

CATEGORY	AMOUNT
Income transfers	
child allowance	2.8
tax relief for children	1.5
housing subsidies	0.5
child-maintenance allowance	0.2
survivors' pensions	4.0
child care allowance	0.2
maternity, paternity, parent's benefits	2.2
home care allowance	0.8
SUBTOTAL	11.4
Services	
day care centers	2.5
family day care	1.7
school meals	1.1
home help	0.4
child welfare	0.8
other	0.1
SUBTOTAL	7.4
TOTAL	18.8

responsibility for children and their families originated in the trenches of past wars. As far as children are concerned, the first manifestation was the creation of maternal and child health centers and the system of child allowances, followed by other income transfers for families. As a result, infant mortality dropped, and the positions and possibilities of families with limited means and of one-parent families were generally improved despite the difficult postwar circumstances.

A new stage in the development of Finnish family policy started at the end of the 1960s and the beginning of the 1970s, when the system of maternity allowances was developed and the purchasing power of the child allowance was increased considerably. Family policy developments were accelerated, partly due to population concerns and partly to economic factors. For a long time the birthrate had been declining, and labor shortages were developing. The declining birthrate had its impact primarily on the increase in the actual value of the child allowances and the lengthening of the period of maternity allowance. The labor shortage led to the expansion of day care in 1974.

Political debates within the Finnish government resulted in the creation of the system of home care, first as a complement to the system of child care services and later as its alternative. As a whole, the development of the child care system has been related to the continued growth in female labor force participation and to the necessity of ensuring the care of children. Additionally, increasing affluence has given parents who want it the ability to take care of their children themselves, although the home care allowance does not totally compensate for the wages lost. As their financial resources have grown, families want to make their own choices concerning the care of their children.

By adopting and accepting the twofold strategy—the simultaneous development of day care and payments to support home care—the investment in child care has grown considerably, increasing the choices. In the late 1980s, there were also other efforts to coordinate the demands of the workplace with those of family life through such means as flexible working hours, partial child care leaves, and partial home care allowances.

Have these objectives been achieved? It is impossible to measure the increase in female labor force participation that resulted from the policies established when the employment situation deteriorated in the fall of 1975. The day care situation has clearly improved, however.

It is even more difficult to estimate the effects of the measures taken specifically for pronatalist purposes. There has been much discussion about the fact that the birthrate rose from the late 1970s until the mid-1980s because the large baby boom generation had deferred having children until these years. If the most important measures concerning family policy are placed on curves representing the birthrate and net reproduction, the result should be considered at least satisfactory from the point of view of population policy in the 1970s. On the other hand, better coordination between working life and family life does not seem to have been achieved as successfully.

Use of Partial Child Care Leave and Partial Home Care Allowance

During the first year following the introduction of this new system, only 25 percent of those expected to use the entitlement to partial child care leave did so. Almost all of the users were women who were somewhat older and better educated than the eligible population as a whole. Some fields of work or personnel in some fields (health, public administration, finance, and insurance) accommodate to the leave more readily than others.[2]

The care allowance was used more often in that first year by a parent of a 2-year-old than a 3-year-old. Perhaps the users of partial care leave wanted to continue their link with their jobs instead of leaving working life completely. Previously it appeared that parents wanted the home care leave to last from six months to a year. To date, there are no data to indicate whether the policy satisfies current preferences.

Most of the parents (88 percent) who took partial leave reduced their working hours to the maximum permitted by law (thirty hours per week). Of these, 41 percent deferred their starting time, 27 percent reduced their hours at both the beginning and end, and 11 percent reduced their hours at the end of the day; 21 percent reduced their working hours by whole days.

As noted above, the majority of eligibles did not apply for or were ignorant of the partial leave benefit. According to one study, if the benefit value were greater, the use of the partial home care allowance would increase. Thirty-eight percent of the employed mothers of very young children and 12 percent of their fathers stated that they would reduce their working hours if the financial support were larger.

Employees' difficulties were considerably less than expected. Twenty-nine percent said they had no difficulties in the management of their duties, 61 percent had some difficulties, and only 10 percent had a lot of difficulties. The difficulties were related to the supply of qualified substitutes.

New Challenges

Finland now faces the same kind of demographic and economic situation as it did two decades ago: the birthrate has declined, and the shortage of female labor is tangible. During the next five years, the number of employed women is expected to decrease by about 40,000, whereas, for example, about 50,000 new employees will be needed in the nursing sector alone, of whom the majority would be women.

Many of the proposed responses resemble the traditional solutions. The purchasing power of child allowances has been raised more than 10 percent per year, and it has been decided to increase the child care supply. Corresponding decisions regarding home care allowances have not yet been made. What is unique, however, is Finland's 1990 legislation to phase in for all children below compulsory school age (7) the right, as of 1995, to a place in an all-day municipal child care center. The family will have the choice between drawing upon the home care allowance or the center. For 3-year-olds, the guarantee will be in effect by 1993; the under 3s are already covered.

Yet the situation is not actually the same as that of the early 1970s; then the aim was to encourage women who were taking care of their children at home to enter the labor force. One result of that policy was an increase in the difficulties in coordinating work and family life. In the 1990s, on the other hand, many in Finland view the main problem as deferred childbirth, perhaps the result of prolonged education or an inadequate supply of housing. The policy strategies used earlier will not meet this definition of the problem—and it is unclear just what the impact will be of the new commitment to child care availability and the home care allowance alternative.

NOTES

1. For further detail, see Jiris Niemi and Hannale Pääkkönen, *Time Use Changes in Finland in the 1980s* (Helsinki: Tilastokeskus, Central Statistical Office of Finland, 1990).
2. Riita Säntti, Planning Department, Ministry of Social Affairs and Health, Helsinki, 1989.

7

SWEDEN: SUPPORTING WORK, FAMILY, AND GENDER EQUALITY

Marianne Sundström

Over the past two decades, the Western world has witnessed rapid increases in women's gainful employment, changes in family composition, and changes in the ways in which young children are cared for and reared. When it comes to the much-debated effects of the increase in paid work among mothers of young children, Sweden is of particular interest since it combines a relatively high fertility rate with the highest female labor force participation rate in the OECD area. Also, Sweden is unique for having changed the parenting role of men. As a foundation for these achievements, Sweden's strong economic growth up to the 1970s and its advanced economic and social policies, including the full employment policy, the separate taxation of married couples, and parenting policies, have been crucial.

Swedish parenting policies, the focus of this chapter, have four major components. First, there is the extensive economic support to families with children, of which the most important ingredient is the child allowance. Second, Sweden has a comprehensive system of heavily subsidized public child care, including day care centers, family day care, and after-school facilities. Third, Sweden's parental insurance benefits offer five options: (1) leave benefits for the care of newborn children; (2) cash benefits for the occasional care of children; (3) pregnancy benefits; (4) ten days of leave for fathers at childbirth; and (5) benefits to allow time for parental contact with child care or school staffs. Fourth, the parental insurance benefits are linked to a series of employment benefits that give parents the right to a leave of absence from work when they draw insurance benefits and a little beyond that. Also, parents have the right to reduce their hours of work to care for young children.

FAMILY AND WORK DEVELOPMENTS IN CONTEMPORARY SWEDEN

Patterns of Marriage and Fertility

In the period from 1900 to 1930, the proportion of Swedes who married declined. Consequently, up to the 1940s, only 65 percent of women ages 40 to 64 were married, and more than 20 percent had never married. Also, women's average age at marriage, 26.5 years, was high. At the end of the 1930s, marriage rates began to rise markedly, peaking in 1970 when 77 percent of women 40 to 64 years were married and only 9 percent had never married. Meanwhile, women's average age at first marriage decreased to 23.4 years in 1976.[1] After 1967 marriage rates declined again, while cohabitation without marriage increased, especially among women under 30 years. The number of marriages doubled in 1989 compared to 1988. This was an anomaly, reflecting the desire of some women to qualify for widows' pensions for women born after 1944 at their last opportunity. The benefit was eliminated the following year.

Women born in the 1950s moved away from home and began living in consensual unions earlier than had previous cohorts. It should be noted, however, that consensual unions are not new in Sweden. At the age of 20, almost 50 percent of women born between 1956 and 1960 had begun their first cohabitation, but only 7 percent had married, as compared to 30 percent and 25 percent, respectively, among women born between 1936 and 1940.[2] Also, women's average age at first marriage had increased to 27.7 years by 1987. Further, the 1974 divorce law led to a leap in divorce rates (table 7.1), which have remained high ever since, although they have decreased slightly in recent years. In addition, the dissolution of consensual unions is high and increasing.[3] Consequently, at the age of 25, women born in the 1950s had lived in a greater number of unions than had those born earlier. However, they had also spent a longer time in such unions, since these start earlier and last longer now.[4]

Over this century large changes have also taken place in patterns of fertility and childbearing. Following the low levels of fertility in the 1930s, childbearing increased significantly during the 1940s but dropped again in the 1950s. In the mid-1960s there was again a peak in fertility, but birthrates subsequently declined, and by the late 1970s, they were as low as in the 1930s. Swedish rates, however, were never as low as those of West Germany and Italy. By contrast, Swedish fertility has recovered since 1984, and in 1989 the rate reached 2.0, the third highest in Europe. For 1990 the total fertility rate is projected to exceed 2.1, the replacement rate.

The decline in birthrates after 1966 is partially explained by fewer women giving birth to more than two children and partially by young women deferring

Table 7.1
Fertility and Divorce Rates in Sweden, 1963–1990

Year	Total fertility rate	Divorces per 1000 married women
1964	2.48	5.0
1966	2.36	5.4
1968	2.07	5.9
1970	1.92	6.7
1972	1.91	8.0
1974	1.87	14.3
1976	1.69	11.8
1978	1.59	11.2
1980	1.68	11.2
1982	1.62	12.0
1984	1.65	11.9
1986	1.79	11.4
1988	1.97	10.7
1989	2.0[a]	
1990	2.1[b]	

Source: *Population changes*, pt 3, Statistics Sweden.

[a] Preliminary figure.

[b] Projection based on data for the first six months.

childbirth until older ages. But whereas the first phenomenon is part of a general trend throughout the industrialized world, the second is a phenomenon of the late 1970s. That is, women born in the 1950s have postponed the birth of their first child, and childbearing among teenagers has fallen drastically, thereby raising the average age of first-time mothers from 24.4 years in 1974 to 26.7 years in 1987.[5] The recovery of fertility of the late 1980s took place in all age groups, except among teenagers, and was most marked among women above 30. Consequently, the childbearing period in women's lives has been substantially compressed over time, and births have been more closely spaced.[6] In particular, the parental insurance system provides incentives for both postponing childbirth and spacing children more closely.

Hence, there are no indications that more women will remain childless throughout their lives. In fact, 88 percent of each cohort of women born between 1936 and 1945 have given birth to at least one child.[7] Interestingly, this statistic represents a decrease in the proportion of childless women as compared to the cohorts born in the end of the last century, of which more than 20 percent remained childless throughout their lives. (Twenty-eight percent of women born between 1894 and 1899 reported in the 1968 Level of Living Survey that they had never had a child.) But the recent cohorts of women do bear fewer children. While women born in 1890 and 1891 gave birth to an average of 2.5 children and women of the cohort of 1930 and 1931 gave birth to an average of 2.1 children, women born in 1945 and 1946 have given birth to only 1.9 children.[8]

Almost half of all children and two-thirds of the firstborn are born outside marriage by parents living in consensual unions, at the same time as childbearing by single mothers outside conjugal unions has fallen drastically.[9] In fact, more than 90 percent of all Swedish children under 3 years live with both biological parents. Of course, these new patterns of childbearing presuppose the use of modern contraceptive techniques. Also, legal abortions have increased from about 3,000 in 1960 to more than 30,000 in each year since 1975, when the law granting free abortion was passed. In 1980 the total abortion rate was .61, which can be interpreted as the average number of abortions Swedish women would have during their lives if the abortion pattern of 1980 were to persist.[10]

Trends in Women's Labor Force Participation

Contrary to what is often assumed, the high rate of labor market activity of married women in Sweden is a fairly recent phenomenon. In the 1950s, never-married women still constituted the majority of the female labor force, and it was not until 1965 that the proportion of married women exceeded 50 percent (table 7.2). This development reflects rising labor force participation for married women but also the larger proportion of married women in the population generally. In the 1970s, labor force participation of married women rose steeply (table 7.3), and in 1975 the rates for married women surpassed those of non-married women. Further, the proportion of women with children in the labor force has increased significantly in the last two decades. Whereas in 1965 only a third of women in the labor force had children under 17 years, this was true for 41 percent in 1988.

A major characteristic of the labor market in the 1970s was the dramatic rise in employment among mothers of preschool children. Their proportion of the female labor force (16 to 74 years) rose from 15 percent in 1965 to 20 percent in 1988. (The proportion of women with children under 17 in the female population 16 to 74 years was about 34 percent in both years, but the proportion with children under 7 declined from 18 percent in 1965 to 16 percent in 1985.) To illustrate the significance of the entry of married women and women with children into the labor market, consider the following figures. Between 1965 and 1980, the labor force expanded by 573,000 women, of whom 35 percent had children under 7 years and 34 percent had children 7 to 16 years. Married women accounted for 60 percent of the expansion.

To a large extent, this steep rise in female labor force participation took the form of part-time work (less than thirty-five hours and more than one hour weekly). In fact, from 1970 to 1980, the increase in the number of women employed part time was three times that of the number employed full time.[11] Thus, full-time work expanded at a slower rate, raising the proportion of employed women who worked part time from 38 percent in 1970 to 46 percent in 1980 and 47 percent in 1982 (table 7.4), which are high rates when international comparisons are made.[12] However, both the proportion and the number of part-

Table 7.2
Women in the Labor Force, 1920–1985

	1920	1930	1940	1950	1960	1965
Women employed (no.)	775	898	810	819	966	1,160
Prop. women in the labor force	29.8	31.0	27.0	26.4	29.8	33.7
Prop. married of female labor force	5.0	10.2	15.5	28.8	44.1	51.3
LFPR all women	26.9	30.7	29.3	29.5	32.0	35.0
LFPR married women	3.8	8.0	9.3	14.1	23.3	29.9
LFPR never married women	52.4	56.8	58.2	61.7	53.8	50.7

	1970	1975	1980	1985
Women employed (no.)	1,207	1,618	1,802	1,912[c]
Prop. women in the labor force	35.4	42.1	45.0	47.1[c]
Prop. married of female labor force	57.8	59.2	70.5[a]	68.2[a]
LFPR all women	38.0	54.4	59.6	62.6[c]
LFPR married women	37.5	53.0	62.2[a]	68.4[a]
LFPR never married women	44.0	51.3	40.3[b]	44.9[b]

Source: Censuses, 1920–1985.

Note: For 1920–1965, all persons over 14 years are included and for 1970–1985, all over 15 years. Female family members in agricultural work are excluded for 1920–1965. Persons working less than 20 hours per week are excluded 1920–1970.
LFRP = labor force participation rate.

[a] Including nonmarried cohabitating women.
[b] Noncohabitating women.
[c] Due to change in methods, the 1985 figures have been recalculated to obtain over-time comparability.

time workers have been falling since 1982. Also, hours worked among part-time workers have risen strongly and continuously over time and often approximate what is classified as full-time elsewhere.[13]

Despite the strong increase in participation rates, average hours actually worked per Swedish woman were almost constant until 1983 (table 7.5). This

Table 7.3
Labor Force Participation Rates for Women 16 to 64 Years, 1965–1989 (Percentage)

	All women	Married women	Women with children 0-16 years	Women with children 0-6 years
1965	53.8	47.2	46.6	36.8
1970	59.3	56.1	57.6	49.7
1975	67.9	66.2	69.0	60.5
1980	75.1	75.6	80.5	75.4
1985	79.2	82.0	87.6	84.0
1989	82.2	N.A.	90.2	86.9

Source: Labor Force Surveys, 1965–1989.

Note: These data differ from those in table 7.2 because table 7.2 includes those over 64 years, table 7.3 includes the unemployed and those working less than 20 hours per week, and the census measures employment during the census week, while the Labor Force Surveys mirror the situation all weeks of the year, on average.

Table 7.4
Part-Time Employment among Women 16 to 64 Years, 1970–1989

	Part-time workers (thousands)	Prop. employed part time (%)	Prop. 20-34 h/w of part-time workers[a] (%)
1970	570	38.3	63.0
1974	643	39.6	68.4
1978	802	44.6	74.7
1982	896	46.5	79.7
1986	870	42.8	84.4
1989	826 (892)	38.9 (41.7)	86.1

Source: Labor Force Surveys, 1970–1989.

Note: Because of a new method used from 1987 (which produces the official figures in parentheses), I have recalculated the figures for 1988 to obtain comparability over time.

[a] h/w = hours per week.

paradox is resolved by the decline in average hours worked by employed women up to 1982. This decline was the result of the growth in part-time work, an increasing absentee rate among employed women, and reductions in the standard workweek. The increase in the proportion of women absent from work is explained mainly by longer vacations and the extended parental leave (during which parents are classified as in the labor force). Therefore, the sharp rise in participation does not correspond to an equally large increase in the proportion who are actually at work. Because of the parental leave, the difference between work force participation and presence in the workplace is the largest for mothers of young children. Whereas 77 percent of women with children under 1 year were employed in 1988, only 11 percent were at work (15 percent of the employed).

Table 7.5
Average Hours Worked Per Week, Absentee Rates, and Proportions at Work among Women 16 to 64 Years, 1965–1989

	Hours per woman in population	Hours per employed woman	Prop. absent of empl. wom. %	Prop. at work of women in the population %
1965	16.8	31.7	11.7	46.6
1970	16.6	32.9	13.5	50.4
1975	17.7	31.6	15.9	56.0
1980	18.0	31.0	20.5	58.3
1982	18.5	31.2	20.0	59.4
1984	19.5	31.7	18.8	61.4
1986	20.3	32.3	19.1	63.0
1989	21.3	33.1	20.4	64.5

Source: Labor Force Surveys, yearly averages.

Note: Numbers for 1989 recalculated to ensure comparability over time.

Among mothers of children 1 and 2 years old, 84 percent were employed and 61 percent were at work (72 percent of the employed). But employed mothers with children over 2 did not on average have higher absentee rates (17 percent) than those of other employed women.[14] Finally, the increase in hours worked among part-time workers and those in full-time work from 1983 is reflected in rising hours worked per employed woman from that year on.

Family and Work Patterns

Most Swedish children live with both their biological parents; in 1985 80 percent of all children under 18 were in this category. But the proportion who live with a single parent is rising and amounted to 12 percent (of which 15 percent lived with their father). The proportion living with both parents is higher among young children (85 percent among those from birth to six years) than among teenagers (72 percent of the 16- and 17-year-olds). However, a rising proportion of children (about 8 percent in 1985) live in reconstituted families—with one parent and a stepparent.

Looking at the work patterns among married and cohabitating couples, the proportion of households where both parents work (the sum of the three left columns in table 7.6) is seen to be high and to vary with the age of the youngest child, from 76 percent among families with a young child up to 3 years old to 90 percent of families with children between ages 12 and 16.

Consequently, the proportion of mothers who stay at home is highest in families with under 3s, and the proportion of households where both parents work full time increases with the age of children. Also, it is almost twice as common that the woman works part time in families with children as in families without children. Turning to table 7.7, we see that single fathers work part time to a

Table 7.6
Combinations of Hours Ordinarily Worked for Married and Cohabitating Men and Women, 1987 (Percentages)

	Both full time	Husband fulltime wife part time	Husband parttime wife employed	Husband fulltime wife not employed	Other combination. of husband or wife not employed		Nos. (000s)
Age of youngest child:							
0-3 years	25	46	2	19	8	100%	330
4-6 years	28	53	1	13	5	100%	143
7-11 years	35	48	1	10	6	100%	202
12-16 years	46	42	2	7	3	100%	216
No children	42	26	3	10	19	100%	915
All	36	39	3	12	10	100%	1810

Source: Author computation from Government Commission report, SOU, *Arbetstid och Välfärd*, No. 53 (1989), Appendix I, pp. 48, 100–101.

Notes: Data refer to self-employed and employees, including those absent from work due to leave, vacation, illness, or other reason. At least one of the spouses is 16 to 64 years old. Full time is defined as at least 35 hours per week and part time as less than 35 hours. The numbers of households are rough estimates.

Husbands refers to the male member of the couple, married or not.

Table 7.7
Hours Ordinarily Worked among Single Men and Women 16 to 64 Years, According to Presence and Age of Youngest Child in 1987 (Percentages)

	SINGLE MEN					SINGLE WOMEN				
	Full time	Part time	Not empl	Sum	000s	Full time	Part time	Not empl	Sum	000s
Age of youngest child:										
0-3 years	*	*	*	*	4	35	38	26	100	27
4-6 years	*	*	*	*	4	32	54	14	100	26
7-11 years	79	16	4	100	9	54	37	10	100	39
12-16 years	87	7	8	100	11	64	28	8	100	44
No children	60	7	32	100	944	46	21	34	100	700
All	61	7	31	100	970	48	24	30	100	827

Source and Notes: See table 7.6.

Note: Asteriks indicate too few observations; data unreliable.

greater extent than do married or cohabitating fathers. Moreover, full-time work is more frequent among single mothers than among married ones. Nevertheless, a substantial proportion of single mothers work part time, which might be taken to indicate that the economic support to single mothers is at least partially successful.

Perhaps it is not fully clear from the data presented that the hours that fathers work are also affected by the age of the youngest child. Interestingly, this effect

Table 7.8
Uses of Time among Men and Women in 1984 According to Presence and Age of Children (Hours per week)

	No. children	Age of youngest child			
		0-2	3-6	7-12	13-17 years
Men					
Market work	22.9	31.7	34.4	38.4	40.3
House work	7.1	8.2	6.9	6.7	6.4
Maintenance, repairs	5.1	4.9	5.9	5.7	5.2
Active child care	0.3	8.2	5.6	1.9	0.4
Women					
Market work	15.8	11.8	20.9	22.1	25.5
House work	19.3	21.5	19.0	23.1	21.4
Maintenance, repairs	2.2	0.5	1.2	1.2	1.7
Active child care	0.6	13.4	10.6	4.1	0.6

Source: L. Flood and A. Klevmarken, ''Arbete och fritid. Svenska hushålls tidsahvándming 1985'' (Work and Leisure. The Uses of Time of Swedish Households 1984) in A. Klevmarken et al., *Tid och råd. Om hushållens ekonomi* (Time and Means. About the Economy of Households). (Stockholm: The Industrial Institute for Economic and Social Research, 1990).

is more pronounced if we examine 1989 time budget findings by Klevmarken and Flood on hours actually worked. We can see in table 7.8 that not only mothers, as expected, but also fathers work fewer hours in the labor market when they have young children. Fathers with infants spend more time in housework and active child care than do fathers with older children. In fact, the hours Swedish men spend on housework are very high when international comparisons are made.[15] This phenomenon results from a reallocation of time in Swedish households so that women spend more time in paid work and less time in domestic work, while the opposite holds for men.[16]

Factors Influencing the Allocation of Time to Paid Work and Housework among Swedish Men and Women

A 1987 study demonstrated that factors on both the supply side and the demand side of the labor market contributed to the increase in paid work among Swedish women. Beginning with the supply side, the female wage rate in manufacturing doubled between 1963 and 1978, thereby reducing the male-female wage gap from 28 percent to 10 percent. Married women's paid work was further encouraged by the separate taxation of spouses, which was introduced in 1971; until that time, wives' earnings were taxed on top of their husbands' in the highly progressive Swedish tax system.[17] Significantly, the marginal tax rate of, for example, a woman working half-time with a full-time employed husband, both with average blue-collar worker wages, fell from 55 percent to 32.5 percent from 1970 to 1971. Also, whereas marginal tax rates for part-time workers remained low on average throughout the 1970s, they rose steeply for full-time workers. It became more profitable for households to allocate more of the wives' time to paid work, especially part time, and less to housework, and vice versa for the husband. Consequently, when marginal tax rates were cut in 1982, women's full-time participation in the labor force increased.

In addition, the rapid expansion of public day care decreased the profitability of domestic work as compared to paid employment for women. Also, the parental leave benefits introduced in 1974 provided women with strong incentives to be employed before having children.

The number of part-time workers increased not only because of the favorable tax treatment but also because of the full social benefits granted to part-time workers[18] and several other reforms that increased employees' opportunities for reducing their hours of work. (Part-time workers are eligible for statutory benefits but must work sixteen hours a week to be eligible for the benefits gained through collective bargaining and at least twenty-two hours a week to be eligible for a partial pension at age 60.) From 1974 on, parental leave could be used on a full-time or part-time basis any time before the child was 8 years old. In addition, in 1979 parents who worked full time in all sectors of the economy received the right to reduce their hours to thirty hours per week until the child was 8 years old, with a corresponding cut in pay.

Turning to the demand side of the labor market, taxation reform and other measures that have increased the supply of labor can be seen partly in the light of the continuous high demand for labor and low levels of unemployment during the whole postwar period (the peak rate was 3.5 percent in 1983). These conditions were, in turn, due to the high priority given to the goal of full employment[19] and concern about slow population growth. As a result of demographic changes, the high demand for labor could not be met solely from the traditional sources for recruitment: men and never-married women. Consequently, employers turned to immigrant labor; from 1960 through 1970 net immigration rose to 234,000. However, as government bodies and the general public became increasingly aware of the social costs of immigration, policies facilitating married women's entry into the labor market gained increased political support.

Additionally, legal reductions in standard working time during the 1970s accentuated labor shortages. Thus, the standard workweek was reduced from 42.5 to 40 hours in 1972, the age of general retirement was reduced from 67 to 65 years in 1976, and the minimum vacation increased to five weeks in 1978 and to five and a half weeks in 1990. Consequently, employers became gradually more willing to employ married women, who would often work part time. In fact, my 1987 study found that the increase of women's part-time work in the 1970s was not explained by disproportionate employment growth in industries with above-average proportions of part-time workers, such as the service industries. Instead, the proportion employed part time rose in all industries as a consequence of the changed composition of the labor supply. Also, as the part-time labor supply decreased in the 1980s, the proportion of part-time workers fell in all industries.

The Swedish Political Debate on Parenting Policies

To understand Swedish politics, it is essential to comprehend the dominant role played by the labor movement. The Social Democrats, with strong support from the largest trade union, have been in power for fifty-two of the last fifty-eight years. Only between 1976 and 1982 did a nonsocialist coalition assume the reins of government.[20]

In spite of the general political unity on parenting policies in Sweden, there are and have been considerable differences in opinions and priorities among political parties. Social Democrats have been eager to encourage mothers to enter the labor market (but have perhaps shown less concern over their achievements once there) and to safeguard the interests of working parents. Thus, they have given high priority to expanding public day care and prolonging parental leave benefits. The nonsocialist parties (Conservatives, Liberals, and Center party) have had the interests of full-time homemakers very much at heart and have emphasized parents' freedom of choice with regard to staying home versus working and private alternatives to public child care. Also, the Conservatives in particular have been strongly opposed to high taxes and the large public sector.

In the election campaign of 1988, the nonsocialist parties jointly proposed a taxable caring allowance (child rearing) of Skr (krona) 15,000 per year for a child ages 1 to 7 (the parental leave was then one year), as opposed to the extension of parental leave benefits to eighteen months, as proposed by the Social Democrats. The caring allowance was to be paid to all parents, whether or not they worked, and to be combined with a right to deduct verified child care costs from taxable income at a maximum of Skr 15,000 a year per child. (As reported by OECD, the average exchange rate for 1989 was Skr 6.446 = U.S. $1.00.) The cost of the program was estimated at Skr 9 billion and was to be financed mainly through cuts in government subsidies to public day care—that is, through increased day care fees.

Additionally, one of the major political issues of the Liberal party in the 1976 election campaign was a ban on discrimination according to gender. This campaign issue resulted in the 1978 Act on Equality between Men and Women at Work, which became effective on January 1, 1980.[21] Moreover, it was the Liberals who initiated the right of parents of preschool children to reduce their weekly working hours to 75 percent of full time, effective January 1, 1979. Social Democrats and especially the trade unions had previously been more critical of provisions facilitating part-time work but changed their attitudes in the 1980s.[22]

SWEDISH PARENTING POLICIES

Economic Support to Families with Young Children

A cornerstone of the Swedish universal social welfare system is the nontaxable child allowance, which is paid to all 1 million families with 1.6 million children from 0 to 16 years, regardless of income, at a rate of Skr 560 per child per month (6,720 per year in 1990 and 9,000 from 1991). The one-child allowance has been about 5 percent of the average wage.

In recognition of the heavier economic burdens of families with several children, the nonsocialist government in 1982 introduced child allowance increments of 25 percent for the third child and 50 percent for the fourth and fifth children. These allowances were raised by the Social Democrats in 1989 to 50 percent for the third child, 190 percent for the fourth, 240 percent for the fifth, and 160 percent for the sixth and additional children.[23] From 1991 the increment is 100 percent for fourth children and 150 percent for fifth and subsequent children. The government's cost for child allowances was estimated to reach Skr 10,350 million in fiscal year 1989–1990, or about 3 percent of total government expenditures and about 0.8 percent of the gross national product (GNP) of Skr 1,300 billion. Also, all families with children over 16 years who attend high school receive student grants equal to the child allowance until the child leaves high school but not beyond age 20. The total government cost for student grants exceeded Skr 2,000 million in 1989–1990.

Additionally, single parents with children under 18 years can receive an advanced maintenance (child support) payment (in 1990 Skr 990 per month and child, tax free) on application if the noncustodial parent fails to pay the maintenance allowance. These allowances are determined by voluntary agreement or court order and depend on the incomes of both parents. The advance must be reimbursed by the nonpaying parent. If the earnings of the noncustodial parent are such that the maintenance allowance is less than the advance, a reduced benefit to fill the gap can be obtained. In this case, reimbursement is not demanded. Both the advance and the allowance are indexed. The custodial parent receives the payment even if she or he lives in a new conjugal union. In 1980 56 percent of single custodial parents and 54 percent of those living with a partner received a maintenance advance.[24] Total government costs for the advanced maintenance payment amounted to almost Skr 2,000 million in fiscal year 1989–1990 (0.6 percent of government expenditures and 0.15 percent of GNP). In addition, the administrative costs of the advance, including work by local government officials in the courts and other settings, were estimated at Skr 51 million in 1981.[25]

Moreover, low-income families with children can obtain a nontaxable monthly housing allowance. The size of the allowance depends on family income, number of children, and housing costs. In 1980 80 percent of single parents received a housing allowance as compared to about 30 percent of married or cohabitating parents. The allowance covered 40 percent of the rent for the recipients who were single parents and about 13 percent for those living in unions.[26] The total government cost for housing allowances was about Skr 1,500 million in 1989–1990.

In addition, survivor benefits for dependent children under social security were raised to a minimum of Skr 4,464 per month in 1989. These pensions are taxable. Finally, parents who take care of a handicapped or severely ill child at home can obtain a caring allowance, for which the total government cost was about Skr 600 million in 1989–1990.

Child Care

Since the end of the 1960s, the Social Democrats have placed a high priority on expanding public child care. This basic position results primarily from the political involvement and activity of women across party lines and in the Social Democratic party in particular.[27] Public child care is provided by the 285 Swedish municipalities with the aid of large government subsidies, which were raised considerably in the 1970s. Places in public child care facilities quadrupled in that decade and in 1988 could accommodate 48 percent of all children from birth to 6 years (54 percent if the places in part-time preschools are included) and 33 percent of all children 7 to 10 years.[28] Due to the extended parental leave opportunities, a declining proportion of children under 1 year use public child care; only 2 percent did so in 1987. Thus, disregarding the infants, 69 percent of children aged 1 to 6 years had access to public child care, including part-time preschool, in 1987. Compulsory elementary school begins at age 7.

Public child care takes a variety of forms. Day care centers are open all day and provide high-quality care and education for children between 9 months and 6 years of age whose parents are employed or in school and for children in need of developmental support. The centers have a cognitive and a developmental program and a trained staff of preschool teachers and nurses. The average ratio of children to annual employees was 4.3 to 1 in 1985.[29] Expanded sibling groups, which also include young school children, are common. There are also a few night care centers for parents with inconvenient working hours. In 1988 31 percent of all children to 6 years old and 38 percent of the 3- to 6-year-olds had a place in a day care center.

Family day care is provided by child minders employed by the municipalities who take care of children up to the age of 12 in their own homes and typically have young children of their own. To some extent they also provide child care for parents with inconvenient working hours. Eighteen percent of all children to 6 years old, 20 percent of the 3- to 6-year-olds, and 13 percent of the 7- to 10-year-olds were in family day care in 1988.

Part-time preschools ("play schools") provide educational activities for three hours per day free of charge for children aged 4 to 6 years who are not in day care centers. A law passed in 1975 requires municipalities to provide preparatory school training for all 6-year-olds at day care centers or part-time schools. In 1987 63 percent of the 4-year-old children attended part-time preschools. One-third of these children also had a place in family day care.

Open preschools are run by preschool teachers and provide activities in which preschool children who are cared for by parents or family day care providers can participate periodically and for various periods together with their caregiver. Twenty-two percent of all children age 6 and under visited an open preschool sometime during 1987.

After-school homes provide care outside school hours and during school holidays for children 7 to 10 years old whose parents work or go to school or who need special developmental support. In 1988 20 percent of all children in this age group attended an after-school home.

There is also private child care—care provided by relatives, au pair girls, or at private day care centers. These centers, which are often run as parent cooperatives, can also receive public subsidies if they follow the program of the day care centers, take children from the municipality waiting list, and are not run for profit. The proportion of children up to 6 years old in private day care declined from 20 percent in 1980 to 10 percent in 1988. By contrast, the proportion of government subsidies to private child care increased from 1 to 2 percent, to which should be added municipal subsidies.

Finally, and obviously, most child care is still provided by parents. In 1988 37 percent of all children from birth to 6 years were cared for mainly by their parents, including working couples who took turns taking care of their children in shifts and mothers who were also providers for other people's children; 4 percent of the children were in this latter category.

Public child care is provided by the municipalities with large government subsidies, which were estimated to reach Skr 10,330 million in 1989–1990. Parents' fees, which cover only an average of 10 percent of costs, normally depend on family income and number of children but also vary. Single parents pay a lower fee. Total costs per place vary from one form of child care to another, as does the size of government subsidies. In general, cost levels decrease in the following order: day care centers, full-time family day care, part-time family day care, after-school homes, and part-time preschools. National government and municipalities share center costs almost equally, but municipality costs are somewhat higher for all other forms of care.

Parents who are white-collar workers use public day care for their children to a greater extent than do blue-collar worker parents. In 1984–1985 71 percent of children from birth to 6 years with parents who were senior white-collar workers were in public day care, as compared to 58 percent of children of white-collar workers at low and middle levels and 46 percent of children of blue-collar workers. Also, children of white-collar workers more often attended day care centers, while children with blue-collar parents more often were in family day care.[30] This uneven distribution is partly the result of a large variation across municipalities in the availability of public day care; it is greatest in the Stockholm area, which has an above-average proportion of white-collar workers.

Analyzing local child care markets and their impact on female labor supply in 1989, Gustafsson and Stafford found, first, that the proportion of female elected municipal officials and the tax revenue per inhabitant had positive effects on the availability of spaces. The number of available spaces was only slightly higher in municipalities controlled by the Social Democrats. Second, the availability of spaces per capita was found to have a large impact on the probability of substantial labor force participation and the use of public day care. In the absence of rationing, a lower fee significantly increases the probability that parents would work and use public day care.[31]

There was an estimated shortage of almost 50,000 places in day care centers and 5,000 places in family day care—enough space for 8 percent of all children from birth to 6 years in 1988. In this situation a rationing system is applied by allotting children a place on the waiting list according to their date of birth, but children of single parents and those with special needs receive priority. Significantly, in 1985, the parliament resolved to expand public day care to make spaces available in 1991 (later postponed to 1992) to all children over 18 months whose parents are working or in school. However, the recent baby boom has increased the difficulties for the municipalities in reaching this goal.

Parental Insurance Benefits

In Sweden employed women have had the right to maternity leave at childbirth since 1931. At that time the leave was only one month and the pay was low, but it was raised in 1937.[32] In 1955 a new law granted employed women a six-month leave of absence at childbirth, of which three months was with some pay; in 1962 a cash benefit for the entire six months was added. With the aim of promoting equality between women and men in both the labor market and the home, in 1974, Sweden was the first country in the world to introduce a system of parental leave that enabled either the mother or the father to stay home from work and take care of the baby or to share the six months as they desired. The leave could be used on a full-time or part-time basis any time before the child was 8 years old. Income replacement was raised to the level of the sick pay—about 90 percent of the pretax earnings reported to the National Insurance System in the 270 days (later, 240 days) prior to childbirth. All nonemployed mothers would receive a payment at the rate of the basic sick pay, that is, a per diem allowance of Skr 25 (from 1987, Skr 60). The design of the system encouraged women to be employed full time and to earn a high wage before having a child.

By 1975 leave benefits were extended to seven months, and they have since been extended stepwise. In 1978 benefits were extended to nine months, with the ninth month compensated at the same flat rate for everybody; in 1980 the increase was to twelve months and in 1989 to fifteen months. Since 1980 the

Table 7.9
Months of Parental Leave Benefits Within 24 Months of Childbirth among Employed Married Parents of Children Born in 1981

Months of Benefit Receipt	%	Prop. shared, %
0	0.5	-
up to 6	3.2	17.9
more than 6, less than 9	14.7	48.5
9 months	7.8	20.8
more than 9 less than 12	52.3	31.8
12	21.3	13.7
All		28.9
Total %	100 %	
Total number	49,791	14,402

Source: National Insurance Board, ''Statistisk information,'' 1986:12.

last three months of salary have been replaced at the flat rate, and the remainder is wage related.

Benefits also apply to parents with young adopted children, and multiple births give parents a right to six months of extra benefits for each additional child. Additionally, a woman who gives birth to another child within thirty months will receive parental benefits at least as high as that received during the previous parental leave, even if she is on unpaid leave or works fewer hours than before the previous birth. The ''thirty-month'' rule, which has applied since 1986, was an extension of the twenty-four-month limit that applied from 1980. Because thirty months is a more realistic target than twenty-four months, the new rule encourages closer spacing of children and is likely to have contributed to the recent increase in fertility, since second and third births have come earlier.[33]

By far the major share of the parental benefits for care of newborn children has been used by mothers. Among married and employed parents of children born in 1981, the mothers who used benefits did so for an average of 290 days compared to 48 days for the fathers who used benefits.[34] However, campaigns have been conducted to encourage fathers to make greater use of parental benefits. Thus, of the total number of days for which income was replaced, fathers used 7.5 percent in 1987, a slight increase from 4.3 percent in 1978; and 24.5 percent of fathers used some benefits in 1987, an increase from 20.4 percent in 1978. Fathers who received benefits were on leave for an average of 29 days in 1987 compared to 11 days in 1978.[35] However, among married employed parents, the proportion who shared the leave was higher—almost 29 percent for children born in 1981 (table 7.9).

It is clear from table 7.9 that about 80 percent of the employed couples had used all nine months with full pay before the child was 2 years old, but only 20 percent had used all twelve months. The proportion of couples who had shared the leave was lower among those who had received benefits for more than nine months than among those who had used less. The willingness of fathers to use the parental leave has been found to depend more on mothers' earnings than on their own; the higher the pay of the mother, the larger the proportion of fathers who had received benefits, regardless of the fathers' earnings.[36] Based on a 1986 sample of parents of 1,000 children, fathers employed in the public sector were found more likely to have used at least one month of full-time benefits than were those employed in the private sector. Fathers who had management positions had used the full-time leave option to a lesser extent than had others. By contrast, fathers who had been on parental leave for at least one month more often worked at worksites with a majority of women workers.[37] Additionally, the vast majority of mothers had substantial earnings before giving birth since only 8 percent of mothers who received benefits in 1985 had a sick pay rate that was lower or equal to the per diem allowance.[38]

Four Additional Options

The benefit for occasional care of children was also introduced in 1974. Called "sick pay for the care of sick children," it gave families with children under the age of 10 the right to ten days of benefits per year, regardless of the number of children, for the care of sick children or for fathers who stayed home from work to care for older siblings on the birth of a child. The benefit was renamed in 1977 when it was extended to twelve days for one-child families, fifteen days for two-children families, and eighteen days for three-children families. It could also be used when the child's normal caretaker was sick, for taking the child for medical care, and (one day per year per child) for visits to public child care. Along with extending this benefit, municipalities have reduced the number of nurses' aides employed to care for sick children at home while their parents work. In 1977 the communes had 3,488 of these nurses' aides, who helped 82,769 families; by 1984 the number had declined to 1,363 nurses who served 27,857 families. Recently the press has reported that some companies are employing nurses to care for the sick children of their employees.

Benefits were extended in 1980 to 60 days per year per child under the age of 12, to 90 days per year in 1989, and to 120 days in 1990 out of concern for the needs of parents of handicapped and severely ill children. A certificate from a medical doctor is needed if the child is sick for more than a week at a time. In 1986 this benefit was used for 48 percent of all children under 12 years, for an average of 7 days. Benefits were used to a larger extent by parents with children ages 1 to 4; 41 percent of those who received benefits were men, and they used 34 percent of the paid days. Only 1 percent of the eligible families had received benefits for 40 days or more.[39]

Pregnant women who cannot continue to work during the last months of their pregnancy because it is too dangerous or otherwise inadvisable have had the right to pregnancy pay since 1980. Pregnancy pay equals sick pay and is paid out for a maximum of fifty days within sixty days of anticipated delivery. The proportion of pregnant women who receive pregnancy benefits increased from

10 percent in 1980 to 21 percent in 1986. The average number of days replaced also increased, averaging thirty-eight in 1986.[40]

In 1980 the right of fathers to take a ten-day leave of absence within sixty days of childbirth (''daddy days'') was introduced with pay equal to sick pay. This right is widely used; 83 percent of fathers of children born in 1986 used the benefit and were on leave for an average of nine days.[41]

Last introduced (in 1986) is the right to two days per year per child (ages 4 to 12) for parents' participation in day care and school (''contact days''). Benefits can be used as full, half, or quarter days. Only about 5 percent of eligible parents used this benefit in 1986 (for 12 percent of the eligible children), and 68 percent of these days were used for young school children; 31 percent of the paid days were used by men.[42]

In 1989–1990, the government's costs for the parental insurance benefits amounted to about Skr 13,360 million or 3.9 percent of government expenditures and 1 percent of GNP. In 1988, when expenditures were Skr 8,575 million, some 6,415 million was benefits for care of newborns, 1,930 million was pay for occasional care of children (including fathers' ten days), and 230 million was pregnancy pay.

Parental Employment Benefits

In 1939 dismissal from employment because of marriage, pregnancy, or childbirth was prohibited by the Swedish parliament. Employers were also forbidden to dismiss women who stayed home from work for a reasonable period of time due to pregnancy and childbirth. In addition, when the parental leave was introduced in 1974, employment protection was also extended to fathers who used leave benefits. All Swedish employees who have had the same employer for six months were protected from unfair dismissals through the Security of Employment Act, which was passed in 1974 and revised in 1982. Comparing the debates during the 1930s in the United States and Sweden on married women's right to work, B. M. Hobson observed that the Swedish debate acknowledged that preventing married women from working could have negative effects on fertility.[43]

The Child Care Leave Act, passed in 1978 and revised in 1985 and 1989, gives parents of preschool children the right to a leave of absence from work until the child is 18 months old when they receive the parental insurance benefits. The law specifies that the parent's working conditions should not be impaired because he or she used parental rights (by, for example, a transfer to an inferior position).[44] Additionally, in 1979 parents who were employed full time in all sectors of the economy were granted the right to an unpaid partial leave of absence to at most three-quarters of full time until the child was 8 years old. (Civil servants have had this right since 1970). That is, parents could reduce their hours of work to thirty hours per week with a right to return to full-time work after two months' notice to the employer. A prerequisite for using the right is that the employee has been employed full time by the same employer for six months.

There is little information about the use of the partial leave. However, 1990 findings by Nasman and co-workers show that 68 percent of employed mothers who returned to work after childbirth and parental leave reduced their hours, 13 percent worked full time, and 19 percent continued to work part time as they had done prior to birth and leave.[45] Among fathers who had been on full-time parental leave, 86 percent worked full time, 12 percent reduced their hours of work, and 1 percent returned to a part-time job.

IMPACTS

Effects of the Parental Insurance and Employment Benefits on Mothers' Labor Market Activity

I used a data set of fifteen panels over the period 1970/72–1988/90, compiled from the Labor Force Surveys, where each panel contained observations for eight consecutive quarters of a year.[46] I was thus able to observe the changes in employment status among women who gave birth to their first child, as well as among those who gave birth to additional children during the two years they were included in the survey. The results showed that Swedish women increasingly work full time up to the birth of their first child and remain (and are classified as) employed full time while on parental leave. Thus, the proportion of first-time mothers who worked full time for eight consecutive quarters rose from 25 percent in 1970/72 to 48 percent in 1988/90. The first-time mothers show the greatest rise in the proportion continuously employed full time among the groups studied. Most likely, this steep rise is a manifestation of the parental leave and the definitions used. First, the parental leave provides women who plan to have children with a strong incentive to work full time prior to childbirth in order to increase the benefits they will receive. Second, since women on parental leave from a full-time job are classified as employed full time, extensions of the leave will increase the proportion classified as full time. One also sees an increase in the proportion continuously employed full time among women giving birth to additional children. The proportion of continuously nonemployed women has been reduced among both groups but most drastically among second-time mothers.

After parental leave, an increasing proportion of first-time mothers in the 1970s shifted from full-time to part-time work; 24 percent of all first-time mothers in 1979/81 were in this category compared to 12 percent in 1970/72 (table 7.11). (The proportion fell in the 1980s because the leave was extended.) Among other things, the options of combining part-time benefits and reducing hours substantially reduced the proportion of women who left full-time work for nonemployment when they gave birth—from 18 percent in 1970/72 to 5 percent in 1988/90. Thus, among first-time mothers, the option of part-time work has not reduced

Table 7.10
Proportions Continuously Employed Full-Time, Part-Time, and Nonemployed among All Childbearing Women, 1970–1990

		Employed full time	part time	Not employed
Women giving birth to their first child	1970-72	25.4	2.4	7.8
	1978-80	31.9	8.1	5.2
	1979-81	31.1	9.9	6.1
	1980-82	40.3	9.5	2.5
	1981-83	35.1	9.4	5.5
	1982-84	39.8	9.7	3.3
	1983-85	34.4	11.5	3.6
	1984-85	39.2	11.8	6.1
	1986-88	40.7	7.7	0.7
	1987-89	42.1	8.0	2.8
	1988-90	47.8	8.4	1.9
Women giving birth to additional children	1970-72	7.7	8.7	31.4
	1978-80	11.9	28.5	17.5
	1979-81	10.2	35.1	17.8
	1980-82	11.9	36.1	12.4
	1981-83	9.5	38.6	12.9
	1982-84	12.1	36.8	12.0
	1983-85	15.2	38.7	10.2
	1984-85	16.2	37.4	7.7
	1986-88	19.1	29.9	7.8
	1987-89	20.5	25.4	8.9
	1988-90	19.9	25.6	5.9

Source: M. Sundström, *A Study in the Growth of Part-time Work in Sweden* (Stockholm: Center for Working Life and Almqvist & Wicksell International, 1989), p. 109; Swedish Association of Local Authorities, *Svensk Barnomsorg-En Dyrgrip?* (Swedish child care–an asset?) (1988).

the number who work full time but has limited the number who interrupt their participation in the labor force. The large positive net flow from full-time to part-time employment among this group has increased the proportion of second-time mothers who continuously work part time and reduced the proportion who are continuously nonemployed.

Effects on Parents' Work Conditions

In their study of parents of children born in 1986, Näsman and colleagues found that only 4 percent of the parents (fathers and mothers) who had returned to full-time work after full-time parental leave reported that their opportunities for career development had been negatively affected by their leave, as compared to 13 percent among those who had reduced their hours after the leave; 97 percent of those who had returned to full-time work reported no adverse impact on their subsequent earnings, as compared to 90 percent of those who had reduced their hours.[47] Also, very few cases of involuntary job transfers were reported. However, the reduced workload was a problem frequently reported by parents who had reduced their hours from full time to part time. By contrast, a 1984 study

Table 7.11
Changes in Employment Status among All Childbearing Women, 1970–1990 (Percentages)

		Proportions changing from full time to part time	from part time to full time	net part time
Women giving birth to their first child	1970-72	11.5	1.0	+10.5
	1978-80	20.2	2.5	+17.7
	1979-81	24.4	3.9	+20.5
	1980-82	19.2	2.5	+16.7
	1981-83	19.5	1.4	+18.1
	1982-84	15.3	1.7	+13.6
	1983-85	15.0	2.9	+12.1
	1984-85	12.7	0.8	+11.9
	1986-88	12.7	3.9	+8.8
	1987-89	13.1	2.9	+10.2
	1988-90	6.9	2.9	+4.0
Women giving birth to additional children	1970-72	3.3	0.7	+2.6
	1978-80	4.8	2.3	+2.5
	1979-81	4.9	3.7	+1.2
	1980-82	8.3	6.6	+1.7
	1981-83	7.7	5.3	+2.4
	1982-84	7.5	4.9	+2.6
	1983-85	7.4	6.1	+1.3
	1984-85	12.0	2.4	+9.6
	1986-88	8.2	6.0	+2.2
	1987-89	10.3	6.2	+4.1
	1988-90	9.0	5.0	+4.0

Source: Sundström, *A Study in the Growth of Part-time Work in Sweden*, p. 110.

by Herlin reported civil servants' favorable experiences of combining managerial work with partial leave.[48]

Effects on Earnings

From economic theory and previous research, we would expect persons who have been absent from work to earn lower wages than those who have worked continuously, everything else being equal. Consequently, we would expect parental leave to present parents with a trade-off in the form of lower wages after they return to work. Such an earnings penalty, although modest, is indeed found in our 1990 study, which analyzes a five-year panel (administrative data records) of 2,200 randomly selected employees at the Swedish Televerket.[49]

The results show that each day of parental leave has a small but significant negative impact on the growth in wages, and it is larger for men than for women. For women, a year of full-time leave decreases earnings by about 1.6 percent. For those with small amounts of company tenure, the net effect of parental leave is essentially no change in real earnings power at Televerket. The cost of parental

Table 7.12
Proportion of Men and Women Who Consider the Following Way to Reduce Working Hours by 5 Percent to Be Most Important

	(Percents) Men	Women
Daily reduction	7	10
Weekly reduction	22	21
Single days free	9	10
Longer vacation	29	19
Extended parental leave	13	23
Lower age of retirement	17	14
To save for a period off	5	4
	100	100

Source: SOU, *Arbetstid och Välfärd*, 1989:53, Appendix, p. 125.

leave is forfeited growth in earnings but not any special earnings penalty for Televerket women. If men took a full year of leave, which they do not, the cost in earnings would be greater—about 3.8 percent.[50]

Estimated Effects of Extending Parental Leave to Eighteen Months

To provide a basis for political decision making on reducing working hours, the Government Committee on Working Hours in 1988 took an opinion poll of a random sample of 7,000 persons who were representative of the Swedish population between ages 16 and 64. One question asked was that of the ways to reduce total hours worked by 5 percent, which did the subject consider to be of highest priority. Interestingly, the results reveal rather strong public support for an extended parental leave. Support, not surprisingly, was stronger among women than among men (table 7.12).

Further, in 1989 Anxo performed simulations of the effects of the possible reform of working hours on a macromodel of the Swedish economy.[51] The results indicate that an extension of the parental leave to eighteen months would result in a 1 percent lower GNP in the year 2010 and Skr 11 billion lower private consumption, as compared to an alternative without reforms. In a separate 1989 analysis, Eriksson and Hultin estimated that the total labor supply would be reduced by 1 percent if the parental leave were extended to eighteen months.[52]

OVERALL EFFECTS OF THE PARENTING POLICIES

Effects on Parental Well-Being

In 1989 Moen used the three waves of the Level of Living Survey 1968–1974–1981 to analyze trends and patterns in parental well-being as measured by both daily fatigue in the previous two weeks and psychological strain (symptoms of anxiety, depression) over the previous twelve months.[53] She found, first, that mothers at every socioeconomic level were more likely than were fathers to report feeling tired during the previous two weeks. The experience of fatigue by both sexes was differentially distributed by social class; those in the working class were the most prone to fatigue. Second, the proportion of Swedish mothers reporting psychological distress appeared to have dropped from 1968 to 1981. Third, controlling for background factors, fathers had an increased probability (from 1968 to 1981) of reporting feelings of fatigue. Moen noted that the likelihood of psychological distress and fatigue appeared to have become more evenly distributed between fathers and mothers from 1968 to 1981, when parental benefits had been enhanced.

Labor Market Effects

As Leighton and Gustafsson pointed out in 1984, one of the costs of adopting a policy of strengthened job security has been an increase in the number of temporary jobs.[54] Moen suggests that this increase in temporary or part-period work also could be seen as response by employers to parental leave and other family policies that frequently produce a need for temporary workers. Although joblessness decreased, there was an increase between 1968 and 1981 in the proportion of workers holding temporary jobs—from 2 to 6 percent among fathers and from 3 to 6 percent among mothers.[55] The percentages were probably even higher among young people without children.

One could also anticipate another reaction by employers to the extensive parental benefits: avoiding the employment of women of childbearing ages. Isolated cases of such discrimination against female job applicants have been reported in the press, and in at least one case, a job applicant who was pregnant was paid damages by the employer after the trade union intervened.

Effects on Fertility

Judging from the relatively high recent fertility rate, Swedish parents are in favor of the country's parenting policies. However, why the Swedish fertility rate rose in the late 1980s is a different question from why Sweden currently has a higher fertility rate than most other West European countries. In response to the first question, most Swedish demographers seem to view the recent increase in fertility as a recovery rather than a permanent increase and as a result of the simultaneous occurrence of postponed births and earlier birth of second and third children, that is, a closer spacing of births.[56] This simultaneous occurrence might be explained by the cumulative effects of the parenting policies, the design of the benefit system (which encourages postponing childbirth and closer spacing of children), and Sweden's favorable economic climate. Second, generous Swedish parenting policies probably explain why Sweden has a higher fertility rate than do other countries that are similar in other respects. Demographers Hoem and Hoem observe that the contrast becomes particularly apparent when a comparison is made with the most similar country nearby, namely Denmark. Although no real rival to Sweden in terms of early and extensive cohabitation and nonmarital childbearing, by international standards, Denmark scores high on these and on most other scales of liberality and modernism; female labor force participation is very high and the availability of outside child-care is fairly good. Unlike Sweden, Denmark has a very low fertility level, a fact that must surely be connected with the country's policies of parental benefits and parental leaves, which have long been much less generous than those of Sweden. Differentials in the national economic climates will no doubt interfere, and international comparisons of demographic behavior are always fraught with effects of cultural differences, so it is hard to isolate the specific impact of public policies. Nevertheless, we are convinced that a closer scrutiny will continue to demonstrate the advantages for the level of reproduction of the advanced Swedish policies that aim to mitigate the direct costs and opportunity costs of childbearing.[57]

CONCLUSIONS

The parental leave system is valuable for Swedish men, women, and children. It enables fathers to build a close relationship with their children from the time they are infants. For women it facilitates the joint pursuit of a labor market career and raising a family. That Swedish families value the parental benefits highly is demonstrated by the high and rising fertility rate. The system also has some drawbacks, however. First, there seems to be a small increase in the number of temporary jobs and possibly also some increased employment discrimination against women of childbearing age. Second, there is an earnings penalty, albeit a small one, for women who take leave: earnings fail to grow during leave, and the loss of training days leads to a small loss in earnings.

NOTES

1. Census reports. See also A. Arvidsson et al., "Barn-behov eller börda?" (Children–need or burden?), in *Urval*, no. 11 (Stockholm: Statistics Sweden, 1979), p. 41.
2. A. Arvidsson et al., *Kvinnor och barn* (Women and children) (Stockholm: Statistics Sweden, IPF, 1982), no. 4, p. 30; and B. Hoem, "Early Phases of Family Formation in Contemporary Sweden," in *Research Reports in Demography*, no. 47 (Stockholm: University of Stockholm, Section of Demography, 1988), pp. 8–12.
3. Hoem, "Early Phases," p. 18; B. and J. M. Hoem, "Dissolution in Sweden: The Break-up of Conjugal Unions by Swedish Women Born in 1936–60," *Research Reports in Demography*, no. 45 (Stockholm: University of Stockholm, Section of Demography, 1988).
4. Arvidsson et al., *Kvinnor och barn*, p. 32.
5. Statistics Sweden, *Population Changes*, pt. 3 (Stockholm). Unless otherwise noted, data are derived from Statistics Sweden and include the *Censuses*, the 1987 and 1988 *Child Care Surveys*, 1989 *Children's Living Conditions*, *The Labor Force Surveys* and *Population Changes*, pt. 3.
6. S. Martinelle, "Fruktsamheten nu Och i framtiden" (Fertility now and in the future), Välfärdsbulletin, no. 2 (1989).

7. Arvidsson et al., *Kvinnor och barn*, p. 42.

8. Arvidsson et al., "Barn-behov eller börda?" p. 35.

9. E. Bernhardt and B. Hoem, "Cohabitation and Social Background: Trends Observed for Swedish Women Born 1936–60," *European Journal of Population* 1 (1986): 375–95.

10. Arvidsson et al., *Kvinnor och barn*, p. 46.

11. M. Sundström, *A Study in the Grown of Part-time Work in Sweden* (Stockholm: Center for Working Life and Almquist and Wicksell International, 1987); and "Part-time Work in Sweden: Trends and Equality Effects," *Journal of Economic Issues* (1990).

12. *OECD Employment Outlook* (Paris, 1988), p. 149, and M. Sundström, "Part-time Work in Sweden and Its Implications for Gender Equality", in Proceedings of the *International Economic Association IXth World Congress*, vol 4, *Women's Work in the World Economy* (New York: Macmillan, forthcoming).

13. Sundström, "Part-time Work in Sweden."

14. *The Labor Force Surveys, 1988* (Stockholm: Statistics Sweden).

15. F. T. Juster and F. P. Stafford, "The Allocation of Time: Empirical Findings, Behavioral Models, and Problems of Measurement," *Working Paper* (Stockholm: Industrial Institute for Economic and Social Research, 1990); and *Working Paper* (Ann Arbor: University of Michigan, Institute for Social Research, 1990).

16. Sundström, *A Study in the Growth of Part-time Work in Sweden*, pp. 122–24; G. Burtless, "Taxes, Transfers, and Swedish Labor Supply," in B. P. Bosworth and A. M. Rivlin, eds., *The Swedish Economy* (Washington, D.C.: Brookings Institution, 1987); and S. Gustafsson, "Separate Taxation and Married Women's Labor Supply: A Comparison of West Germany and Sweden," in *Working Papers* (Stockholm: Center for Working Life, 1989).

17. A review of the Swedish tax system and its impact on labor supply is found in Burtless, "Taxes, Transfer and Swedish Labor Supply." For a study of the effects of separate taxation, see Gustafsson, "Separate Taxation and Married Women's Labor Supply."

18. Sundstrom, "Part-time Work in Sweden."

19. H. Ginsburg, "Flexible and Partial Retirement for Norwegian and Swedish Workers," *Monthly Labor Review* 108 (1985): 33–43. Also see National Insurance Board, *Annual Statistical Report* (various years).

20. S. Hadenius, *Swedish Politics during the Twentieth Century* (Stockholm: Swedish Institute, 1985).

21. S. Gustafsson, "Equal Opportunity Policies in Sweden," in G. Schmid and R. Weitzel, eds., *Sex Discrimination and Equal Opportunity Policy* (Aldershot, Hampshire: Gower, 1985).

22. M. Petterson-Sundström, *Deltidsarbetet i Sverige* (Part-time work in Sweden) (Stockholm: Center for Working Life, 1981), chap. 2; and Ginsburg, "Flexible and Partial Retirement for Norwegian and Swedish Workers."

23. Ministry of Finance, *Regeringens Budgetförslag 1989/90* (Government's budget proposition 1989/90) (Stockholm: Allmänna Förlgaet, 1989), p. 86. This is the source for 1989–1990 expenditures as reported in this section.

24. S. Gustafsson, "The Labor Force Participation and Earnings of Lone Parents," *Working Papers* (Stockholm: Center for Working Life, 1988). On advance maintenance elsewhere in Europe, see Alfred J. Kahn and Sheila B. Kamerman, eds., *Child Support: From Debt Collection to Social Policy* (Newbury Park, Calif.: Sage Publications, 1988).

25. Ministry of Social Affairs, *Underhållsbidrag och bidragsförskott* (Maintenance allowances and maintenance advance), Ds S, no. 10 (Stockholm: Allmänna Förlaget, 1983).

26. S. Gustafsson, "Labor Force Participation and Earnings of Lone Parents," p. 41.

27. A. Baude, "Public Policy and Changing Family Patterns in Sweden 1930–1977," in J. Lipman-Blumen and J. Bernard, eds., *Social Policy and Sex Roles* (London: Sage, 1978), pp. 145–74.

28. The data sources for this section, unless otherwise stated, are *The Child-care Surveys*, 1987 and 1988, Statistics Sweden.

29. National Board of Health and Welfare, Stockholm, *Barnomsorgen i Sverige 1985–86* (Child Care in Sweden), Rapport till Nordiska Kontakskommutteens Möte (May 1986). Kitchen and administrative staff excluded.

30. S. Nelander, *LO-medlemmar i Välfärden* (LO-members in the welfare state) (Stockholm: Landsorganisationen, 1987).

31. S. Gustafsson and F. Stafford, "Daycare Subsidies and Labor Supply in Sweden," *Working Papers* (Amsterdam: Department of Economics, University of Amsterdam, 1990).

32. For a review of the early maternity reforms, see SOU, *Arbetstid och välfärd* (Working hours and welfare), no. 53 (Stockholm: Allmänna Förlaget, 1989), pp. 112–13.

33. J. M. Hoem, F. Stafford, and M. Sundström, "Parental Leave Policy and Women's Careers in Sweden," *Working Papers* (Stockholm: Center for Working Life, 1990).

34. National Insurance Board, Stockholm, Statistical Report No. 4 (1985).

35. National Insurance Board, Stockholm, Statistical Report No. 24 (1989).

36. National Insurance Board, Stockholm, Statistical Report No. 4 (1985).

37. E. Näsman et al., "Föraldraledighetslagen i tillämpning" (The Swedish law on parental leave in practice) (Stockholm: Center for Working Life, forthcoming).

38. National Insurance Board, Stockholm, Statistical Report No. 7 (1986).

39. National Insurance Board, Stockholm, Statistical Report No. 8 (1989), p. 8.

40. Ibid.

41. Ibid.

42. Ibid.

43. B. M. Hobson, "The Debate over Married Women's Right to Work, in Sweden and the U.S. during the 1930s," in S. Koven and S. Mitchell, eds., *Gender and Origins of Welfare States in Western Europe and North America* (London: Routledge, forthcoming).

44. E. Näsman and E. Falkenberg, "Parental Rights in Work and Family Interface," *Working Papers* (Stockholm: Center for Working Life, 1989).

45. Näsman et al., "Föräldraledighetslagen i tillämpning."

46. Sundström, *A Study in the Growth of Part-time Work in Sweden.*

47. Näsman et al., "Föräldraledighetslagen i Tillämpning."

48. H. Herlin, *Chef på deltid—går det?* (Manager on part time—does that work?) (Stockholm: FOA, 1984).

49. Hoem, Stafford, and Sundström, "Parental Leave Policy."

50. For more detail about the method and calculations, write to the author.

51. D. Anxo, "Samhällsekonomiska följder av kortare arbetstid" (Economic consequences of reduced working hours), in SOU, *Arbetstid*, appendix.

52. H. Eriksson, and M. Hultin, "Vad betyder kortare arbetsvecka, längre semester

och längre föräldraledighet för utbudet av arbetskraft?'' (What does shorter workweek, longer vacation and extended parental leave imply for the supply of labor?), in SOU, *Arbetstid*, appendix.

53. P. Moen, *Working Parents: Transformations in Gender Roles and Public Policies in Sweden* (Madison: University of Wisconsin Press, 1989).

54. L. Leighton and S. Gustafsson, ''Differential Patterns of Unemployment in Sweden,'' in *Research in Labor Economics*, vol. 6 (1984), pp. 251–85.

55. Moen, *Working Parents*, p. 84.

56. Martinelle, ''Fruktsamheten nu och i framtiden.''

57. B. and J. M. Hoem, ''The Swedish Family: Aspects of Contemporary Developments,'' *Journal of Family Issues* 3 (1988): 397–424.

BIBLIOGRAPHY

Anxo, D. 1989. ''Samhällsekonomiska följder av kortare arbestid'' (Economic consequences of reduced working hours). In SOU, *Arbetstid och Välfärd* (Working hours and welfare), no. 53. Stockholm: Almänna Förlaget.

Arvidsson, A. et al. 1979. ''Barn—behov eller börda?'' (Children–need or burden?). *Urval*, no. 11. Stockholm: Statistics Sweden.

———. 1982. *Kvinnor och barn* (Women and children). Stockholm: Statistics Sweden, IFP, no. 4.

Baude, A. 1978. ''Public Policy and Changing Family Patterns in Sweden 1930–1977.'' In J. Lipman-Blumen and J. Bernhard, eds., *Social Policy and Sex Roles*, pp. 145–74. London: Sage.

Bernhardt, E., and Hoem, B. 1986. ''Cohabitation and Social Background: Trends Observed for Swedish Women Born 1936–60.'' *European Journal of Population* 1: 375–95.

Björklund, A. 1989. ''Potentials and Pitfalls of Panel Data. The Case of Job Mobility.'' *European Economic Review* 33: 537–46.

Burtless, G. 1987. ''Taxes, Transfers, and Swedish Labor Supply.'' In B. P. Bosworth and A. M. Rivlin, eds., *The Swedish Economy*. Washington, D.C.: Brookings Institution.

Edlund, S., and Nyström, B. 1988. *Developments in Swedish Labor Law*. Stockholm: Swedish Institute.

Eriksson, H., and Hultin, M. 1989. ''Vad betyder kortare arbetsvecka, längre semester och längre föräldraledighet för utbudet av arbetskraft?'' (What does shorter workweek, longer vacation and extended parental leave imply for the supply of labor?). In SOU, *Arbetstid och Välfärd*, no. 53. Stockholm: Almänna Förlaget.

Forsebäck, L. 1980. *Industrial Relations and Employment in Sweden*. Stockholm: Swedish Institute.

Ginsburg, H. 1983. *Full Employment and Public Policy: The United States and Sweden*. Lexington, Mass.: D. C. Heath & Co.

———. 1985. ''Flexible and Partial Retirement for Norwegian and Swedish Workers.'' *Monthly Labor Review* 108:33–43.

Gustafsson, S. 1985. ''Equal Opportunity Policies in Sweden.'' In G. Schmid and R. Weitzel, eds., *Sex Discrimination and Equal Opportunity Policy*. Aldershot, Hampshire: Gower.

———. 1988. "The Labor Force Participation and Earnings of Lone Parents." *Working Papers*. Stockholm: Center for Working Life.

———. 1989. "Separate Taxation and Married Women's Labor Supply: A Comparison of West Germany and Sweden." *Working Papers*. Stockholm: Center for Working Life.

Gustafsson, S., and Stafford, F. S. 1990. "Daycare Subsidies and Labor Supply in Sweden." *Working Papers*. Amsterdam: Department of Economics, University of Amsterdam.

Hadenius, S. 1985. *Swedish Politics During the 20th Century*. Stockholm: Swedish Institute.

Hamermesh, Daniel, 1987. "Why Do Fixed Effects Models Perform So Poorly? The Case of Academic Salaries." Working Paper No. 2135. Cambridge, Mass.: National Bureau of Economic Research.

Herlin, H. 1984. *Chef på deltid—gär det?* (Manager on part time—does that work?). Stockholm: FOA.

Hobson, B. M. 1990. "The Debate over Married Women's Right to Work in Sweden and the U.S. during the 1930's." In S. Koven and S. Mitchell, eds., *Gender and Origins of Welfare States in Western Europe and North America*. London: Routledge.

Hoem, B. 1988. "Early Phases of Family Formation in Contemporary Sweden." *Research Reports in Demography* 47. Stockholm: Section of Demography, University of Stockholm.

Hoem, B., and Hoem, J. M. 1988. "The Swedish Family: Aspects of Contemporary Developments." *Journal of Family Issues* 3:397–424.

———. 1988. "Dissolution in Sweden: The Break-up of Conjugal Unions to Swedish Women Born in 1936–60." *Research Reports in Demography* 45. Stockholm: Section of Demography, University of Stockholm.

Hoem, J.; Stafford, F.; and Sundström, M. 1990. "Parental Leave Policy and Women's Careers in Sweden." *Working Papers*. Stockholm: Center for Working Life.

Klevmarken, A., and Flood, L. 1989. "Tidsanvändningen i Sverige 1984." (The uses of time in Sweden). Mimeo. Department of Economics, University of Gothenburg.

Juster, F. Thomas, and Frank P. Stafford. 1990. "The Allocation of Time: Empirical Findings, Behavioral Models, and Problems of Measurement." Working Paper, Industrial Institute for Economic and Social Research, Stockholm, and Working Paper, Institute for Social Research, University of Michigan.

Leighton, L., and Gustafsson, S. 1984. "Differential Patterns of Unemployment in Sweden." *Research in Labor Economics* 6:251–85.

Martinelle, S. 1989. "Fruktsamheten nu och i framtiden" (Fertility now and in the future). *Välfärdsbulletinen*, no. 2.

Ministry of Finance. 1989. *Regeringens budgetförslag 1989/90*. (Government's budget proposition 1989/90). Stockholm: Allmänna förlaget.

Ministry of Social Affairs. 1983. *Underhällsbidrag och bidragsförskott* (Maintenance allowances and maintenance advance). Ds S, no. 10. Stockholm: Allmämma förlaget.

Moen, P. 1989. *Working Parents: Transformations in Gender Roles and Public Policies in Sweden*. Madison: University of Wisconsin Press.

Nelander, S. 1987. *LO-medlemmar i välfärden*. (LO-members in the welfare state). Stockholm: Landsorganisationen.

Näsman, E., and Falkenberg, E. 1989. "Parental Rights in the Work and Family Interface." *Working Papers*. Stockholm: Center for Working Life.

Näsman, E. et al. 1990. *Föräldraledighetslagen i tillämpning*. (The Swedish law on parental leave in practice). Stockholm: Center for Working Life.

OECD. 1988. *Employment Outlook*. Paris: OECD.

Pettersson-Sundström, M. 1981. *Deltidsarbetet i Sverige*. (Part-time work in Sweden). Stockholm: Center for Working Life.

SOU. 1983. *Ensamföräldrarna och deras barn* (The single parents and their children). No. 51. Stockholm: Allmänna förlaget.

SOU. 1989. *Arbetstid och välfärd* (Working hours and welfare). No. 53. Stockholm: Allmänna förlaget.

Sundström, M. 1987. *A Study in the Growth of Part-time Work in Sweden*. Stockholm: Center for Working Life and Almqvist & Wicksell International.

———. 1990. "Part-time Work in Sweden and Its Implications for Gender Equality." In B. Bergmann and N. Folbre, eds., *The Roles of Men and Women in the Economy of the Future*. New York: Macmillan.

———. 1990. "Part-time Work in Sweden: Trends and Equality Effects." *Journal of Economic Issues*.

Swedish Trade Union Conferation (LO). 1987. *LO and Family Policy*. Stockholm: Landsorganisationen.

Trost, J. 1978. "A Renewed Social Institution: Non-marital Cohabitation." *Acta Sociologica* 21:303 + 15.

PRINTED DATA SOURCES

National Board of Health and Welfare, Stockholm

Barnomsorgen i Sverige 1985–86 (Child care in Sweden). Rapport till nordiska kontaktkommitteens möte maj 1986.

National Insurance Board, Stockholm

Föräldraledighet i samband med barns födelse. Barn födda 1978–1982. Statistik rapport 1985:4.

Föräldraförsäkringen 1985. Statistik rapport Is-R 1986:7.

Föräldrapenning med anledning av barns födelse. Barn födda 1978–83. Statistisk information Is-I 1986:12.

Föräldraförsäkringen 1986. Statistik rapport Is-R 1989:8.

Föräldrapenning med anledning av barns födelse 1987. Statistik information Is-I 1989:24.

Statistics Sweden

The Censuses.

The Child Care Surveys 1987 and 1988.

Children's Living Conditions 1989.

The Labor Force Surveys.

Population Changes. Part 3.

Swedish Association of Local Authorities

Svensk barnomsorg—en dyrgrip? (Swedish child care—an asset?). 1988.

8

Trends, Issues, and Possible Lessons

Sheila B. Kamerman and Alfred J. Kahn

Something unexpected has been occurring in Europe with regard to public policies toward families with very young children.

When in the 1970s there was a perceived need to respond more adequately to the explosion in female labor force participation rates, the strategy universally considered relevant was an expansion and improvement of child care services. Already in place were maternity benefits, job-protected leaves, and cash to replace wages lost during the "disability" period right after childbirth (and in some places in the weeks before).

Preschool programs did more or less well in the mid-1970s in providing child care for children ages 3 to 5, often serving those children with an at-home parent too, and were marked for growth. By now preschool development has become almost universal in Europe. Most children ages 2 ½ or 3 are participating in such programs (nursery schools, prekindergartens, kindergartens) and continue until they reach compulsory school age. Coupled with a policy of much longer paid vacation than for U.S. workers, this constitutes adequate child care for children of working parents in many places, although there are still content and quality issues. A short school day in other places leaves the child care issue still unresolved for some working parents. The only major laggard countries—Britain, Australia, and the United States—are also moving in this direction. It is for the under 3s that child care coverage was very limited in the 1970s, remains poor today, and for whom the appropriate design of the system remains uncertain.

Nonetheless, the pattern was there in the 1970s: preschool teamed with maternity disability leaves and the gradual development, shaping, and expansion of child care services for toddlers. This pattern obtained almost universally despite country variations in demographic structure and female labor force participation rates and varied gaps. It appeared to be the dominant societal response as of the early 1980s too. Gradually, as measures in a number of countries were observed and summed up, however, one noted that a basic shift was occurring. Public parenting policy was undergoing a change. The policy focus was becoming one of targeting new financial support on families with very young children, the under 2s and under 3s, and ensuring employed parents of access to more extensive job-protected leaves. The leaves were long enough to offer new options to parents and thus signaled a major qualitative policy change. Whether this development is temporary, transitional, or permanent remains to be seen. But its existence and interest in its meaning is the topic of this book. What can be learned from this experience by examining it in detail? What, if any, are the lessons for the United States?

TRENDS AND ISSUES

Goals and Objectives

There is no single, overarching purpose directly addressed by these new parenting policies other than supporting the possibility of an at-home role for a parent for at least one and a half years after childbirth. Beyond this, the countries all have multiple goals and objectives in establishing their policies—some explicit, some implicit, some much discussed, others taken for granted. These motives vary significantly across countries and often even within them, at least over time. A list would include the following:

- To encourage higher birthrates.
- To provide greater recognition for ''family work'' and to support traditional husband-wife families.
- To provide economic support for families with young children.
- To encourage women to enter (or withdraw from) the labor force.
- To support good child development.
- To provide a less expensive alternative to high-cost infant and toddler care.
- To facilitate a better—and more easily maintained—balance between work and family life.
- To support gender equity.
- To facilitate and support parents' choice between an at-home role or a labor force role.

Obviously some of these goals are in tension or even mutually contradictory. Ultimately the country policy packages reflect compromises, often between potentially conflicting purposes.

We have summed up the country goals and objectives in table 8.1. The one

Table 8.1
Parenting Policies: Goals and Objectives

	PRO-NATALISM	FAMILY WORK	ECOMOMIC SUPPORT	WOMEN TO WORK	WOMEN TO STAY HOME	CHILD DEVELOP-MENT	ALTERNATIVE TO CHILD CARE	WORK/ FAMILY BALANCE	GENDER EQUITY	CHOICE
AUSTRIA	?	Y	Y				Y	Y		Y
FINLAND	?		Y	Y		Y	Y	Y	Y	Y
FRANCE	Y		Y				Y	Y		Y
F.R. GERMANY	Y	Y	Y		?					
HUNGARY	Y		Y	Y	Y		Y	Y		
SWEDEN	?		Y	Y		Y		Y	Y	

Note: This table summarizes the editors' reading of country author interpretations. Y = yes; ? = uncertain, possibly; blank = not explicit or implicit.

objective supported in all countries is to provide economic support for families with very young children as a response to their continued economic vulnerability. Here, improving the economic situation of these families involves compensating them for some of the financial costs incurred in rearing and caring for children; it does not necessarily mean reducing the poverty rate of these families. In Finland and Sweden, and to a lesser extent Austria, in fact, child poverty is not a problem. France, on the other hand, is concerned with child poverty and sees these policies as helpful in improving the economic situation of poor, large families in particular. Despite the existence of child poverty, reducing poverty is not a goal for Germany where the parenting policy is targeted mostly to traditional families and offers no real help to poor, single mothers. Finally, in Hungary, the economic situation at the time of writing was so chaotic that no such policy could solve the economic problems of families without further attention to wages, cost of living, and other aspects of the social infrastructure for children and their families.

Helping parents balance work and family life more easily is the second most prevalent objective and holds true for all the countries except for Germany. This comes as no surprise since the growth in female labor force participation rates has been dramatic in most of these countries, leading to pressures for policy response. In contrast, Germany has the lowest proportion of women with young children in the labor market among these countries and has been motivated to develop its policies for different reasons.

Pronatalism is an explicit concern of at least three countries and an implicit concern at least for conservatives in the others as well. The goal of encouraging childbirth is manifested in either public discussion or the policy provisions in which larger families receive higher benefits. As our authors observe, there seems to be a general conviction that although these benefits may have no direct impact on the reproductive decisions of adults, in a context in which more and more women are likely to be in the labor force, making it difficult for women to manage both work and family life can only lead to lower birthrates.

Developing a less expensive alternative to infant and toddler care is part of the motivation in Austria, Finland, France, and Hungary. Austria's policy specifically extends its parental benefit to low-income women who are unable to obtain child care, and the Hungarian policy was developed initially with this goal in mind. In contrast, in Finland and France, the intention is to expand child care services, but until there are sufficient numbers of places, the policy is to provide support for an at-home parent role. This is an attractive alternative, which, it is assumed in these countries, a significant proportion of parents will always prefer. Therefore, both possibilities may be preserved, to allow choice.

Labor market motives have been of great significance in the development of these policies, although the specifics have changed over time and across countries. Hungary (and possibly Germany) at different times has deliberately designed its policy to encourage low-wage, uneducated, poorly skilled women to leave the work force, and the government has set the benefit level with this group in mind. Indeed, when Hungary initially developed its child caring grant policy, the goal of coping with an excess of unskilled female labor was central and was reinforced by concern for the high costs and poor quality of infant and toddler care.

From a contrasting perspective, Finland, Hungary, and Sweden at various times have explicitly announced their need for more women to enter the labor force and have developed policies that would support this goal. In prior years, this would have meant increasing the supply of child care services and expanding access. Now it also means providing generous leaves and cash benefits at the time of childbirth but limiting these to women who have had extensive prior work histories.

Interest in providing recognition and support for family work is clearly among the factors driving Austria and Germany. The latter country has designed its policy so that it specifically benefits traditional families, and Austria is moving in this direction as well. Thus, in Germany, the benefit has no real value for single mothers, though their incomes may be very low, and in Austria, a benefit that was designed first to protect low-income single mothers has now been expanded to cover income-qualified married parents too.

Supporting parental choice is an important motive in Austria, Finland, and France, but especially in the last two. Sometimes choice is the goal; at other times it begins as a way to span competing policies but then develops a life of its own. The Finnish policy is explicitly designed to permit parents to choose either a subsidized place in child care or an at-home role or to purchase private child care. France, with its multiple, complicated amalgam of policies, has tried through a variety of incremental measures to support parents' decisions to remain at home or enter the labor force. Unlike Finland, however, the French have not fully committed resources to either option, and therefore choice exists as a principle but not as a real option.

Finally, and of some interest, Sweden and Finland include as motivating factors the goal of promoting gender equality, and Finland also identifies enhancing child development as an important objective. It is of some interest that a country clearly enunciating child development as an objective also stresses the importance of gender equity as a compatible goal.

Strategies and Instruments

Given the circumscribed nature of the policy, providing support to parents of very young children, the range of policy instruments employed is truly astonishing:

Earnings-related cash benefits
Flat-rate cash benefits

Income- or means-tested cash benefits

Tax benefits

Job-protected leaves from work

The right to part-time work

Partial cash benefits (combined with wages for part-time work)

Services

All countries here reported provide something in the way of a paid and job-protected maternity leave, but some have transformed this almost completely into a parental benefit (Sweden and Finland). Some have supplemented the initial maternity "disability" benefit (to cover the weeks of physical recuperation after childbirth) by a more extensive parental benefit (Austria, Germany, France, Hungary), while others extended their original parental benefit (Finland and Sweden).

Some countries have also concentrated on expanding their supply of child care services for the under 3s (Finland, France, Sweden). Only Finland now guarantees a child care place for all parents wanting one for their children under age 3 on the assumption that about half the parents will prefer to be supported at home. Sweden expects to have guaranteed places in child care for all children 18 months and older within the next few years. Finland's guarantee will extend to age 7 in 1995.

These strategies come together in interesting ways (tables 8.2 and 8.3). In some countries the parenting policy involves only one option: support for an at-home role for a parent. In others, however, there are parallel complementary policies of paid and job-protected leaves and subsidized services (Finland, France). In still other countries the concept is one of sequential policy in which the leave comes first and is followed by the child care service (Sweden, Hungary). Of some interest, job protection, a major feature of the right to a leave, is rigorously implemented and enforced only in Finland and Sweden; and only in Sweden, but soon Finland, are employed parents also guaranteed the right to reduce their working hours to thirty hours a week when children are under compulsory school age.

Eligibility Criteria

The qualifying conditions for these benefits vary among benefits and across countries (table 8.4). Three types of criteria are applied in determining which parents are eligible. In addition to the fact of childbirth (or adoption), these include gender and role, prior work history (and complete or partial abstention from work while in receipt of the benefit), and income.

All the countries offer a basic benefit that includes a leave covering the immediate pre- and postchildbirth period (usually four to six weeks before childbirth and eight to ten weeks "maternity disability" after birth) and a

Table 8.2
Parenting Benefit Levels and Duration

COUNTRY	EARNINGS-RELATED (% OF EARNINGS)	FLAT-RATE	DURATION[a]
AUSTRIA			
Basic Benefit	100		16 weeks
Extended Benefit		50% of average wage	2 years[b]
F.R. GERMANY			
Basic Benefit	100		14 weeks
Extended Benefit		600 DM per mo.	18 months
FINLAND			
Basic Benefit	80[c]		10 1/2 months
Extended Benefit		d	until child's 3rd birthday
FRANCE			
Basic Benefit	84		16 weeks
Extended Benefit		e	e
HUNGARY			
Basic Benefit	65-100[f]		24 weeks
Extended Benefit	65- 75[f]	25% of average wage	until child's 3rd birthday
SWEDEN			
Basic Benefit	90[c]		g
Extended Benefit	90[c h]		15 months

[a] All basic benefits are longer in the case of multiple or complex births.
[b] Plus one more year for low-income parents who have no access to child care.
[c] Taxable.
[d] Varies depending on income level and number of children.
[e] Varies depending on benefit.
[f] Depending on prior work history.
[g] Integrated with extended benefit.
[h] Last three months at flat-rate minimum; benefit and leave can be prorated and stretched out over time.

cash benefit that replaces all or some portion of wages forgone. Eligibility for this combined benefit and leave is conditional on a prior employment history. In Sweden and Finland, even those few women (or parents) who were not in the labor force at the time of childbirth can qualify for a minimum-level benefit. Only Germany, however, now—as part of the new policy thrust—provides the same parental benefit to all regardless of labor force status. France provides a series of alternative benefits, some of which are

Table 8.3
Parenting Policy Strategies

COUNTRY	MATERNITY/ DISABILITY BENEFIT (LEAVE & PAY)	EXTENDED PARENTING BENEFIT (LEAVE & PAY)	EXTENDED PARENTING BENEFIT OR CHILD CARE SERVICES	EXTENDED PARENTING BENEFIT THEN CHILD CARE SERVICES
AUSTRIA	Y	Y[a]		
FINLAND	Y		Y[a]	
FRANCE	Y		Y[a]	
F.R. GERMANY	Y	Y[a]		
HUNGARY	Y	Y[a]		
SWEDEN	b			Y[a]

[a] Right to work part-time and receive a partial benefit for at least some portion of leave.
[b] Included as first part of extended benefit.
Y = available.

available regardless of labor force status and some that are limited to those who are currently employed.

Austria, Sweden, and Hungary limit the extended parental leave/benefit to employees with a prior work history. All the countries permit part-time work for part of the leave, but working hours are restricted if individuals wish to qualify as well for some portion of the benefit (for example, nineteen hours a week is the part-time work maximum in Germany). In contrast, only Sweden actively encourages part-time work. It does this by guaranteeing working parents the right to reduce their work hours, requiring employers to allow it, and permitting the parenting benefit to be prorated and extended throughout a child's preschool years, so that the income lost by the reduced hours is largely recouped.

Although Austria limited its extended benefit to single mothers initially, eligibility was extended to low-income two-parent families beginning in 1990. In contrast, although Germany's extended benefit is available to parents in both husband-wife and single-parent families, the level of the benefit makes it unlikely that single mothers will gain any advantage from it.

Most of the benefits are available regardless of income. Although Austria, Finland, France, and Germany income test some portion of their extended parental benefit, the income ceiling is set at a sufficiently high level everywhere so that most parents of very young children qualify. Indeed, the fact that most young parents qualified even for the income-tested part of the benefit caused great surprise in Germany and served as a reminder of just how vulnerable these

Table 8.4
Parenting Benefits: Eligibility Criteria

COUNTRY	MARITAL STATUS	PRIOR WORK	ABSTENTION FROM WORK	INCOME	OTHER
AUSTRIA					
Basic Benefit	Maternity	Y	Y		a
Extended Benefit	Parental	Y	Y	b	
FINLAND					
Basic Benefit	Maternity/ Parental	Y[c]	Y		a, d
Extended Benefit	Parental	c	e	f	d′
FRANCE					
Basic Benefit	Maternity	Y	Y		a
Extended Benefit	Parental	g	e	g	a, d, h
F.R. GERMANY					
Basic Benefit	Maternity	Y	Y		
Extended Benefit	Parental		e	i	d
HUNGARY					
Basic Benefit	Maternity	Y	Y		a
Extended Benefit	Maternity/ Parental	Y	e		
SWEDEN					
Basic Benefit	Maternity/ Parental	Y[c]	e		d
Extended Benefit	Parental	Y[c]	e		d, k

[a] A special benefit is contingent on receipt of prenatal care.
[b] The third year of the benefit is limited to low-income parents.
[c] A special minimum benefit is available to those with no prior work history, but the earnings-related benefit is limited to those with prior work history.
[d] Adopted very young children are covered as well.
[e] Part-time work, with a reduced benefit, is permitted.
[f] The benefit is higher for low-income families.
[g] For certain benefits.
[h] One benefit is limited to those with three or more children.
[i] After six months, the benefit is income tested.
[j] The basic benefit and the extended benefit are linked together.
[k] Guaranteed right to reduce working hours at end of extended benefit, until youngest child is 8 years old.
Y = applicable.

families are economically. In Finland, low-income families may be entitled to an additional supplement to the basic parental benefit, and in Austria, Germany, and Finland, some localities also provide a supplementary benefit on an income-tested basis.

Benefit Levels

Benefit levels vary across countries and, for the five countries that distinguish between a basic benefit and an extended benefit, between the two benefits.

The basic benefits, all earnings related, are pegged at some portion of pre-childbirth wages—usually between 80 and 100 percent (table 8.2). As social insurance benefits, they are designed to protect family income against temporary loss as a consequence of maternity.

The extended benefits, central to the new policies featured in this book, are earnings related only in Sweden and, partly, in Hungary. In these countries, the function of the benefit is the same as the basic benefit: to protect against the loss of income as a result of childbirth. The dominant pattern among these extended benefits, however, is a flat-rate payment that varies in value between one that is inadequate to maintain a family unless there is also at least one full-time wage earner in the household (Germany and France), to one that does make an at-home role viable even for a single mother if packaged with other child and family benefits (Finland and Austria). Only the Swedish benefit is fully adequate to support a single mother at a comfortable standard of living, but is is wage related, assumes a firm attachment to the labor market, and is predicated on a full employment economy. Obviously each of these benefit patterns creates its own policy, whether or not intended or explicitly stated.

The flat-rate benefits are often discussed in the context of a ''mother's [now parent's] wage'' and some policy recognition of the economic value to the society of parenting and family work. Family work, however, is expected to be paid for at a level well below that of labor market work. In contrast, the earnings-related benefit is more closely linked to an expectation of wage work and a definition of maternity and parenting as a social risk that the society should help pay for.

The Hungarian benefit, whether the earnings-related or the flat-rate one, is especially vulnerable now because both are contingent on prior work history and labor force attachment. Unemployment is rising, placing both benefits at risk. The flat-rate benefit was especially vulnerable during completion of chapter 5 because inflation was increasing dramatically and the rate of indexing had not kept up with changes in real values.

To be adequate, earnings-related benefits require a healthy economy with a low unemployment rate, and flat-rate benefits are contingent on adequate benefit levels and a policy of indexing that links benefits to wages or prices, preferably whichever is higher.

Benefit Duration

The basic benefits tend to limit duration to the period of maternity disability, covering between four to six weeks before childbirth and eight to ten weeks after, with adjustments in the case of multiple or complex births. Even the

Swedish parenting benefit includes the option of a prebirth leave for women and a guaranty of at least six weeks postchildbirth even if a mother does not have custody of her child. Finland too reserves the first part of its longer parental leave for women. Only Hungary among these countries has a significantly longer basic benefit, a pattern typical of the East European countries. A few Western countries and most East European countries in fact mandate the prechildbirth leave.

In contrast, the extended parental benefit ranges from fifteen months in Sweden (soon to be eighteen months, as in Germany) to two to three years in Austria, France, and Finland. Moreover, two or three years seems to be the objective in all these countries except Sweden, and even there the issue is debated and posed as an option—if only by conservatives. In all the countries, a leave longer than three years is considered as penalizing women in the labor market and unnecessary for child development purposes because children will benefit more from a good preschool experience by that age. Several countries assume that by the third year (the second in Sweden) women (parents) will already be returning to work part time. All the countries now permit part-time work and partial receipt of the cash benefit even in the initial period. From various surveys, part-time work, beginning relatively early, appears to be women's preference while children are very young, but the problem is that some countries do not have enough part-time jobs available, some do not provide adequate social benefits and wages for such work, and some still do not have enough toddler child care services in place to provide care for the children involved. It is also likely that a pattern of extensive part-time work in connection with extended leave would undermine the objectives of some champions of the leave.

Financing

The basic maternity-parental leave is financed in all countries but Germany in the same way as are all other social insurance benefits, as a contributory benefit, often with a governmental supplement, but contribution sources and proportions vary. Thus, in Finland and Hungary (for the maternity benefit and the child care allowance), the benefits are financed through contributions of employees, employers, and government. In Sweden, the contributions are provided by employers and government. In Austria, half the costs are paid by the national Health Insurance Fund and half by the Family Allowance Fund; these in turn are funded by employer and government contributions. In France, employers' contributions pay for the whole benefit; and in Germany, the employer tops off the government-provided benefit in cases where the employee's salary is above the maximum government benefit.

Governments provide more of the funds to pay for the extended benefits. Thus, in Finland and Germany, the benefits are paid for out of general revenue. In Hungary (for the child care grant) and Sweden, the financing is by employer and government contributions. In France, all the various benefits are paid for through the Family Allowance Fund, which is funded by employers' contributions. And in Austria, one extended benefit is paid for half by the Family Allowance Fund and half by the Unemployment Insurance Fund, while the second is paid for completely out of the Unemployment Insurance Fund.

The costs of these policies are quite modest in all the countries, constituting at most 4 or 5 percent of total public social welfare expenditures, which in turn constitute about 24 percent (Finland) to 34 percent (France) of gross domestic product in 1989, in comparison with 18 percent for the United States. Adamik points out that in Hungary the total costs of the child care grant and allowance are less than what the cost of unemployment insurance would be for the women involved and far less than the cost of good quality infant care.

Coverage and Participation

The basic maternity or parenting benefits are available to all employed women or parents who have worked for at least one year and usually all those currently receiving unemployment insurance benefits as well. Hungary expands this coverage to include all full-time students. Just about all who qualify for the basic benefit use it. In Austria and Germany, working women are required by law to take these leaves (including prechildbirth leaves) and related benefits, and full participation is assumed in France and Hungary. The culture is such that in Finland and Sweden too, although not mandated, parents (overwhelmingly mothers) make full use of the benefit; albeit in Sweden, where it is an option, many women use the benefit to help cover the costs of reduced working hours for some time, even some years, rather than for full withdrawal from the labor market.

Access to extended parental leaves is extensive though not as complete as for the basic benefit, and use is high too. Although all countries also provide a partial benefit combined with part-time work, only in Sweden is this right extensively used. A problem in the other countries may be the lesser availability of part-time jobs, that the right to reduce working hours is not guaranteed, or other attendant conditions outlined in several of the chapters.

In Germany, 97 percent of women who gave birth in the late 1980s received the child rearing allowance. This included 98 percent of married mothers and 84 percent of single mothers. Less than 2 percent of eligible men used the benefit, largely unemployed fathers. Less than half the women users (46 percent) had been employed at the time of childbirth, employment not being an eligibility requirement in Germany.

At the end of the first six months, when entitlement to the universal benefit ended, 79 percent of the mothers still qualified for the income-tested full benefit and another 11 percent qualified for a partial benefit. Schiersmann writes, however, that high participation in this benefit in Germany should not be construed to mean that all women prefer this policy to any alternative. The reality is that, without an adequate supply of affordable child care services, they may have no alternative.

In Austria, as in Germany, the basic leave is mandated, so all employed women make full use of it at the time of childbirth. The two-year extended maternity (now parental) leave and benefit is now available to about 60 percent of all new mothers, and 95 percent of those eligible take advantage of it. The supplementary extended leave provided to low-income single working mothers (and covering all low-income parents beginning with children born in 1990) is used by 53 percent of the above or about 25 percent of all new mothers (and just about all single mothers). Provincial supplements now available to moderate-income husband-wife families in some parts of Austria are taken up by 85 percent of those who qualify.

In Hungary, all working mothers and full-time students—almost all new mothers—claim the basic maternity benefit. Eighty-nine percent also claim the child care grant (or allowance) after six months, when the basic leave ends. Initially the benefit attracted low-wage women far more than higher-paid women. Of some interest, between 1969 and 1986 the rate at which well-educated (well-paid) as compared with poorly educated (low-paid) mothers took advantage of the benefit more than doubled, and after passage of the child care allowance (the earnings-related benefit), participation by older mothers increased significantly as well.

In Finland and Sweden all parents are covered with at least a minimum-level benefit while those who are in the labor force (the vast majority) have almost their full earnings protected. As a result, participation is almost 100 percent for the extended benefit as well. In Sweden in 1981, when the full parent insurance lasted for one year (rather than the current fifteen months) 75 percent of parents used the benefit for between nine and twelve months and another 23 percent for six to nine months. Very few parents took less than six months of full-time leave, but some saved a portion to use in their child's second year, often to offset a shorter workday. Only 21 percent of women used any of the two months of prematernity leave they are entitled to. Twenty-five percent of fathers used some part of the parent insurance benefit in 1987, and 83 percent used their full entitlement to the two-week paternity leave following childbirth. Of some interest, 41 percent of the parents using the right to a paid sick leave to care for an ill child in Sweden were fathers, and they used 34 percent of the days taken by both parents.

In contrast, only one-third of eligible fathers used the two-week paternity leave in Finland, but only 8 percent of women (or their spouses) did not use the full nine and a half months of basic maternity-parental leave.

OUTCOMES AND IMPACTS

The contributors to this book report on evidence that country intentions are or are not achieved with regard to parenting policies. While one assumes that political leaders and administrators ask about achievements frequently, there is little by way of ambitious formal evaluation here. Those evaluation studies carried out by social scientists are reviewed by our authors, as available, and relevant statistical data in the form of program and outcome indicators are considered. It is easier to discuss achievement of some of the objectives than others.

Well-being of Children and Their Families

Providing economic support for families with young children was identified as the major overarching objective behind the development of these policies. The chapter authors considered whether there is evidence that these policies have visible consequences for the economic well-being or the development of children in these countries. More is said about economic impacts than about child development.

Neither Sweden nor Finland suffers from a child poverty problem. Indeed, Sweden has the lowest child poverty rate of any of the major industrialized countries that have made comparable data available.[1] In the early 1980s, the Swedish child poverty rate (5 percent) was less than one-third that of the United States (17 percent), and it now is probably less than one-quarter of the U.S. rate. Sundstrom's thesis is that Swedish labor market policies stressing full employment, coupled with Sweden's family policies (child allowances, individualized income taxes, advanced maintenance, housing allowances), including its special parent insurance policies, are a major factor in ensuring the economic well-being of children, especially when they are young.

Other positive child development impacts are noted by Swedish researchers: Swedish child care services are world renowned for their quality and have had demonstrably positive consequences for child development, especially for those children entering care at about age 1.[2] Finally, while the consequences are not clear and documented, there is strong evidence that Swedish fathers have significantly increased the time they spend in child-related activities since passage of the parent insurance law; most child development experts would agree that this should have positive consequences for children.

Nonetheless, in Sweden as in Germany, and all the other countries here discussed, there is no requirement that any part of the cash benefit be spent directly on the children or that the newly available parental time be spent with children either. Schiersmann points out that in Germany, the benefit is specifically designed neither to provide adequate financial support nor to help pay for child care. According to her, ''Neither child care leave nor the payment of the child care benefit has been found to have any direct effect on parents' attitudes toward their children, responses to their needs, or stimulation of their development. The impact is limited to the framework of the child care task, in particular, on the factors of money, time, and social recognition of family tasks.'' The net effect is that the benefit represents a modest amount of assistance for families, especially husband-wife families, for a limited and brief period of time.

The Expert (Scientific) Advisory Board to the German minister of family affairs has strongly recommended an extension of the child care leave from the present eighteen months to three years. It bases this proposal on the findings of child development researchers who report that the first three years of life are of central importance for subsequent development. The board rejects any suggestion of a longer leave, holding that it would adversely affect women in the labor market without any concomitant positive consequences for children who, after age 3, would be better off in kindergarten anyway.

In Hungary, where child-related benefits are indexed to changing wage levels, the official estimate of the average cost of a child increased more rapidly than did the value of the grants. The value of the child care grant declined from 40 percent of the average female wage in 1967 and 31 percent of average wages generally to about 30 percent of the average female wage in 1987 and 25 percent of average national wages. Moreover, since wages are not necessarily above the poverty threshold, even benefits linked to wages do not ensure above-poverty income to the child.

Adamik points out that child poverty is rising in Hungary but not because of inadequacy of benefits. It is the decline in real wages and the rise of inflation that are the major factors. Child allowances and child care grants are set at a level linked to the minimum wage, regardless of whether the "cost of a child" is above that level. Any increase in unemployment would worsen this imbalance between family needs (the cost of a child) and wage and benefit levels. Thus one result in Hungary—as a consequence of its major social, political, and economic transitions—may be that women and children are worse off than ever, despite a seemingly generous child care benefit.

In France, family benefits have been linked to changing levels of prices rather than to wages. Since wages increased at a far higher rate than prices in the period here in focus, family allowances have declined as a percentage of family income. As a result, family benefits generally play a smaller role in compensating for the economic costs of children. In the end, all transfer measures considered, some horizontal redistribution has been accomplished, and families with children clearly benefit, but vertical redistribution has been limited to large families and low-income, lone-parent families. Despite the fact that family benefits are substantial in France, they offset only a small part of the cost of a child. Continued lack of family allowance coverage of the first child in the family severely limits the extent to which these benefits could compensate for the added costs of children.

In Finland, the home care allowance is very modest, equaling only about 20 percent of average wage; however, supplements are available for low-income families and families with more than one child. And there are additional supplements provided in some major cities where the cost of living is significantly higher (or the child care shortage looms as a major potential problem). In Helsinki, a supplementary benefit is available for nine months (until a child is 18 months old) and more than triples the value of the basic benefit, and a more modest supplement until the child is 3 years old more than doubles the benefit. The result is that in Helsinki the extended parental benefit is worth between 40 and 70 percent of an average wage, depending on the age of the child.

In Austria, as in most of the other countries, the macroimpact of these benefits (or family benefits generally) may be modest—they may constitute only a small portion of social welfare expenditures generally—but the microimpacts, for an individual family, may be quite significant. The result of a combined federal and provincial parenting benefit, for example, may be an increase of an average family's income of more than 20 percent.

Gender Equity

A policy development that either permits or encourages at-home care for infants and toddlers, even if available to either parent as it is in some places, is taken up largely by mothers. In contrast to a four- to six-month maternity leave, will a one-, two-, or three-year leave, even if job protected, affect labor force roles, wages, and status of women? What, if any, are the intra-family impacts of such policy? Is there in fact a conflict between child policy and women's policy?

A review of the parenting policies in several countries suggests that it is possible to develop parenting policies that are more (or less) sensitive to gender issues but that it requires explicit attention and careful monitoring. Gender impacts seem to depend on the policy intent, both manifest and latent, and on the nature of the policy(ies) and how it (they) are implemented.

We illustrate the point by contrasting the German policy, which thus far does not appear to advance gender equity, with the Swedish alternative. We add some observations relevant to the Hungarian experience, but the latter country was engaged in a monumental transition when the chapter was written.

Germany and Austria structure their policies around providing recognition and support for "family work" as a counterpart to the more conventional support provided for work in the paid labor market. Although this is important in raising public consciousness regarding the activities of women in the family and the household, it may not result in any greater equality for women in the labor market. It could reinforce contrary stereotypes.

The modest, flat-rate, income-tested benefit available in Germany for one and a half years (after a six-month wage-related start for those with a work history), as long as the at-home parent works no more than nineteen hours a week, illustrates the dilemma. The German parenting–child rearing policy is gender neutral in its qualifying conditions, and one might anticipate its use by some fathers. However, because the cash benefit for the extended leave is not linked to wages and is set at a low level, the policy is clearly geared to women. Its job protection provisions are not yet adequately tested. Working single mothers derive no advantage from the benefit, since it is not adequate as a replacement or substitute for wages. As a result, single mothers cannot realistically avail themselves of this benefit unless they choose social assistance ("welfare" in

U.S. terms) over a job and use the child rearing benefit to supplement a meager public assistance benefit. In effect, the most important impact of the policy as now designed is to support traditional gender roles within traditional husband-wife families.

While parents on leave may work part time during the extended leave, the employer is not required to offer part-time work, and they cannot go elsewhere because of the job guarantee. Child care is inadequate even for the 3s to 5s since despite good nursery school coverage, it is only for Germany's very short school day. The current political debate in Germany counterposes conservatives, who want to see the leave policy extended until the child's third birthday, with political liberals and feminists who support the idea of a three-year leave but stress ensuring job protection for the full period of the leave, expanding available part-time jobs (and having them covered by fringe benefits), and expanding publicly subsidized child care services in order to extend the range of choices available to women. This, they are convinced, would make for a policy that would be much more sensitive to women's status in the labor force as well as in the family and home. The Austrian policy also would appear to reinforce traditional gender roles, for similar reasons.

Despite a job-protected, three-year leave and a cash benefit that is wage related for one and a half years and set at a flat rate for another one and a half years, the Hungarian experience is that once a woman is home for three years, traditional intra-family gender roles become reinstituted and are hard to reverse subsequently. The original Hungarian policy, enacted in 1967, was in fact a response to both an excess of unskilled women in the labor force in a society that guaranteed employment and recognition of the high costs of good-quality child care. It was copied in much of Eastern Europe subsequently, usually in the form of two-year leaves, for similar reasons but also in the context of major concern about birthrates and (in some places) enactment of abortion restrictions. Since the original Hungarian program provided a flat-rate benefit until a child was 3, it attracted proportionately fewer high-earner women, who also had career concerns. Now, with benefit levels wage-related for the initial one and a half years, one sees a not-surprising doubling of participation by better-educated career women. How the ultimate pattern will work out (when benefits revert to the flat rate after one and a half years) cannot be predicted on the basis of current experience in abnormal times.

In Finland and Sweden, despite high proportions of women in the labor force generally, those who are in managerial positions tend to work in the public sector, where work time and leave adaptations can be imposed through government action. Such adaptations are exemplary.

Sweden is the best example of those countries that structure their policies specifically around gender equity (preferring the term gender equality). The results appear to warrant close attention. In a report of research carried out by two Swedish researchers and an American,[3] Sweden is described as characterized by high female labor force participation rates, high female labor force attachment rates, higher part-time employment rates for women than in most other countries, relative equality of post tax male-female wage rates, and high fertility rates for second and third births of educated women. The researchers attribute this pattern, which they find unique in the industrialized world, to Sweden's parental leave policy in combination with other policies such as subsidized child care and individually based income tax rates.

The Swedish parental leave policy gives parents the right to a paid and job-protected leave from work for up to fifteen months. The leave can be shared by the parents, can be taken on a full- or part-time basis, and can be used at any time (translated into shorter workdays) until the child is 8 years old. Eligibility for the benefit is contingent on a work and wage history. A parent with no work history receives only a very small benefit, while others receive a benefit equal to 90 percent of gross earnings.

The researchers point out that since these benefits are based on earnings and since earnings usually rise more rapidly during the early years of work experience, the Swedish leave policy emerges as a significant factor contributing to the postponement of entry into motherhood until a woman has an established labor market position. Moreover, the availability of extensively subsidized child care makes it easier for women to continue a career after parental leave, and the tax system limits the effects of the spouse's income. The researchers go on to indicate that the joint influence of these policies results in a very different pattern than in the United States, where fertility is higher among less educated and younger women and where childbearing is likely to result in lower lifetime career attainment.

In an analysis of the use of the parental leave benefits and its impact on earnings for mid-level employees of Sweden's telephone company over a five-year period (1983–1987), the researchers found that the availability of a one-year paid parental leave to working mothers, and their ability to use the leave flexibly to phase in a return to full-time work after a full-time spell at home, permits women to balance work and family life in a more satisfactory way than in any other country (and than earlier in Sweden). As Sundstrom reports, women who are in the labor force and have children, and who take the leave, do experience a modest earnings penalty; earnings fail to grow while they are on leave, and the loss of training days leads to some real earnings reductions. However, these are modest losses indeed and not enough to be serious or prohibitive. The net result is that Swedish women want the leave benefits and have an incentive to enter full-time work early and defer childbearing. And they rarely leave the labor force after childbirth but rather reduce their hours of work somewhat.

Because of the overall Swedish policy and the policy environment, Swedish men are far more involved in parenting than men in other countries. About 25 percent of eligible fathers use some portion of the parent insurance benefit, and 83 percent of eligible fathers use the full two-week paternity leave to which they are entitled to stay home when a child is born; 41 percent of the users of the paid leave to care for an ill child are men. As a result, Swedish men are also found to spend more time in housework and child care when they have very young children and significantly more than men do in most other industrialized countries.

The evidence provided here is only preliminary and incomplete. Nonetheless, it does suggest that policies that support a much more extensive at-home role for parents of newborns can be designed in such a way that family income and family time at childbirth are protected and that there is some protection of gender equity both within the family and in the labor market. Moreover, the economic costs to women are modest, and the apparent rewards for children and parental preferences are high. The Finnish policy seems to reinforce choice, an important value for many, but the impacts on women's careers and wage patterns are not clear. The German policy appears to support the predominant value in that society—traditional families—but raises questions about consequences for women.

To pose the questions as we did earlier: Can the well-being of children be enhanced without impinging on or sacrificing the well-being of women? The answer would appear to be yes. Is there an inevitable conflict between the interests of children and that of their mothers as individuals in their own right? The answer would appear to be no. But, of course, our clear cases are few in number.

Other Impacts

Depending on the particular policy objectives in the different countries, other outcomes may be sought and may or may not be achieved. Countries seem to have had some modest success in achieving desired changes or modifications in behavior, but the analytic work has not been carried out rigorously, and the conclusions are not all firm.

Although no country in this group claims that its policies lead directly to higher birthrates, and all have fertility rates that are below replacement level, several suggest that these policies coupled with others may facilitate, support, or sustain the birthrates that otherwise might be even lower (Austria, France, Finland, Hungary, Sweden). In several of these instances the pronatalist goal is used to sell the policy; in others it is not.

Almost all the countries are convinced that linking a maternity-related benefit to obtaining prenatal care has led to higher rates of early and sustained prenatal care and better pregnancy, maternity, and infant and neonatal outcomes as a result. Again, one cannot disaggregate this from other factors, but the data on participation and well-being are impressive.

Only Austria has established a policy specifically limited to single-parent, mother-only families. Of some interest, Austrian research suggests that following the establishment of its single-mother extended maternity policy, an unanticipated outcome was that the rates of unwed childbirth increased, and there was evidence of a marriage delay until these single mothers completed their three-year extended maternity leave. In part because of this, the policy was changed in 1990 to apply to all low-income families, husband-wife as well as single-mother families. It remains to be seen whether the policy change will have any impact on Austrian marriage and out-of-wedlock birthrates.

Austria, Germany, and Hungary have implemented policies that were designed to facilitate labor force withdrawal by women following childbirth. The policies appear to have been successful in that both the Austrian and German benefits are used overwhelmingly by those women who qualify, and about 60 percent of new mothers stay out of the labor force for the full three years that their benefits permit in Hungary. On the other hand, the German analysis (the only one reported) suggests that these labor force withdrawals make only a small contribution to the solution of the unemployment problem.

In contrast, in Finland, Sweden, and Hungary, the stress was on the creation of incentives for early attachment to the labor force, and they have apparently succeeded in advancing this goal. Of some importance, linking more generous paid and job-protected post maternity leaves to prior work history seems to have had the result of decreasing very young parenthood. Young women defer their decision to have a baby until they qualify for a more generous, wage-related cash benefit and leave. The success of such a policy, however, is contingent on there being sufficient job opportunities available.

A final question has to do with the extent to which those countries that decided on the expansion of parental choice as their primary objective have achieved their desired goals. Finland has established a holistic family policy package and France an incremental policy amalgam, each stressing choice as a goal in order to respond to diverse values and concerns. Here we note that only Finland appears to have gone beyond the rhetoric of choice and deliberately committed its resources to facilitating choice between a parental role in the workplace and one at home and between child care at home or out of home. It seems to be well on the way toward achieving its objective.

A Note about Impact Evidence

We are discussing legislation and program development that has often been incremental, may be piecemeal, is not deliberately meshed, is periodically adjusted or expanded, and is often administered in a decentralized system. The same strategies and instruments may be serving different objectives, or different hierarchies of objectives, in different countries. With few exceptions, there was and is no consideration of built-in evaluation. While the authors of the chapters in this book do consider the manifest or obvious implicit objectives of these policies and programs and ask what can be said about efficacy, they do not exaggerate the levels of confidence to be attributed to the conclusions. This is not a domain of controlled experimentation or even of standardized data collection across countries so as to permit observations about experiments while controlling for relevant variables.

In short, the innovations in parenting policies and their evolution are largely to be explained by cultural and value systems, political and economic strategies, interest groups, and the influence of leaders and experts. Policies are sustained and expanded by the same forces, perhaps, as well by popular (voter) response. These matters may or may not be important enough in the political debate to become considerations affecting election results, so ultimate public response is often unmeasured.

Inevitably, then, a discussion of outcomes and impacts is ''soft,'' by social science criteria. Nonetheless, our chapter authors do review the more rigorous research and relevant data where they exist and ask about the fulfillment of country-specific goals. We have attempted to summarize and characterize the results. The sum total of the discussion suggests that there is information here relevant to U.S. policymakers and others who are concerned with these issues but that—as in most other policymaking—we will need to design our own combinations without certainty based on research evidence and, eventually, monitor our own results. In any case, given our own societal characteristics and the nature of our polity, this is what we would expect to do. We do not behave differently in other policy domains.

If that policy analysis undertaken before choice is made among available options may be characterized as anticipatory evaluation, we might add for the U.S. discussion and evaluation the relevance as well of universalism as a strategy. More specifically, if the parenting and child rearing benefits are universal, as they are in several of these countries, what are the consequences for poor children? Are poor—and minority—children better off as a result of universal policies (that target all children while stressing certain groups) or selective policies (that target only the poor)? Are specific antipoverty policies the most effective strategy for improving the situation of children in poor families, or are they helped more through general child and family policy strategies? Does the politics of child and family policy result in more widespread and stronger political support for universal programs, or would it short-change poor and minority children? We believe on the basis of our own studies that assessments along these lines could shift the U.S. preference in certain fields from antipoverty targeting toward more universal provision in parenting policy, as seen in most of the countries reported.

OBSTACLES AND CHALLENGES TO U.S. POLICY DEVELOPMENT

It will not be easy to increase policy attention to very young children in the United States. There are obstacles to substantive agreement and to implementation. One immediate issue is that among the cohorts of children born each year, the United States has a disproportionately large group of children born to never-married women who are not living with their child's father, and a significant group among these women are teenagers. Growing up with an adolescent mother creates an even more severe handicap for the very young child. Clearly any policy initiative focused on very young children must be designed in such a way that it discourages teen parenting. Several countries have discovered that limiting eligibility to paid parental leave policies to women with a prior work history creates strong incentives for young women to enter the labor force early and defer childbearing.

Many Americans reject all child policy proposals as likely to benefit minority children, a large group among the most deprived, and to encourage out-of-wedlock childbearing by minority women. This often implicit argument must be confronted directly as inconsistent with American values regarding equality and respect for differences—and as probably factually wrong as well. On the pragmatic side, one should remind Americans of our growing dependence on minorities in the work force.

Even if one overcomes prejudice and racism, however, there is the fact that the United States is truly a large and heterogeneous country whose population holds allegiance to pluralistic value systems. Among the states within our own country, we include some of the variability that produces the differences among the European countries. Our tradition of federalism will insist that for some purposes at least, states continue to carry the program and policy leads and reflect our diversity. This does not, however, mean that we do not require national leadership and participation.

Then there is the tradition in the United States of church-state separation, a doctrine that has often helped the country to avoid facing complicated issues of family policy. The abortion fight has shown how difficult things may become if we forget or cannot avoid challenging the tradition of respect for family privacy. Furthermore, there is a preference for market solutions to problems where they are available or can be encouraged. Whether real or not, proposals along such lines serve to block public action. Nor do we in this country have the powerful labor movements that in some other countries have actively moved family benefit proposals. Finally, it is not easy—as was seen in 1989–1990—to overcome diverse values in designing social legislation. Certainly child care proposals were stalled, blocked, and compromised almost beyond recognition as value clashes within and between parties took over. A happy solution emerged as one element in a complex budget deficit reduction package.

Beyond this, certain other values, considered precious by advocates, prove difficult to interpret or to implement. Some conservatives would support family policy initiatives but only if they are limited to traditional families. Some feminists are concerned that policies designed to improve the situation of children may ignore the possible negative consequences for women. Conservatives fear the economic costs to the society of providing paid leaves for working parents, and feminists fear the economic consequences (lower wages, constricted career paths) for the women who take extended leaves. And all these issues are debated in a context in which government has traditionally avoided family issues because of the racial, ethnic, religious, and cultural diversity within the country and the concomitant difficulty in reaching consensus. Nonetheless, we believe that it is urgent for the country to increase its attention to very young children, and the extensive European experience can have some relevance.

Launching the Public Debate

Obstacles apart, Americans who are talking of improved child and family policy, even of a child policy decade, cannot ignore the policy vacuum concerning the under 3s. In considering how to move, several elements in the European story stand out.

First, it makes no sense to deal separately with what are obviously intertwined elements of a policy package. Parenting policy requires attention to economic buttressing of those who rear young children, parental time with children, and child care resources. While the congressional committee system and program delivery bureaucratic boundaries may keep them apart, we need to think holistically about a policy package involving maternity and parental leaves, child care services, and needed income transfers for families with young children. Simultaneous attention to these elements will not occur without considerable public discussion.

Second, parenting policies build on a social policy infrastructure. Our authors note the importance to the parental leave and child care innovations of the basic system of family and children's allowances, tax policies, housing measures, and medical care provisions. Those who would take this matter further in the United States cannot, for example, advocate for child care or parental leave—or even for both as an integrated policy—and ignore the rest. This may pose overwhelming problems or may help focus a systematic effort.

Third, and very important for the United States, conservatives and more radical advocates, where they are truly concerned about the well-being of children and families, can come together around a policy of choice. Political and cultural diversity, ethnic and regional differences, do not need to be homogenized to move on children's policy. Federalism may facilitate implementation of a policy of federal underpinning and infrastructure, plus local diversity. It is possible to have and to respect traditional families with at-home mothers, two-earner families, and single-parent families with the adult either at home or in the labor force while adjusting resource and program responses to the scope and scale of each group's needs. And it is certainly possible to recognize that family role patterns will change as parents and their children move through the life cycle. Special considerations when children are below age 3 seem both merited and manageable without penalizing children, women, or men.

Finally, but inevitably, questions of cost will influence the debate over child and family policies. Clearly we must make choices rather than pretend that the society can do everything at once. Yet we should also remember that countries not as wealthy as ours do all these things and more.

NOTES

1. House Committee on Ways and Means, *The 1990 Green Book: Background Material and Data on Programs within the Jurisdiction of the Committee on Ways and Means* (Washington, D.C.: U.S. Government Printing Office, 1990), p. 1036.

2. B. E. Andersson, *Effects of Various Forms of Public Child Care: A Longitudinal Study* (Stockholm: Institute of Education, University of Stockholm, 1988, 1990).

3. J. Hoem, F. Stafford, and M. Sundström, "Parental Leave Policy and Women's Careers in Sweden," *Working Papers* (Stockholm: Center for Working Life, 1990).

Index

About the Editors and Contributors

SHEILA B. KAMERMAN is Professor in social policy and planning at the Columbia University School of Social Work and is co-director of the Cross-National Studies Research Program. Her research interests include comparative work in family and child policy, income transfers, child care, parental leave, and personal social services. She is co-author (with Alfred J. Kahn) of many books, including *Mothers Alone: Strategies for a Time of Change* (Auburn House, 1988) and *The Responsive Workplace: Employers and a Changing Labor Force* (1987).

ALFRED J. KAHN is Professor Emeritus in social policy and planning at Columbia University School of Social Work and is co-director of the Cross-National Studies Research Program. His research interests encompass U.S. and comparative work in family and child policy, personal social services, social expenditures and related subjects. He is the co-author and co-editor (with Sheila J. Kamerman) of over fifteen books, including *Child Care: Facing the Hard Choices* (Auburn House, 1987) and *Privatization and the Welfare State* (1989).

MARIA ADAMIK is a lecturer in the Department of Social Policy, Institute of Sociology and Social Policy of Eötvös University (Budapest). She is involved in setting up the first women's studies program in Hungary. Her research interests encompass women's studies generally and the income maintenance and transfer system affecting families and children.

CHRISTOPH BADELT is Professor of Economics and Social Policy at the Vienna University of Economics and Business Administration. His main research areas are the social services, family policy, the handicapped, and the non-profit sector. He is author (in German) of *Political Economy of Volunteer Labor* (1985) and *Market Incentives in the Public Sector* (1987).

MARIE-GABRIELLE DAVID is a Program Director at the Center for the Study of Incomes and Costs (CERC), based in Paris. Her research interests are household income, social policy, and retirement. She is the co-author (with Christophe Starzec) of ''Mères de Famille: Coûts et Revenus de l'Activité Professionnelle'' (1985).

MATTI MIKKOLA, Doctor of Laws, is legal advisor at the Ministry of Social Affairs and Health in Helsinki. He is also Assistant Professor of Labor and Social Law at the University of Helsinki and teaches social law in Sweden as well. His main research interests are social law and employment. He is author (in Finnish) of *On the Terms of Unemployment Security* (1979) and *Work, Working Hours and Social Security* (1986).

CHRISTIANE SCHIERSMANN is a Professor affiliated with the Seminar on Developmental Theory at the University of Heidelberg. Much of her contribution to this volume was completed at the Institute for Research on Women and Society, University of Hannover. Her research focuses on women, education and various sociological topics. She is author, with others, of *Berufliche Wiedereingliederung von Frauen* (1990).

CHRISTOPHE STARZEC is a Research Director at the National Center for Scientific Research (CNRS), based in Paris. His interests are in the areas of household income, social policy, and retirement. Based at CERC, he is the co-author (with Marie-Gabrielle David) of ''Familles Nombreuses, Mères Isolées, Situation Economique et Vulnérabilité'' (1987).

MARIANNE SUNDSTRÖM is Senior Researcher at the Swedish Center for Working Life (Stockholm). Her main research areas are labor economics and social policy. She is the author of *A Study in the Growth of Part-Time Work in Sweden* (1987).